Hull

PEVSNER ARCHITECTURAL GUIDES

Founding Editor: Nikolaus Pevsner

PEVSNER ARCHITECTURAL GUIDES

The *Buildings of England* series was created and largely written by Sir Nikolaus Pevsner (1902–83). First editions of the county volumes were published by Penguin Books between 1951 and 1974. The continuing programme of revisions and new volumes has been supported by research financed through the Buildings Books Trust (now the Pevsner Books Trust) since 1994.

The Pevsner Books Trust gratefully acknowledges
Grants towards the cost of research, writing and illustrations
for this volume from

ENGLISH HERITAGE
GEORGIAN SOCIETY FOR EAST YORKSHIRE
HULL CITY COUNCIL
ALEC-SMITH FAMILY TRUST
SONJA BOEHMER-CHRISTANSEN

ENGLISH HERITAGE

Hull

DAVID AND SUSAN NEAVE

PEVSNER ARCHITECTURAL GUIDES

YALE UNIVERSITY PRESS

NEW HAVEN & LONDON

For Emma, Joseph and Esther

The publishers gratefully acknowledge help in
bringing the books to a wider readership from
ENGLISH HERITAGE

YALE UNIVERSITY PRESS
NEW HAVEN AND LONDON
302 Temple Street, New Haven CT06511
47 Bedford Square, London WC1B 3DP

www.lookingatbuildings.org
www.pevsner.co.uk
www.yalebooks.co.uk
www.yalebooks.com

Published 2010
10 9 8 7 6 5 4 3 2 1

Printed in Italy by Conti Tipocolor

Library of Congress Cataloging-in-Publication Data
Neave, David.
  Hull / David and Susan Neave.
      p. cm. -- (Pevsner architectural guides)
  Includes index.
  ISBN 978-0-300-14172-6 (alk. paper)
  1. Architecture--England--Hull--Guidebooks. 2. Hull (England)--Buildings,
structures, etc.--Guidebooks. 3. Hull (England)--Guidebooks. I. Neave,
Susan. II. Title.
NA971.H84N43 2010
  720.9428´37--DC22
                            2010031302

Contents

Acknowledgements viii
How to use this book x

Introduction 1

Major Buildings 37
Holy Trinity 38
St Mary 48
Guildhall 53
Queen Victoria Square 60
Trinity House 71
University of Hull 77

Walks 85
Walk 1. The Old Town: High Street 86
Walk 2. The Old Town: West of High Street 97
Walk 3. Waterfront 111
Walk 4. Queen's Gardens and the Northern Suburb 121
Walk 5. City Centre West and Park Street 132
Walk 6. Beverley Road, Pearson Park and Spring Bank 141
Walk 7. The Avenues, Newland and Newland Park 155
Walk 8. West: Anlaby Road and Hessle Road 162
Walk 9. East: Holderness Road and Garden Village 172
Walk 10. Sutton-on-Hull 181

Excursions 187
Hessle and the Humber Bridge 188
Cottingham and West Hull Villages 194
East of Hull: Hedon and Burton Constable 203
Beverley 211

Further Reading 231
Glossary 234
Index of Artists, Architects, Patrons and Others 240
Index of Localities, Streets and Buildings 247
Illustration Acknowledgements 254

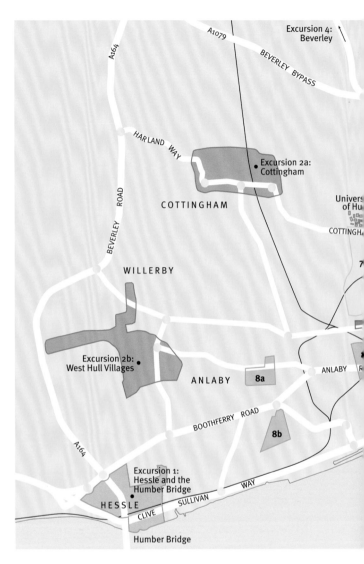

1. Hull, showing areas covered by walks

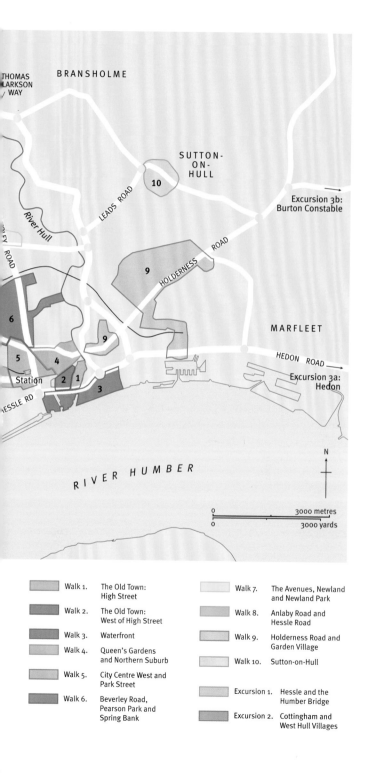

BRANSHOLME

THOMAS
CLARKSON
WAY

SUTTON-
ON-
HULL

River Hull

LEADS ROAD

10

Excursion 3b:
Burton Constable

HOLDERNESS ROAD

9

MARFLEET

ROAD

6

9

HEDON ROAD

5

4

Excursion 3a:
Hedon

Station

2 1

3

HESSLE RD

N

RIVER HUMBER

| 0 | | | 3000 metres |
| 0 | | | 3000 yards |

	Walk 1.	The Old Town: High Street
	Walk 2.	The Old Town: West of High Street
	Walk 3.	Waterfront
	Walk 4.	Queen's Gardens and Northern Suburb
	Walk 5.	City Centre West and Park Street
	Walk 6.	Beverley Road, Pearson Park and Spring Bank

	Walk 7.	The Avenues, Newland and Newland Park
	Walk 8.	Anlaby Road and Hessle Road
	Walk 9.	Holderness Road and Garden Village
	Walk 10.	Sutton-on-Hull
	Excursion 1.	Hessle and the Humber Bridge
	Excursion 2.	Cottingham and West Hull Villages

Acknowledgements

Our first debt is to Sir Nikolaus Pevsner whose original survey of the architecture of Hull in his *Buildings of England: Yorkshire: York and the East Riding* (1972) was the starting point for the more detailed account in the second edition (1995) revised by David and Susan Neave. The present volume is based on this revised text which benefited greatly from the advice and editorship of Bridget Cherry, to whom we owe so much. Others who made a major direct contribution to the revised Hull text were Chris Ketchell, who generously shared his exceptional knowledge of the buildings, streets and architects of the city, and the late Sandy Chamberlain who helped with research.

For this present guide particular thanks are due to Christopher Wilson who kindly contributed much to the entry on the architecture of Holy Trinity church, and to Robert Barnard and Philip Hampel, the city's Senior Conservation Officer, for reading and commenting on our text. The responsibility for any errors remains that of the authors and we would welcome corrections and additions.

This book has drawn on the publications of others, in particular Ivan and Elisabeth Hall's *Georgian Hull* and Ivan's contribution to the *Victoria County History* volume edited by Keith Allison whose own published work has been invaluable. Other printed sources used are detailed in Further Reading but we wish to acknowledge especially Ian Goldthorpe's study of the city's Victorian architecture. Others whose writings have contributed to our knowledge of Hull buildings include Rupert Alec-Smith, Robert Barnard, Clive Barnby, Bernard Blanchard, Arthur Credland, Dave Evans, Paul Gibson, Rosemary Horrox, Edward Ingram, Ken MacMahon and John Markham.

Original research was carried out in Hull City Record Office and Hull Local Studies Library and we are most grateful to Martin Taylor, City archivist, and David Smith, senior local studies librarian, and their staff for being so helpful at a time when they were preparing for their move to the new Hull History Centre. The resources of the Treasure House, Beverley, the Brynmor Jones Library, University of Hull and the King's Manor Library, University of York were also drawn upon and we thank their staff.

We would like to thank the following who supplied information about individual buildings: Robin Diaper (Guildhall), Canon Stephen Deas (Charterhouse), Geoff Brandwood (St Mary's, Sculcoates), Arthur

Credland and Susan Capes (Maritime Museum), Vanessa Salter (Wilberforce House), Sidney Tasker (Crown Court), Reece Andrew (University of Hull), Zoë Opačić and Emily Keane (Holy Trinity), Matt Woodworth (Beverley Minster), David Connell (Burton Constable), Chris Mead (Anlaby Park) and Gordon Stephenson (Reckitt Benckiser). Gerardine Mulcahy kindly helped with queries on sculpture and Audrey Howes generously loaned us material on her grandfather Joseph Hirst. We also thank Tim Barnett, Geoff Bell and Ed Dennison for their help in various ways.

Our thanks go to those who have welcomed us to their homes particularly Kevin Barnes, John Bernasconi and Ivor Innes and those who arranged access to various buildings and permitted photography especially S. Pinder and Capt. J. Robinson (Trinity House), Canon Michael Loughlin (St Charles Borromeo), East Riding of Yorkshire Council and Fiona Jenkinson (Beverley Guildhall), Jeremy Fletcher (Beverley Minster), National Trust (Maister House), University of Hull, Hull City Council and Mike Lister and Tony Ridley (City Hall), Sue Sedgwick (Hull Guildhall) and Simon Green (Hull Museums).

This publication would not have been possible without a major grant from English Heritage, secured through the good offices of Colum Giles, for which we are most grateful. Most of the photographs were provided by English Heritage, taken especially by Bob Skingle who produced so many excellent images despite the restrictions of a long grey winter. The historic images come chiefly from Hull Museums and Art Galleries courtesy of Hull City Council who, through the welcome support of Simon Green, assistant director of Culture and Lifestyle, and Martin Taylor, City archivist, also made a grant towards the cost of drawing the maps.

Vital financial help was received from the Alec-Smith Family Trust via Alex Alec-Smith to whom we give thanks. Of particular assistance was the generous grant from the Georgian Society for East Yorkshire that was instrumental in ensuring that this publication got under way when other funding was elusive. The pioneering Georgian Society founded in 1937 by Rupert Alec-Smith, then aged only 24, Hull Civic Society founded 1964 and Help! Conservation Action Group, active for over twenty years from the mid 1970s, along with the city's conservation officers, have played a major role in ensuring that so many historic buildings remain to be included in this guide.

Special thanks go to the staff at Yale University Press: Charles O'Brien who actively promoted the project and saw it through to the last stages, Sophie Kullmann who ably edited the final text and designed the volume, Louisa Lee, picture researcher who coordinated the images and plans which were skilfully drawn by Martin Brown, and the commissioning editor Sally Salvesen who oversaw the whole production. We also wish to thank the Pevsner Books Trust and its secretary Gavin Watson for their support.

How to use this book

This book is designed principally as a guide for exploring the buildings of central Hull, and selected suburbs or outer areas. The divisions between the sections are shown on the map on p. vi–vii.

After a chronological introduction, the gazetteer begins on p. 37 with seven Major Buildings in central Hull (including three buildings in Queen Victoria Square), along with a section devoted to the University of Hull and its campus and buildings. The next section covers central Hull and selected suburbs in ten Walks. Each Walk has a street map, with the main buildings and landmarks marked and arrows indicating the suggested route. A final section describes four Excursions further afield. Readers should note that the description of the interior of a building does not indicate that it is open to the public.

In addition certain buildings, topics and themes have been singled out for special attention and presented in separate boxes:

Architects and Sculptors: Hull's Victorian Sculptors, p. 56; William Catlyn and Artisan Mannerism, p. 90

Building Materials and Types: Medieval Brick, p. 6; Court Housing, p. 16; Board Schools, p. 18

Docks: The Georgian Docks, p. 14

Fortifications: Town Wall, p. 5; Hull Castle and Citadel, p. 118

Lost Buildings: Cuthbert Brodrick's Town Hall, p. 54

Public Services: Hull Telephone Boxes, p. 32; Springhead Pumping Station, p. 171

Introduction

Medieval Hull 4

The Sixteenth and Seventeenth Centuries 9

Georgian Hull 10

Victorian Hull 15

Civic Pride: The Late Victorian and Edwardian City 20

Between the Wars 24

The Post-war City 29

Regeneration Post 1980 35

HVL

Introduction

The city of Hull, or more correctly Kingston upon Hull, with a population of around 260,000, is by far the largest settlement in East Yorkshire. Sited on low-lying land where the River Hull joins the broad Humber estuary, it is one of only a handful of English cities that have experienced an unbroken position as a leading centre of population and economic activity from the Middle Ages to the present day [2]. This continuity, reflected in its buildings and urban form, derives from Hull's role over nine centuries as one of the country's major ports, trading chiefly with NW Europe.

The great medieval church of Holy Trinity, much of it brick, lies at the heart of the Old Town, an area once surrounded by the town walls and later the Georgian docks. Here there are C17 buildings, their architecture strongly influenced from the Low Countries, splendid Georgian merchant houses and Italianate Victorian commercial buildings. To the N are the remnants of the grand terraces of the Northern Suburb, St Charles Borromeo R.C. church with its lavish interior, and the delightful Georgian Charterhouse Hospital.

Hull was at its most prosperous and self-confident in the years before the First World War, as evidenced by the monumental Edwardian Baroque Guildhall and City Hall. The city suffered severely during the Second World War and rebuilding was slow and piecemeal, and there are few buildings of note from the later C20, except at the University of Hull. At the beginning of the C21 Hull appears to be undergoing a renaissance, with a kick start from Terry Farrell's aquarium, The Deep. It is at last appreciating the unique character of its townscape, with former docks, river and estuary waterfronts in or close to the city centre being transformed and enhanced by quality buildings.

The city's boundary is tightly drawn and encompasses only one sizeable former suburban village, Sutton-on-Hull, but from the C18 onwards many of the middle classes who worked in Hull lived across the border in the East Riding, and their homes and other buildings are covered by the excursions at the end of this guide.

2. Detail from plan of Kingston upon Hull, *c.* 1540, showing ships on the River Hull (British Library, Cotton Augustus I.i., f.83)

3. Holy Trinity, from the sw; nave c. 1380–1420; tower c. 1490–1520

Medieval Hull

The city of Kingston upon Hull had its origins in the port of Wyke established by the Cistercian abbey of Meaux by 1193 on the w side of the old Hull river near its junction with the Humber estuary. Evidently in the mid c13, because of problems with silting up, a new channel was cut utilizing a creek further e creating the present route of the River Hull, and Wyke was resited alongside. Evidence of continuous settlement from the 1260s has been found on High Street, originally Hull Street, which follows the line of the river.

Trade flourished and soon Wyke upon Hull was the third major wool port in England, after Boston and London, with exports chiefly to the Low Countries and Italy, and in 1279 the right to hold a weekly market and an annual two-week-long fair was granted. In 1293 Edward I, in need of a northern base for provisioning his military campaign against the Scots, acquired Wyke from the monks of Meaux. He immediately changed the name of the port to Kingston upon Hull, granted it two weekly markets and a six-week annual fair, built a new quay and laid out roads leading to Beverley, Hessle and York. A sizeable town was planned and a grid-like pattern of streets was added to the original more irregular layout which had been dictated by the line of the river. In 1299 Edward granted the town borough status.

At first the town was slow to develop but the building of two churches, Holy Trinity [3] and St Mary [32], and the founding of two friaries,

Carmelite and Augustinian, by the early C14 were indications of the port's growing prosperity. Wool was joined by cloth and lead as the main exports from the mid C14, and the major imports were timber, corn and flax from the Baltic, herrings from Iceland, iron from Sweden and wine from Gascony. The town concentrated on trade and manufacturing was limited, with only a handful of craft guilds. With access via the rivers Hull, Ouse and Trent to a vast hinterland, the port was considered as the 'key to the adjoining country and whole county of York'.

Hull's strategic importance was recognized in 1321 when Edward II licensed the building of a ditch and wall around the town. Built in stages over many decades, the wall enclosed an area of some 80 acres, the present Old Town (*see* topic box below).

Town Wall

4. Beverley Gate, *c.* 1770 by Benjamin Gale, engraving from J. Tickell, *A History of the Town and County of Kingston upon Hull*, 1798

Between the late 1330s and 1410 a town wall made up of at least 4,700,000 bricks was constructed at Hull. It stretched round three sides of the town, open only to the E along the River Hull providing access to the merchants' wharves or 'staiths'. It had thirty interval towers and posterns and four main gates. The most important was Beverley Gate [4], guarding the main entry to the town from York and Beverley. Originally a free-standing timber gate, it was rebuilt in brick in the later C14. The lower section of its northern half and part of the adjoining wall, excavated in 1986–7, are displayed at the W end of Whitefriargate. Finally demolished in the late C18–early C19 for the construction of the docks, the line of the town wall is marked out in darker brick along the E side of Princes Dock and The Marina.

Charterhouse, a house of Carthusian monks founded in 1379 by Michael de la Pole, 1st Earl of Suffolk and Chancellor to Richard II, and the adjoining hospital founded by his father William in 1354, were the only major buildings outside the town walls in the Middle Ages. The de la Poles were financially, politically and socially the most successful of the merchant families that emerged from the new town of Hull. Their initial wealth was made through trade in wine, wool and lead but their real fortune was made by large-scale moneylending, particularly the vast sums lent by William to Edward III to meet the costs of his Scottish campaigns and those of the royal court. By the mid 1340s the de la Poles were the main landowners in Hull, and despite having his main residence elsewhere, Michael probably rebuilt the manor house near St Mary's church, which had twenty rooms, a chapel, a hall and a tower in 1388, and built three other brick houses in the town as well as contributing to the rebuilding of the nave of Holy Trinity church. Michael's grandson William de la Pole, 1st Duke of Suffolk, through his influence over Henry VI, secured for Hull the rare distinction of independent county status in 1440. The jurisdiction of the county of Hullshire was enlarged in 1447 to include Hessle, North Ferriby, Swanland, West Ella, Kirk Ella, Tranby, Willerby, Wolfreton, Anlaby and Haltemprice to the w of the town.

The **topography** of the medieval town of Hull is better preserved than in many other cities; former docks and Humber Street mark the line of the town wall and, with the River Hull, contain the Old Town where many of the streets follow their original route. However, with the exception of the two churches and one small timber-framed structure, nothing remains of the town's early buildings. This is partly due to

Medieval Brick

Hull and Beverley are pre-eminent in the history of the use and manufacture of brick in medieval England. Although bricks were almost certainly being made in East Anglia in the last quarter of the c13, the earliest documentary reference to brickmaking comes from Hull in 1303. At this date there was a large brickworks sited at the western edge of the town producing up to 100,000 bricks a year.

John Leland was struck by the number of brick buildings when he visited in 1541, noting that Holy Trinity church was 'most made of brike' and that the town wall was built 'al of brike'. Charterhouse, the prison and many houses were brick, including four formerly belonging to the de la Poles 'whereof every one hath a tour of brike'. Hull bricks must also have been used for St James's, Sutton, built in the 1340s, and the clerestory at nearby St Peter's, Wawne.

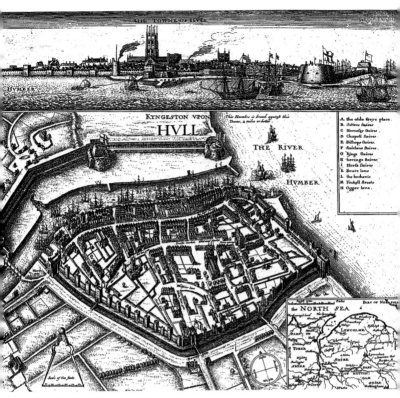

5. Plan of Hull by Wenceslaus Hollar, *c.* 1640

post-medieval prosperity leading to rebuilding, but also to destruction in the Second World War and more recent demolitions. Lack of good natural **building materials** in and around Hull, particularly timber and stone, may also have been a factor.

Little woodland was recorded in the area in Domesday Book and the limestone from the Jurassic belt on the western edge of the southern end of the chalk Wolds, some 10 m. w, the only reasonable local building stone, was rarely used in the town. There was plenty of clay, used in its natural state for the humblest buildings which would have been mud-built, as was common further N along the Hull Valley, or from the late C13 made into bricks and tiles for the grandest buildings (*see* topic box, p. 6). Brick was expensive and evidence, chiefly pictorial and archaeological, suggests that the majority of the buildings of medieval Hull were timber-framed but of varying quality. Timber reached the port via the river system, and from across the North Sea. Baltic oak was used for mid- and later C14 coffins at the Augustinian Friary and in the C15 for large wooden vats uncovered alongside the River Hull.

6. King's Head,
High Street,
drawing by F.S.
Smith, *c.* 1880s

Simple single-storey post-and-wattle buildings and more substantial structures of post construction with the main upright timbers standing on padstones have been excavated on sites on or near the High Street and date to the late C13 and early C14. The only surviving **timber-framed building** in Hull, No. 5 Scale Lane [63], and others recorded by survey or in drawings or photographs, appear to be of the C15 and are similar to buildings in Beverley and York. The timber-framing would generally consist of a series of main posts rising from the ground sills to the wall-plate, through two or three storeys. Most of the buildings had at least one jettied wall with separate posts to each storey. Between the posts the framing consisted of upright studs, infilled with bricks on edge, to the full height of each storey, which was demarcated by timber sills. Braces curving downwards from a post to the sill are associated with jettied walls, and braces curving upwards from the post to the wall-plate or tie-beam with unjettied walls. The roofs are likely to have been of crown-post construction. No. 85 Queen Street, demolished in the 1970s and partly reconstructed in the Hull and East Riding Museum, had a crown-post roof. It was a tall narrow building with its gable-end to the street as at No. 5 Scale Lane, but unlike the three large timber-framed buildings that survived on High Street into the C20: Nos. 139–41 (King's Head), Nos. 169–71 (George Yard) and No. 179, which had wide jettied-frontages to the street with tunnel entrances [6].

The Sixteenth and Seventeenth Centuries

Hull, along with most English ports, suffered a decline in trade in the late c15, and there had been only limited recovery by the late 1530s when the impact of the Reformation was felt in the town. The **dissolution** of the two friaries and the Carthusian priory (but not the hospital), and later the extinction of the many chantries in the two churches, led to the destruction of buildings or their fittings and meant a great reduction in the number of priests and other religious, which adversely affected the town's economy. Hull had not initially supported the Pilgrimage of Grace, the rising in 1536 against the government of Henry VIII, but eventually the town surrendered and was occupied for a short time by the rebels. There were two consequences of the rising for the town. One was a visit from the king in 1541, the other the revitalizing of the Council of the North which was to meet periodically at Hull up to 1556.

The visit of the king was particularly important as he then decided to strengthen the existing walls and build defences on the E side of the River Hull (*see* topic box, p. 118). The new works carried out in 1542–3 were partly of brick and partly of stone from Meaux Abbey and St Mary's church, Hull. Bricks were again being made in Hull and by the 1570s, as a fire precaution, the council was encouraging the use of brick, rather than timber, and ordered that all thatched buildings should be roofed in tiles. The Old Grammar School, South Church Side, was one of the new **brick buildings**, erected in 1583–5 with a schoolroom on the ground floor and merchants' exchange above [76]. It was largely paid for by William Gee, a merchant who had prospered by the great improvement in trade in the later c16. The town's chief benefactor was Thomas Ferres (d.1631), a shipmaster, who gave Trinity House the site of the Carmelite friary, founded an almshouse, and left money for repairing the North Bridge and the town defences, and for rebuilding the Guildhall. The last was carried out in 1634–6 by the bricklayer *John Catlyn sen.* who was also probably its designer. The town at this time is superbly portrayed in a bird's-eye view by Hollar [5]. It has the appearance of a Dutch town with its brick walls, surrounding moat and gabled houses along the River Hull.

On the eve of the Civil Wars the castle at Hull was one of the two principal stores of arms in England, the other being the Tower of London, but when Charles I tried to enter the town on 23 April 1642 he was denied entry by the Governor, Sir John Hotham. This led to the first siege of the town by Royalist forces in July 1642, prior to which Hotham had the Charterhouse and other extramural buildings blown up. Hull stayed loyal to the Parliamentarian cause throughout the Civil Wars, enduring a second much longer siege in September–October 1643.

From the 1650s there was much building in the town. The Charterhouse was rebuilt in three stages 1650–73, the Guildhall restored, a new market cross in cupola form erected 1682, chapels were built for the Presbyterians and Independents in the 1690s, and a tower was added to St Mary's church to replace one that had 'fallen down' in the early C16. Merchants rebuilt their houses in a distinctive 'Artisan Mannerist' style that suggests strong Dutch influence (*see* topic box, p. 90).

There are plenty of other signs of the impact on the buildings of Hull of the close trading connections with the Low Countries, features such as the shaped gables on the Master's House, Charterhouse, and the demolished Old Dutch House, Dagger Lane [7]. At Wilberforce House there are small yellow Dutch clinker bricks and Delft tiles in the fireplaces, imported from Holland in the C17 along with bricks and large quantities of pantiles. The most unusual goods imported from the Low Countries were gravestones, the 'black' Tournai marble ledger stones to be found in large numbers in Holy Trinity church. The work of Hull monument makers, such as the one visited by Abraham de la Pryme in 1699, is to be found in churches on both sides of the Humber. They evidently added the inscriptions and arms to the roughly prepared slabs.

It was war with the Dutch rather than trade that resulted in the town's largest C17 building, the Citadel, a great triangular fortification on the E bank of the River Hull (*see* topic box, p. 118).

Georgian Hull

The building of the Citadel added a further restriction to the **growth of the town**, which was still largely confined within its medieval walls at the beginning of the C18. Defoe noted in the 1720s that Hull was 'exceedingly close built' and 'extraordinary populous, even to an inconvenience, having really no room to extend itself by buildings'. Despite its population doubling to some 18,000 over the next fifty years there was virtually no development outside the walls, and many were housed in poorly built cottages crammed into the yards off the w side of High Street.

7. Old Dutch House, Dagger Lane, drawing by F.S. Smith, *c.* 1888

8. Maister House, High Street, staircase, 1744–5

The wealthy merchants, who continued to dominate the economic and cultural life of the port, still lived chiefly on the High Street where their homes doubled as business premises with warehouses behind and private staiths, or wharves, on the River Hull. This arrangement can be seen at Wilberforce House, where William Wilberforce, the emancipator, was born in 1759. He recalled that in his youth Hull 'was then as gay a place as could be found out of London. The theatre, balls, great suppers, and card-parties were the delight of the principal families in the town.' The merchants were more cosmopolitan than might be expected; many had spent part of their lives as representatives of the family firm in Amsterdam, Stockholm or St Petersburg, and made frequent trips to London. Some were there more regularly, representing the borough in the House of Commons. This is probably how George Crowle and Henry Maister, who served together as M.P.s for the town 1734–41, became part of the 3rd Earl of Burlington's local circle. Crowle was a frequent visitor when Burlington was at his East Yorkshire home at Londesborough, and when Henry Maister was rebuilding his house in the High Street in Hull in 1744 he sought the architect-earl's advice.

It is probable that the design of the magnificent staircase hall at Maister House owes more to Burlington than *Joseph Page* (d.1776) who was the stuccoist and oversaw the building work [8]. Page, apprenticed to a Hull bricklayer in 1733, may have penned the epitaph on his own gravestone in the churchyard of St Peter's, Barton-on-Humber, which proclaims that he was an 'architect and master builder, of an extensive

9. Prince Street, by Joseph Page, 1770s

genius in the liberal arts superior to many and excell'd by few'.
Producing modest Palladian-influenced buildings, Page was the leading architect of mid-Georgian Hull.

The example set by Maister House no doubt encouraged other merchants to rebuild or improve their High Street homes and *Page* was
probably responsible for the building of Blaydes House and Nos. 23–24

High Street, as well as the additions, including the grand staircase, at Wilberforce House *c.* 1760. *Page* designed Nos. 9–12 King Street, with the archway leading to the delightful Prince Street [9], and the splendid court and council rooms at Trinity House, 1773–4, the first buildings in the Adam style in Hull [51–2]. The rebuilding of the almshouses at Trinity House [50] in 1753 is attributed to *Jeremiah Hargrave* of Hull, who carved the Rococo relief in the pediment, and the chapel of 1772 (dem. 1844) was designed by *Sir William Chambers* who had local connections. *Joseph Hargrave*, son of Jeremiah, was architect of the handsome rebuilt Charterhouse and its chapel, 1778–80 [93–4].

The trade of Hull was booming in the third quarter of the c18. The port provided the link between Northern Europe and the rapidly expanding industrial hinterland covering Yorkshire, Nottinghamshire, Derbyshire, Warwickshire and Staffordshire, served via the Humber and the Ouse and Trent rivers and an ever-increasing network of canals. Many of the raw materials vital for the mills and factories of the industrial revolution were imported via Hull and the finished products exported. More and more ships were using the port, including the growing whaling fleet from the 1760s, and the Old Harbour, the lower reach of the River Hull, was often congested. This and the government's wish for a legal quay, where the customs officers could act more effectively, led to pressure for a purpose-built dock that was opened 1778 (*see* topic box, p. 14).

The construction of the dock was the signal for Hull to break out of its retaining walls and expand to the N and W. The Northern Suburb was laid out to the N of the new dock with grand three-storey terraces on George Street and its continuation, Charlotte Street. Here *Charles Mountain sen.* of Hull designed an eleven-bay mansion (dem.) for J.R. Pease, and was probably responsible for the surviving Nos. 83–85 George Street (formerly Charlotte Street) [88]. Mountain, whose style was Late Palladian with Adam interiors, also designed Hesslewood Hall, Hessle, for Pease. It was one of the many country mansions that merchants erected in the villages to the w of Hull in the late c18 and early c19. A visitor in the 1790s commented that here 'the whole country seems an extended range of pleasure-grounds, so richly has it been cultivated and adorned by mercantile opulence'.

Although the merchants and professionals abandoned High Street, not all rushed to the country. The Northern Suburb expanded with the development of Albion Street, Baker Street, Wright Street, Jarratt Street and the laying out of Kingston Square, and in the early decades of the c19 tall terraces and neat Regency villas spread out along Beverley Road, Anlaby Road and Spring Bank. Within the Old Town *Charles Mountain sen.* and *Thomas Riddell* laid out Parliament Street in 1796 [73]. This is Hull's most complete Georgian street, linking the new dock with Whitefriargate, where the brethren of Trinity House built the impressive Neptune Inn (now Boots), 1794–7, by *George Pycock* of Hull, with its great Adamesque banqueting room. Pycock was architect of

The Georgian Docks

The first three docks were constructed along the line of the walls around the Old Town.

Queens Dock (Queen's Gardens): Designed by *John Grundy*, with modifications by *Henry Berry* and *Luke Holt*, the Dock (later Old Dock, finally Queens Dock) was opened in 1778. Covering some 11 acres (4.5 ha) it was the largest inland dock in Britain when built. Closed in 1930, it was infilled and laid out as Queen's Gardens, 1935. The entrance from the River Hull still survives.

Humber Dock (The Marina), opened 1809, by *John Rennie* and *William Chapman*. The 7-acre (2.8-ha) dock is entered via a dock basin direct from the Humber. An extension **Railway Dock**, 3 acres (1.2 ha), by *John B. Hartley*, was opened in 1846.

Princes Dock, originally called Junction Dock, as it linked the Humber and Queens Docks, opened 1829, by *James Walker*. It covers 6 acres (2.4 ha). Much of it is now taken up by the Princes Quay Shopping Centre, 1990.

10. E view of the bridge and new dock at Kingston upon Hull, painting by Robert Thew, 1786

some of the town's major buildings in the late C18 including the Hull General Infirmary, 1784, the Gaol on Myton Gate, 1786, and Marfleet church, 1793 (all dem.).

The area of the Old Town was extended s when Nelson, Wellington and Pier Streets were laid out on land reclaimed from the Humber as a second dock, Humber Dock (The Marina), opened 1809, was being constructed. Here *Charles Mountain jun.*, who had inherited his father's business in 1805, designed the Theatre Royal, Humber Street, 1809–10 (dem.) and *John Earle* of Hull, sculptor and architect, the handsome Pilot Office, 1819. Mountain and Earle were also responsible for the redevelopment of the Trinity House estate between Whitefriargate, Posterngate and the new Junction (Princes) Dock. Mountain generally worked in a Greek Revival style; his last Hull building was the Assembly Rooms (now New Theatre), Kingston Square, 1830–34, left uncompleted when he moved to Malton.

Victorian Hull

At the beginning of the Victorian period Hull was undergoing its sharpest rise in population, which doubled in a decade to reach 65,670 in 1841. The age of the merchant had passed and the future lay with the industrialist and shipowner. Hull's **industries** were closely linked to the trade of the port. Seed crushers and paint manufacturers, depending on imported linseed, were numerous in the 1840s but the chief employers then were shipbuilders and the recently established, but comparatively short-lived, cotton mills. The city's best-known firms of Reckitt, originally starch manufacturers, Rank, corn millers, Needler, confectioners, and Smith & Nephew, medical goods, did not emerge until later in the century.

The opening of the Hull to Selby railway line in 1840, linking the port to the West Riding, and the arrival in 1845 of trawlermen from Devon and Kent who came to exploit the newly discovered Silver Pits fishing ground, laid the foundations of Hull's fishing industry. Whaling, for which Hull was the main British port in 1820, had all but ceased by the 1840s and fishing took its place. By 1882 there were 736 trawlers registered at Hull, and the fishing industry gave rise to a whole group of related trades and processing industries. New docks were built along the Humber: Victoria Dock to the E for the all-important timber trade, and to the W Albert Dock and St Andrew's Dock, used successively for trawlers, thus concentrating the fishing community along Hessle Road. A fourth dock, Alexandra Dock, was built further E by the Hull and Barnsley Railway Co. in 1885, primarily for the export of coal.

The population of Hull had reached 200,000 by 1891 and the town had spread N, E and W along and off the main arterial roads, Hessle Road, Anlaby Road, Spring Bank, Beverley Road and Holderness Road, reaching further out after the arrival of the first trams on these roads in the 1870s. Although the middle classes still lived in the grand Georgian terraces and Regency and Early Victorian villas near to the centre, the majority then moved further out, escaping the great spread of working-class terraces and court housing (*see* topic box, p. 16). Their destination was the new developments around Pearson Park, The Avenues and Newland Park, or villages to the W such as Hessle, Brough, North Ferriby and Cottingham that had railway stations. Some chose to commute from Bridlington and Withernsea.

The rapid expansion of the town provided much work for builders and architects. Of the many building firms in Victorian Hull, two were of more than local significance: *George Myers*, originally *Myers & Wilson*, who was A.W.N. Pugin's loyal builder, and *Simpson & Malone* who did much church work around the country for J.L. Pearson and G.E. Street. Myers was the contractor for most of the early buildings designed by *Henry Francis Lockwood*, who rapidly established himself as Hull's leading architect soon after arriving from York in 1834. Although he designed the Tudor Kingston College, Beverley Road, 1836–7, and two imposing Gothic churches, St Mark and St Stephen (both dem.), Lockwood's forte was the Greek Revival. The two

Court Housing

Court housing was Hull's distinctive contribution to working-class housing [11]. It seemingly originated in the infilling of the courtyards off High Street and elsewhere in the Old Town, where terraces of two-storey, often one-up one-down, cottages were ranged facing each other across a narrow yard accessed by a tunnel entrance from the main street. Local Board of Health bylaws of 1854 prohibited tunnel entrances and restricted new courts to a maximum length of 120 ft (36.5 metres) and minimum width of 20 ft (6.1 metres). Further bylaws in 1893 required larger houses and front and rear gardens. Forty years ago there were over 20,000 houses in such cul-de-sac courts around the city. Many courts, or 'terraces' as they are known locally, still survive running at right angles to the main street. Good examples can be seen off the streets on the s side of Holderness Road, the w side of Newland Avenue, the e side of Hawthorn Avenue and the n end of De la Pole Avenue.

11. Smoke houses and court housing, West Dock Street, photograph by H.I. Cartlidge, 1967

Nonconformist chapels that were his Hull masterpieces have gone, Albion Independent and Great Thornton Street Wesleyan [12], both 1841–2, but his spectacular interior of Trinity House Chapel survives.

Lockwood left Hull in 1849 to become, with his partner William Mawson, the architect of Victorian Bradford. His place was taken by his former pupil *Cuthbert Brodrick*, the most celebrated Hull-born architect whose surviving buildings in the city are the much altered former Christ Church Schools, John Street, a modest row of shops and offices at Nos. 4–6 Silver Street, and the grander Wellington House, Wellington Street. Brodrick had set up practice in Hull in 1845 and the following year he designed lodges and a chapel for the General Cemetery (dem.). Then followed various minor local works until 1852 when he was commissioned to design the Royal Institution at Hull, a magnificent Greek Revival building on Albion Street, destroyed in the

12. Great Thornton Street Wesleyan Methodist Chapel, by H.F. Lockwood, 1841–2

Second World War [13]. That same year he won the competition to design Leeds Town Hall which gained him national recognition. Nothing further came his way in Hull until he was selected as architect for the new Town Hall (dem.) in 1861 (*see* topic box, p. 54).

The commission for the Corn Exchange (now Hull and East Riding Museum), High Street, 1856, had gone to *Bellamy & Hardy* of Lincoln, and Brodrick was probably offended when his rather conventional design for the Dock Office was rejected in favour of the far more original scheme by a little-known London-based architect *Christopher G. Wray*. Completed in 1871, the ornate Venetian-style Dock Office (now Maritime Museum), with three great domes and lavish sculptural detail, stands right in the centre of the city at the junction of two former docks [40].

13. Royal Institution, Albion Street, by Cuthbert Brodrick, 1852

14. Stepney Primary School, Beverley Road, by Botterill & Bilson, 1886

Some of the best Victorian architecture is to be found in the Board Schools built after Forster's Education Act of 1870. During its short life (1870–1902) Hull School Board built thirty-seven schools, of which fourteen remain, six still in use as schools. The architect to the Board was *William Botterill*, from 1881 *Botterill & Bilson*. The style of the first schools was Gothic; examples include Blundell Street, 1878, and Charterhouse Lane, 1881. (Also Gothic were St George's Road and the former Somerset Street schools, both 1881, by *William Freeman* for Newington School Board.) At this point Gothic was abandoned and the Queen Anne style favoured by the London School Board took its place. *John Bilson*, now effectively the School Board architect, had been working in London and had recently travelled in France and Belgium. Shaped gables are the distinguishing features and appear at Newington Primary, Dairycoates Avenue, 1885, Stepney Primary, Beverley Road, 1886 [14], and the Avenues Adult Education Centre, 1888, with stepped gables on Malton Street, 1888. All of red brick and slate with pretty cupola-topped bell-turrets. The later Board Schools, Thoresby Street and Mersey Street, both 1902, are enlivened by tall narrow towers, rather Arts and Crafts, that hide the boiler chimney.

In 1870 Cuthbert Brodrick gave up architecture and went to live in France. His practice was taken on by his nephew *Frederick Stead Brodrick*, who went into partnership with *Richard George Smith*, who had succeeded *David Thorp* as Borough Surveyor in 1865. There are indications that Smith was not the greatest of architects, but the firm *Smith & Brodrick,* who were joined by *Arthur Lowther* in the early 1890s, was probably the most prolific in East Yorkshire. Of their many buildings in Hull the most memorable are the Northumberland Court almshouses [113] and the Punch Hotel, Queen Victoria Square [48], and further afield the County Hall, Beverley, 1890. The firm also designed offices, shops, private houses and St John the Baptist church, St George's Road, 1878, one of only three Victorian Anglican churches surviving in the city. The others are St Matthew, Anlaby Road, 1870 by *Adams & Kelly*, and St Giles, Marfleet, 1883 by *J.T. Webster* of Hedon. They cannot compete with the striking Baroque interior of St Charles Borromeo R.C. church, Jarratt Street [91].

Hull was strongly Nonconformist and there were ninety Victorian chapels, chiefly Methodist, of which around fifteen remain, only three in use as places of worship. From mid century Gothic was favoured by the Wesleyans and the older dissenting churches. Wycliffe Congregational chapel (dem.) on Anlaby Road, 1868, by *W.H. Kitching*, had nave, transepts, small chancel and full traceried windows, and later a tower with spire. The Primitive Methodists preferred a version of the Italianate style as at Sutton-on-Hull, 1876, the only one to survive of *Joseph Wright*'s six Hull chapels. Wright had been a pupil of Cuthbert Brodrick.

Of Anglican churches, the greatest losses are All Saints, Margaret Street, 1869, by *G.E. Street*, with vicarage, school and church hall, and St Augustine, Queen's Road, 1897, by *Temple Moore*. The original plans for St Augustine, the finest Victorian church in the city, were by *George Gilbert Scott jun.*, who had designed some Queen Anne style houses in The Avenues, nearby, for his cousin John Scott Cooper. Scott's father was responsible for the major restorations of the churches of Holy Trinity and St Mary, the latter for a cousin who was then vicar of St Mary's. The great architect G.F Bodley, another Scott relation, evidently did not work in his native town.

The great mass of buildings of Victorian Hull – houses, shops, offices and chapels – were by local architects and builders. *Botterill & Bilson* were the chief rivals of *Smith & Brodrick*. *William Botterill* arrived in Hull in 1848 as clerk of works for the Royal Station Hotel and had set up his practice by 1851. A capable architect, he designed excellent Italianate commercial buildings, such as the Hull Exchange, Lowgate, 1865, and a fine series of Board Schools (*see* topic box, p. 18). Many of the latter were by his former pupil *John Bilson*, who joined the firm in 1881. Bilson, an able architectural historian, is best known for his Jacobean-style Hymers College, 1893 [112]. A third firm, *Gelder & Kitchen*, founded by *William Alfred Gelder*, was making its impact on the city by the end of the century. *Gelder* designed the Paragon Arcade, Paragon Street, 1892, demonstrating that the westward move of shopping, away from the Old Town, had already begun. *Llewellyn Kitchen*, having joined the firm, designed Hepworth's Arcade, Market Place, in 1894 [72].

15. City Hall, Queen Victoria Square, by Joseph H. Hirst, 1903–9

Civic Pride: The Late Victorian and Edwardian City

The two decades before the First World War saw Hull at the peak of its prosperity and architectural achievements. In the value of trade it was the third port in Britain after London and Liverpool, it was the leading fishing port and its industries were booming. Hull's position was recognized in 1897 when it was granted city status, just four years after Leeds and Sheffield.

The architect *W.A. Gelder* (later Sir Alfred Gelder) was Lord Mayor 1899–1903 and he proclaimed Hull's new status through an ambitious programme of town planning and civic building. A new wide road that bears his name, Alfred Gelder Street, was cut through a maze of yards and slum housing in the N part of the Old Town in 1899–1900, leading from the new Drypool Bridge to the swing bridge between Queens and Princes Docks. Over the bridge further clearances led to the creation of Queen Victoria Square and King Edward Street leading N, from which the new Jameson Street ran w towards Paragon Station.

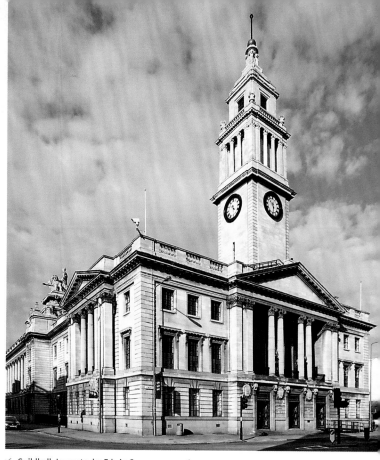

16. Guildhall, Lowgate, by Edwin Cooper, 1904–16

Buildings to grace these new streets were immediately planned. Queen Victoria Square was to be the heart of the city, with a grand City Hall for civic occasions, concerts and public meetings, and a more fitting Guildhall and Law Courts were to be built along Alfred Gelder Street. *Joseph H. Hirst*, the newly appointed City Architect, was entrusted with designing the imposing Baroque City Hall, built 1903–9 [15]. Hirst was articled to the civil engineer and architect, *W.H. Wellsted* of Hull, before joining the Borough Engineer's department as a draughtsman *c.* 1885, advancing to building surveyor in 1892 and City Architect in 1900. As well as the City Hall he designed the Market Hall, North Church Side [75], the former Central Police Station, Alfred Gelder Street (mostly dem.), the great domed Beverley Road Baths [107], and the Northern Cemetery Chapel, Chanterlands Avenue, all Edwardian Baroque. Amongst his other buildings are the charming half-timbered Carnegie Library, Anlaby Road [125], the Tudor-style Pickering Almshouses, Hessle Road [128], numerous schools including Newland High School, various Arts and Crafts-style park and cemetery lodges, and the long-gone half-timbered cabmen's shelters that were dotted around the city.

Hirst contributed more to the landscape of the new city than any other architect but was not considered for the grandest of the Edwardian buildings, the Guildhall. Its design was put out to competition and won by the young *Edwin Cooper*, who produced a monumental classical composition, built 1904–16 [16]. The Guildhall and City Hall are of stone, or stone-faced, as are the vast former General Post Office by *W. Potts*, 1908–9 [69], and various contemporary banks and offices on Lowgate and Silver Street, but some of the most successful buildings of this period are of brick. These include the Central Library, 1900–1, by *J.S. Gibson* [90] and the superb College of Art, Anlaby Road, 1904, by *E.A. Rickards* [102], both Baroque, and the Early Georgian buildings of the Municipal Training College (now University of Hull, West Campus), 1909–13 by *Crouch, Butler & Savage* [60], and the Lee's Rest Houses, Anlaby Road, 1914–15, by *Henry T. Hare* [126]. The use of flint for the former Trafalgar Street Baptist church, Beverley Road, 1904–6, by *George Baines & Son*, London [105], looks out of place, but it is a lively building with an eccentric Perp tower and Art Nouveau touches.

John Bilson was still producing some good buildings but his Late Perp St Nicholas's church, Hessle Road, 1915 (dem.), designed as a memorial to King Edward VII, was somewhat old-fashioned compared with *Temple Moore*'s St Mary, Sculcoates Lane, 1915–16, and the more modest St Michael, Holderness Road, 1915, by *Sir Charles Nicholson*. The vast Wesleyan Queen's Hall, Alfred Gelder Street, in a Free Gothic style by *Gelder & Kitchen*, 1905, with a 'spire' that dominated the E end of the city, has been demolished but the spire of his Princes Avenue Methodist church, 1905, survives. *Gelder & Kitchen* were also responsible for the 'extravagant' Premier Store, Hessle Road, the more refined Neo-Georgian Town Hall Chambers, Alfred Gelder Street, a series of Baroque shops on King Edward Street, and the city's most distinctive industrial buildings, the mill silos of 1912 and 1915 along the River Hull.

Hull's many corn merchants met and traded at the former Pacific Club, High Street, 1899–1901, of red brick and terracotta by *B.S. Jacobs* who had been articled to *William Botterill* and then worked for four years in Austria and Hungary. Also by Jacobs is the Yorkshire Bank branch of 1901 on Queen Victoria Square and the former Western Synagogue, Linnaeus Street, 1902. Amongst the more original of the office blocks are the Norman Shaw-influenced Maritime Buildings, Alfred Gelder Street, and the Baroque Ocean Chambers, Lowgate [71], both by *William Snowball Walker* of *Brodrick, Lowther & Walker*. In 1897 Walker returned to the firm where he had been apprenticed, after fourteen years working in London for George Sherrin and Fred Chancellor, and enhanced the quality of its work. Regent House, on the corner of Carr Lane and Ferensway, 1904, by *John M. Dossor*, who had been articled to Smith & Brodrick, has Arts and Crafts elements and a touch of Art Nouveau. There are Art Nouveau details on the remarkable public

17. Tower Cinema, Anlaby Road, by H.P. Binks, 1914

convenience of 1902 in Market Place and on the charming Tower Cinema, Anlaby Road, 1914, by *H.P. Binks*, the most extravagant of the handful of Edwardian cinema buildings surviving in the city [17].

The need to rehouse those made homeless through the laying out of Alfred Gelder Street and Queen Victoria Square led to the building of Hull's first **council housing**, designed by *Joseph H. Hirst*, City Architect. Forty flats or 'tenement dwellings' in three blocks on Great Passage Street, 1899–1900, no longer exist but some of the seventy-five houses built on Rustenburg and Steynburg Streets and New Bridge Road in 1902–3 still survive. No more local authority houses were built before the First World War but superior housing was provided for his workers by Sir James Reckitt at Garden Village off Holderness Road [132], where some 500 Arts and Crafts-influenced houses were built 1907–13 by *Runton & Barry. Percy T. Runton*, trained by W.A. Gelder, and *William E. Barry*, who had worked for George & Peto, went on to design the private Anlaby Park Estate, 1911–12 [127], and large private houses in the villages to the w of Hull. Within the city the grandest houses were being built on the Avenues and Newland Park, some half-timbered, others more Voysey-inspired by architects such as *John M. Dossor, Freeman, Son & Gaskell* and *Habron & Robson*. Voysey, although born at Hessle, adjoining Hull, did no work in the area.

Between the Wars

Compared to the buildings erected in Hull in the two decades of great prosperity and civic pride prior to the First World War, those built in the following twenty years were far less showy. The best buildings owed much to one benefactor, Thomas R. Ferens (1847–1930), Managing Director of Reckitt's and Liberal M.P. for East Hull. In 1917 Ferens gave the Corporation the site and funds for the superb Neoclassical Ferens Art Gallery, designed by *S.N. Cooke & E.C. Davies*, and built 1924–7 [46], and it was his initiative in buying three fields on Cottingham Road in 1922 and the gift of £250,000 three years later that enabled the founding of the University of Hull in 1928. Ferens evidently suggested *W.A. Forsyth* as a suitable architect for the first university buildings [56].

Thomas R. Ferens's philanthropy was commemorated by the Corporation when they named their great new street Ferensway. Opened in 1931, and predicted by the city fathers to take, in time, 'its place among the famous streets of the world', Ferensway was to be lined with Neo-Georgian shops, offices, hotels and restaurants based on an overall design, the architects of which, selected through a competition assessed by Sir Reginald Blomfield (designer of the comparable Headrow, Leeds), were *Scarlett & Ashworth* [18]. Never completed, this ambitious venture was the 'pivotal centre' of Hull City Council's 'bold and many-sided scheme of reconstruction', which involved 'clearance of slums, building garden suburbs, construction of twelve miles of new roads, erection of new bridges, provision of cheap transport and the conversion of an obsolete dock into a beautiful boulevard'. The last was the infilling of Queens Dock in the heart of the city and its transformation into Queen's Gardens, opened in 1935.

These large-scale undertakings must have helped at a time when unemployment in the city was usually above the national average. Hull was not as badly affected as other north-east towns during the Great

18. Brook Chambers, Ferensway, by Scarlett & Ashworth, 1934

19. Porter Street Flats, by David Harvey, 1938–9

Depression; trade through the port fluctuated and shipbuilding was badly hit, but there was a considerable expansion in the fishing industry. Population continued to rise but at a slower rate, reaching an all-time peak of around 321,500 in 1936. Part of the increase was due to the boundary extensions in 1929 and 1935 which took into the city some 5,000 acres, including most of Sutton parish to the NE and part of Cottingham to the N, and parts of Hessle, Anlaby, Willerby and Kirk Ella to the W. The city then spread rapidly into these areas, with private housing along and adjoining the new or widened arterial roads, such as Willerby Road and Bricknell Avenue, and local authority housing in five large housing estates. Two of these were on the W side of the city (West Hull or Gipsyville, centred on Askew Avenue, and Derringham Bank estates), two to the NW (Endike Lane and North Hull estates), and one on the E side (East Hull estate, either side of Preston Road). In the years 1921–38 around 14,000 houses were built by private enterprise and 10,500 by the Corporation.

Many of the inter-war **council houses** survive. The earliest, of the 1920s, built under the Addison Act, are a mixture of rows of four to twelve houses, and a few semi-detached pairs in low-density cottage estates conforming to the 1919 Tudor Walter Report's recommendations, all with small front and larger back gardens, and many with parlours. Rendering, usually confined to the first floor, hipped roofs and occasional round-arched openings provide some relief to the otherwise uninspired plain brick and tile terraces. Not all were brick for over 1,000 were of concrete and nearly 500 steel-framed. The layout of the estates, initially by *Joseph H. Hirst*, was based on a grid-like plan with long straight streets or geometrical, as at the Quadrant off Inglemire Lane.

The second phase in the 1930s under the Greenwood Act, and linked to slum clearance, resulted in a layout and housing on the Derringham Bank and North Hull estates that was more in keeping with the Garden City ideal. Trees, open spaces, and shops, schools, churches and other communal facilities were more evident, and bay windows and the gabled roofs broke up the façades of the terraces which were enlivened with Rosemary tiles between the bays and painted bands, pilasters and pediments to the doorways. Although the Greenwood Act gave an extra subsidy for multi-storey flats the City Council were not initially enthusiastic. Many of those made homeless by the Ferensway scheme had been housed in the three-storey blocks of flats still standing in Newtown, off Hedon Road, Nornabell Street, off Holderness Road, and New George Street, but it was not until the late 1930s that more flats were built. These were the Porter Street Flats, the most original of the Corporation's housing schemes, and its showpiece. Designed by *David Harvey*, City Architect 1926–39, they consist of three blocks, four and five storeys high, around a large central garden and playground [19]. The complex originally contained eight lock-up shops, communal pram and cycle stores, and a 'social hall' on the fourth floor. The flats had from one to three bedrooms, a living room, scullery, W.C. and bathroom, with balconies to front and rear. Two of the blocks were built 1938–9, the third after the war.

Much of the **private housing** was typical inter-war suburban semis with occasional variety such as the estate of over 250 modest semi-detached houses off Priory Road built in the 1930s to designs by *Allderidge & Clark*. These are flat-roofed, as are the handful of semis at the N end of Ellerburn Avenue. The grander private houses were built in Newland Park and on the W side of Beverley High Road, and in the villages to the W of Hull, in styles ranging from Arts and Crafts to Modern. The best are by *Blackmore Sykes & Co.*, a firm founded in 1913 by the Hull-born architect *Alfred C. Blackmore* and his future brother-in-law *Wilfred E. Sykes*, surveyor [119]. Probably the most prolific, and innovative, inter-war practice in the city, in addition to suburban houses they designed offices, shops, factories, restaurants and cinemas, including the Art Deco Carlton Theatre (former Mecca Bingo), Anlaby Road, 1928. Other Art Deco buildings include shops on Whitefrairgate and Hessle Road and the former Mayfair Cinema (Old Picture House), Beverley Road.

The City Architect's Department under *David Harvey* designed some excellent **schools** between the wars. Of the secondary schools, Malet Lambert, James Reckitt Avenue, 1932, overlooking East Park, is a great two-storey Neo-Georgian brick block, with projecting three-bay centre, with paired Doric columns to the stone entrance, and nineteen-bay wings to left and right. In contrast Pickering (originally Kingston) High School, Pickering Road, 1937–8, is Modern-style, of brick, with an Art Deco entrance flanked by large two-storey semicircular bows. (Demolition pending 2009.)

Harvey's combined schools with infant, junior and senior departments around three linked courtyards are particularly successful.
A good example is Endike Primary School, Endike Lane, 1932–7, of
brick with some rendering, much glass and hipped slate roofs [20]. The
main front has a central two-storey block of nineteen windows, low
single-storey blocks of sixteen windows to either side, and three-bay
links to the end ranges. The last, at right angles to the main block,
contain attractive six-bay Wrenaissance pavilions (just like the early C18
village school at Chippenham, Cambridgeshire). Other primary
schools in a near-identical style include Ainthorpe, Ainthorpe Grove,
1932–6; Foredyke, Flinton Grove, 1931; and Hall Road, 1930–7.

The best of the inter-war Anglican **churches** are by London-based
architects: St John the Evangelist, Rosmead Street, 1925 by *Leslie
T. Moore*, and three by *Milner and Craze*: St Aidan, Southcoates Avenue,
1935, St Alban, Hall Road, 1938, and St Martin, Anlaby Road, 1938–9.
With its narrow aisles, rounded brick arches and white painted walls,
the last has similarities to the same architects' Anglican Shrine of Our
Lady at Walsingham. The chapel complex at the Eastern Cemetery,
Preston Road, 1931, by *Harvey* is in an accomplished Byzantine Revival
on a symmetrical butterfly-shaped plan. St Vincent de Paul, Queen's
Road, 1932–3, by *Jopling & Wright*, the most original of the C20 R.C.
churches, also has a Byzantine flavour. In contrast Newland Methodist
church, Cottingham Road, 1927–8, by *Gelder & Kitchen*, large, octagonal, in an unsatisfactory rather industrial red brick, is still Edwardian
Baroque.

Gelder & Kitchen, largely run by *Llewelyn Kitchen* (d.1947) and Sir
Alfred Gelder's son *Edward Gelder* (retired 1942) and great-nephew
H. Conyers Robinson, continued to be favoured by some of the city's
principal employers. They designed mills around the country for
J.A. Rank, including Clarence Mill, Hull (bombed and rebuilt), and the
now celebrated Baltic Mill at Gateshead, and public houses for
Hull Brewery, typical suburban road houses, usually in the Old
English style, with plenty of mock half-timbering as at the Haworth
Arms, on the corner of Beverley Road and Cottingham Road, 1925, or

20. Endike Primary School, Endike Lane, by David Harvey, 1932–7

21. Bomb damage in Queen Victoria Square, May 1941

Neo-Georgian like the Priory Inn, Priory Road, *c.* 1930. The firm's best-known contribution to the street scene was the distinctive white faience façades with coloured mosaic panels and 'gold' lettering of the shops for local grocers William Jackson & Son Ltd (some now Sainsburys), built all over the city in the first three decades of the C20. More informed, and elegant, are the former Hull Savings Banks, stone-faced in a restrained classical style by *John Bilson*, on Holderness Road (No. 398), 1920, and Anlaby Road (No. 499), 1925, with a third at Derringham Bank built after Bilson's retirement, 1936.

Many inter-war Hull architects had their initial architectural training at the Hull School of Art. It was dissatisfaction with the education provided there that led *G. Dudley Habron* to establish the independent Hull Atelier of Architecture in 1921. Habron, a great teacher and architectural writer, had been pupil then assistant with *Brodrick, Lowther & Walker* before opening a practice on his own in Hull in 1905. There are no buildings of note identified as by Habron in Hull, except some houses on Newland Park, but his initial fellow tutors at the Atelier, *Frederick J. Horth* and *Harry Andrew*, designed the Deaf Institute, 1926, on Spring Bank and Trinity House Almshouses, 1938–40, on Anlaby Road.

The Hull Atelier was the forerunner of the Hull School of Architecture, founded as part of the College of Art and Craft in 1934 with Dr (later Sir) *Leslie Martin*, best known for the Royal Festival Hall, as the first principal. Martin, then only 26 years old, stayed for five years and had a lasting impact on architectural education in the city. He was already deeply involved with the latest architectural ideas and whilst at

Hull he became a member of the Modernist MARS group and edited, with Ben Nicholson and Naum Gabo, the single-issue journal *Circle: International Survey of Constructive Art*, considered to be one of the most important British contributions to the international abstract art movement. Martin persuaded leading Modernist architects and designers such as Serge Chermayeff and Marcel Breuer to visit Hull and lecture to his students. The Second World War intervened before there was any sign of Modernist ideas in the architecture of the city, and it was Leslie Martin himself who was to be responsible for bringing the best post-war buildings to Hull.

The Post-war City

Hull was the most bombed northern city during the Second World War [21]. It suffered eighty-two raids during which some 1,200 people were killed and 152,000 rendered temporarily homeless. Of the city's 92,660 houses only 5,945 were undamaged. The city centre was badly hit with the loss of five main department stores and nearly half the principal shops.

Early in 1944 Hull Corporation commissioned the formidable team of *Sir Edwin Lutyens* and *Sir Patrick Abercrombie* to produce a plan for the reconstruction of the city after the war. Lutyens died soon afterwards and the report is usually known as 'The Abercrombie Plan'. The compilers drew on the findings of the innovative Hull Regional Survey directed 1941–3 by *Max Lock*, then Head of the Hull School of Architecture and one of the principal figures in post-war planning.

Abercrombie's *Plan for Kingston upon Hull 1945* [22] informed and influenced the development of the city over the next forty years but none of its major proposals for a radical remodelling of the city centre, an imaginative integrated traffic system and a new satellite town for 60,000 people adjoining the parkland of Burton Constable Hall, were implemented, with the exception of the divisive Castle Street that was cut through the Old Town in 1981.

The rebuilding of the city centre got under way in the late 1940s. The House of Fraser Department Store (originally Hammonds), Ferensway, 1950 by *T.P. Bennett & Son* [97], with its combination of 1930s and Festival of Britain elements, displayed an individuality when most of the other immediate post-war commercial buildings favoured Neo-Georgian. These include extensions to Crown House and Brook Chambers on Ferensway and Festival House, Jameson Street, 1951–3 by *C. Cowles-Voysey and John Brandon-Jones,* and the most successful, Queen's House, an extensive triangular development fronting Paragon, Jameson and King Edward Streets, 1951–2, by *Kenneth Wakeford* of *Donald Hamilton Wakeford & Partners,* London. Initially Neo-Georgian continued in favour at the University of Hull, where the buildings designed by *Forsyth & Partners* in the 1950s were a version of their original buildings of some thirty years earlier.

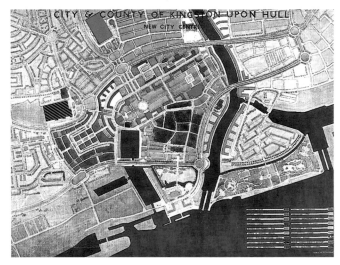

22. Proposal for New City Centre from E. Lutyens & P. Abercrombie, *Plan for Kingston upon Hull*, 1945

The appointment of *Frederick Gibberd*, the leading post-war civic designer, as consultant for the redevelopment of Queen's Gardens in 1952, and *Leslie Martin* as consultant architect at the University of Hull in 1958, apparently signified the acceptance, at last, of the Modern Movement in the city. Gibberd's own contribution was the huge nine-storey Hull College (formerly College of Technology), 1960–2, which, although dismissed by Pevsner as 'run-of-the-mill', makes a dramatic, if

23. University of Hull, Lawns Halls of Residence, Cottingham, by Gillespie, Kidd & Coia, 1963–7

24. St Michael and All Angels, Orchard Park Road, by Francis Johnson, 1957–8

period, backdrop to Queen's Gardens [86]. With the exception of the Central Police Station, by *Lazenby & Priestman*, 1958–9, (demolition pending), none of the other civic buildings, including a museum complex, proposed in Gibberd's plans for Queen's Gardens were built.

Far more exciting were the new buildings at the **University of Hull** in the 1960s (*see* p. 77). Here *Leslie Martin* himself designed Middleton Hall and the Larkin Building fronting the campus, but for the rest he recruited friends and former colleagues from amongst the leading architects of the period. *Peter Moro* who designed the Gulbenkian Theatre on the campus and *Trevor Dannatt*, who extended the Needler Hall student residence at Cottingham, had been in Martin's Royal Festival Hall team. Other buildings on the campus, including the Wilberforce Building, are by the firm founded by *Jack Napper*, of Newcastle, who had taught with Martin at the Hull School of Architecture before the war. The Lawns student residences at Cottingham by *Isi Metzstein* and *Andrew MacMillan* of *Gillespie, Kidd & Coia* are considered the most significant of the University buildings of this period [23].

There was a spate of Anglican **church building** in the 1950s, partly to replace buildings destroyed in the war and partly to provide for the new or enlarged estate communities. *Milner & Craze* completed their 1930s buildings at St Aidan, Southcoates Avenue, and St Alban, Hall Road, to their original designs and designed the new St Columba, Laburnum Avenue, 1958–60. All have impressive brick interiors. The best of the post-war churches is St Michael and All Angels, Orchard Park Road, 1957–8 by *Francis Johnson*, a brick Neo-Georgian church with Scandinavian-style w tower with cupola [24].

Hull Telephone Boxes

No visitor can miss Hull's unique telephone boxes, cream-painted for the city's independent telephone company [25]. The corporation was granted a licence to operate a municipal telephone system in 1902,

and eventually Hull (with surrounding towns and villages) became the only area of the United Kingdom not under the Post Office monopoly. The system was privatized in 1999 and is now operated by Kingston Communications (KCOM Group). There are still plenty of *Sir Giles Gilbert Scott's* 1930s K6 telephone boxes around the city, lacking the crown displayed on GPO boxes, and the increasingly rare late 1960s K8 boxes by *Bruce Martin*. There are good examples of K6 boxes outside the former General Post Office on Lowgate and one of a number of K8 boxes on Holderness Road stands at the entrance to East Park.

25. Hull Corporation K6 telephone box

Of new **schools** the most original was David Lister High School, Rustenburg Street, Hull's first comprehensive school, by *Lyons, Israel & Ellis*, 1964–6 (demolition planned). It consists of series of rectangular blocks, of one, two and three storeys, of white concrete with sawn-board shutter finish. An austere but elegant building by a firm known for its 'brutalist' style. Most of the other schools, the additions to Kingston upon Hull Teacher Training College (now University of Hull West Campus), and the more challenging former Nautical College on George Street, 1974, were by the *City Architect's Department*, whose main work comprised housing and community buildings for the vast post-war municipal estates.

In the immediate aftermath of the war some 2,500 prefabricated bungalows were erected around the city as part of the Temporary Housing Programme, chiefly for those whose houses were destroyed or badly damaged. Many of these **'prefabs'**, some designed by the Hull firms of Tarran Industries, pioneers of prefabricated housing, and Spooner Ltd, others by Arcon Industries and Aluminium Bungalows, were still standing in the 1980s. The last prefab was demolished *c.* 1994.

The proposal in the 1945 plan for housing the overspill population in a new town was rejected by the Corporation but it did undertake the 'rearrangement of the inhabitants' that Abercrombie had declared was necessary 'to achieve a proper healthy and amenable state of living'. This involved the creation of neighbourhood units for 5,000–10,000 people, free from industry or main road traffic, with their own schools, parks, shops, churches, halls, libraries and clubs. The new local authority 'neighbourhoods' were on the E side of the city: Bilton Grange, completed 1955, Longhill, 1958 and Greatfield, 1960. Designed by *Andrew Rankine*, City Architect 1939–61, one-time assistant of John Bilson, these estates are characterized by curving roads, trees, open spaces and a variety of housing types: short terraces, semis and three-storey blocks of flats. Traditionally built of brick and tile, including pantile, in a simple Festival of Britain style, the housing has worn well. For the new residents the change was succinctly summarized in a letter Tom Courtenay received from his mother: 'Longhill isn't so alive as Hessle Road. But there's more sunlight and fresh air and gardens.'

A fourth neighbourhood was created much closer to the centre of the city between Anlaby Road and Hessle Road where new housing was built in the place of 'a chaotic and depressing mixture of bomb damage, factories and old houses'. Here the emphasis was on blocks of flats, initially of three, four and six storeys, but by the end of the 1950s the first high-rise blocks, three of nine storeys and two of twelve, had been built, and five fifteen-storey blocks followed in 1962–70.

By the early 1960s, with a rising population and increased slum clearance, there was an ever-lengthening housing list, and drastic measures were required by the council. Two new estates were begun in 1963, Orchard Park in N Hull and Ings Road in E Hull. The wide-open layout of the immediate post-war estates was abandoned in favour of a tighter development based on the Radburn principle of separating vehicles and pedestrians by providing roads at the rear of houses and footpaths at the front. The Orchard Park estate took the form of four closely linked 'villages' of traditional houses with a twenty-storey block of flats as the focal point for each. Much of the housing on the Ings Road estate was factory-made for quick-build. The houses, called CASPON after the initial letters of the words City Architect (*David Jenkin*) and the Hull firm, *J.L. Spooner*, who jointly designed them, won praise from the National Building Agency and a Good Design in Housing Award from the Ministry of Housing and Local Government and the Royal Institute of British Architects. Erected elsewhere in Britain they are amongst the most notorious of the non-traditional houses built in Britain in the 1960s–70s and the majority have now been demolished.

Another type of quick-build industrialized housing devised by the Yorkshire Design Group (YDG), a consortium of local authority architects from Hull, Leeds, Nottingham and Sheffield, was erected on the Anlaby Road (Thornton) estate in 1967–9. These YDG six-storey deck-housing blocks with high-level walkways were damp and expensive to heat and had 'their own peculiar horrors of interlocked dwellings, public walkways over domestic ceilings, and ground levels given to stores and parking space that were rapidly abandoned to the wreckers' (Alison Ravetz, *Council Housing and Culture*). They were instantly unpopular in all the northern cities where they were built and all but one block in Hull, Rossett House on the Thornton estate, have been demolished, and even this has been radically transformed.

It was unfortunate that all the elements that Alison Ravetz has identified as leading to almost certain failure on local authority housing estates, that is 'flats rather than houses, peripheral rather than central locations, and prefabricated rather than traditional construction', especially when these are combined with the Radburn system with its 'unfamiliar geometries, unclear distinctions between public and private space, and networks of public footpaths that encroached on public privacy', were to be found on the City Council's last and largest housing project at Bransholme. Heralded as Hull's satellite town, to be built in two stages for 45,000 people and begun in 1966, Bransholme is isolated over 3 m. N of the city centre. Much of the original housing was CASPON, now demolished or boarded up, and YDG deck-access blocks, similarly demolished. Other housing has fared better and the vast Bransholme estate with its wide open landscaped spaces has not been a complete failure. The expected increase in population forecast in the 1960s did not materialize and so the development and most crucially many of its facilities were not completed. Nevertheless by the late 1970s almost fifty per cent of Hull's housing was local authority. There was only limited private house building in the thirty years after the Second World War. At one time eight council houses were being built for every one private-sector house.

The skyline of the city was transformed in the 1960s and early 70s with the building of thirty-six high-rise blocks of flats, some now demolished and others scheduled to go, *Gibberd*'s Hull College, the fourteen-storey Hull Royal Infirmary, 1962–7 on Anlaby Road by *Yorke, Rosenberg & Mardall* [121], and Kingston House, an uninspiring fifteen-storey office block on Bond Street by *Fry, Drew and Partners*, 1965–7. *Andrew Rankine*, City Architect, designed Telephone House, Carr Lane, 1961–3, as headquarters for the local telephone service, and on the same street *Gillinson, Barnett & Partners* were responsible for the Allders store (now Primark), 1970, which received mild praise from Pevsner. The 1970s fashion for facing office blocks in reflective glass resulted in Europa House, Ferensway, 1974–5, by *John Brunton & Partners* of Bradford, and King William House, Market Place, 1974–7 by *Elsworth Sykes Partnership*. The latter incorporates at its rear a multi-storey car park, a post-war feature that did much to damage the appearance of areas of our cities, as is very evident from those of the 1960s on Carr Lane, George Street and particularly Pryme Street. Such car parks were part of the council's attempt to manage the increasing traffic which also involved the building of the unsightly concrete viaducts on Hessle Road, 1962, and Anlaby Road, 1965, and the widening of Bond Street for an inner-ring road that fortunately was never built.

26. Hull History Centre, Worship Street, by Pringle Richards Sharratt, 2009

Regeneration Post 1980

The 1980s began with Hull, like many cities, in crisis. The fishing industry had all but ended, manufacturing was in sharp decline, unemployment was well above the national average and poor housing was still a major problem. Great hopes were placed on the Humber Bridge, opened in 1981 [147], but the economic benefits were slow to materialize. However this outstanding structure triggered the local community's re-engagement with the Humber, a factor that has been so important in Hull's regeneration. The conversion of two of the former docks into a lively marina soon followed, but opportunities were lost to make more of this unique city centre environment. Few of the monumental early C19 dockside warehouses were retained, much of the former Princes Dock was taken up with a shopping centre, albeit an effective building by *Hugh Martin & Partners*, 1988–91 [74], and the new South Orbital Road isolated the waterfront area from the rest of the city.

The appearance of the lower stretch of the River Hull was enhanced by the great arch of the tidal surge barrier by *Shankland Cox Associates*, 1980 [81], and on the E bank the former Victoria Dock was infilled, and a large well-planned housing estate was developed, 1989–96, making the most of its setting along the estuary. Elsewhere the emphasis was on housing improvement, including the rehabilitation of older properties such as the important Victorian lower-middle-class houses on Coltman Street [123].

The futuristic Kingswood College (formerly Perronet Thompson School; demolition planned), Bransholme, 1987 by *Peter G.H. Dale*, Humberside County Architect (job architects, *C. Ratcliffe-Springall* and *D. Thomas*), the Crown Court, Lowgate, 1990, by *Building Design Partnership* [70], and the ARCO National Distribution Centre, off the A63, begun 1999, by *Dewjoc Architects,* with its blue external trusses, are amongst the few individual buildings of the 1980s–90s that attract attention.

This is in great contrast to the first decade of the C21 when regeneration really got under way and all over the city there appeared buildings that stand out for some originality in design, ranging from schools, hospitals, health centres and other community facilities to those much celebrated icons, The Deep, *Terry Farrell*'s great aquarium [82], and the KC Stadium, by *Miller Partnership* [124], both opened in 2002. The success, visual and commercial, of these two has been capitalized on by Citybuild, an Urban Regeneration Company, and its successor Hull Forward. Key objectives identified in the City Centre Masterplan, 2004, by *Roger Tym & Partners*, included the reuniting of the city centre with its waterfronts along the Humber and River Hull and an emphasis on buildings of high architectural quality and originality. Promoting quality in architecture is also the purpose of the innovative ARC building, Queen Street, 2006, by *Niall McLaughlin Architects*, the city's most unusual structure [84].

Humber Quays, an attractively landscaped public space overlooking the Humber, with two congenial glazed office blocks, 2005–7 by *DLA Architecture* (a firm also responsible for the eye-catching additions to Hull College and Queen's Court), the state-of-the art footbridge by *McDowell & Benedetti* being built over the River Hull to provide a link to planned development on the E bank, and the St Stephens development, including a large shopping centre and hotel tower, on the w side of Ferensway, 2007–8, have been the flagship projects. Individual elements of St Stephens, particularly the improvements to Paragon Station with a transport interchange by *Wilkinson Eyre*, Albemarle Music Centre by *Holder Mathias* [99] and Hull Truck Theatre by *Wright & Wright* [100], are excellent, but overall the development looks out of place. Hull's attractiveness depends very much on its human scale, something that has been lost here. It is through buildings such as the Hull History Centre, 2009, by *Pringle Richards Sharratt* [26], with its elegant curved timber arcade, that Hull can best demonstrate its architectural and cultural renaissance.

Major Buildings

Holy Trinity 38

St Mary 48

Guildhall 53

Queen Victoria Square 60

Trinity House 71

University of Hull 77

27. Holy Trinity, from the sw

Holy Trinity

Market Place

Holy Trinity [27] is among the greatest of the great town churches of medieval England, although when built it was merely a chapel of ease dependent on Hessle. Remarkably, full parish status came as late as 1661. The choir, along with the slightly earlier nave of St Botolph's church at Boston, Lincolnshire, is a pioneering example of the scheme which was to become the pattern for ambitious Perpendicular parish church architecture, including the nave of Holy Trinity itself: a spacious, light-weight structure consisting of tall, open arcades carrying a low but generously lit clerestory, and outer walls with extremely large windows, the whole covered by low-pitched timber roofs. Holy Trinity's other claim to high importance is its exceptionally early use of brick for the plain walling of the transepts, choir and lower part of the crossing tower. This is by any standard a large church: 285 ft (87 metres) long, 72 ft (22 metres) wide across the choir and nave, and 150 ft (46 metres) to the top of the crossing tower.

A chapel at Wyke, in existence by 1291, was replaced by the present church soon after the founding of the new town by Edward I. In 1327 William Skayll requested to be buried in the 'new chapel of Holy Trinity'. The tracery in the earliest work still surviving, the transepts of c. 1300–20, is in the style of *Michael of Canterbury*, architect of Edward I's chapel of St Stephen in Westminster Palace, and it seems likely on that account that the king played an active role in promoting the project. The original choir was presumably fairly small, for c. 1340–70 it was superseded by the present long aisled choir. The nave followed c. 1380–1420, and the upper stages of the tower, c. 1490–1520.

Holy Trinity underwent 'improvements' in the early-to-mid C18 including refurnishing and the covering of the brickwork of the transepts and choir with stucco. The latter was removed as part of the restoration by *H. F. Lockwood* in 1842–5. A more major, and prolonged, restoration took place 1860–78 under *Sir George Gilbert Scott* when much of the external stone and brickwork of the church was renewed and the choir refurnished. Fortunately Scott opposed moves to face the medieval brickwork in stone. Then in 1906–7 *F. S. Brodrick* oversaw the underpinning of the church. The oak raft on which the tower was built originally was replaced by concrete and the nave piers rebuilt.

Exterior*

The N and S **transepts** are the oldest remaining part of the building, begun *c.* 1300. They have identical and very ambitious end windows. Their six lights are grouped into two-light units under quatrefoils, a design which reproduces almost exactly the central sections of the windows in the lower chapel at St Stephen's, Westminster. The rather bulbous ogee forms of the quatrefoils are used for the large and small trefoils in the upper parts. The main lines of the design are still Geometrical – three piled-up spherical triangles within a large spherical triangle – but some of the interstices have incipiently curvilinear forms. The E and W three-light windows in each transept, with large unencircled cusped trefoils, look earlier. There is a gabled stone porch to the S transept with ogee-arched entrance and pinnacles.

The five-bay **choir** has stonework to the windows, the embattled parapet and the facings to the buttresses between the bays and pinnacles above. The buttresses have canopied niches and along the sides the parapet has a wavy pattern. At the E end the parapets over the aisles are pierced tracery in the form of crenellations while that on the main vessel has blank quatrefoils under cresting and an empty central niche. The clerestory has twice as many windows as there are arcade bays. The windows have flowing tracery throughout. The side aisle windows are of four lights; those to the S are more elaborate than those to the N. The aisle E windows of five lights have at the top in the middle an area of reticulation. E window of seven lights is remarkable for the intimations of Perp in the large overlapping arches enclosing four lights, in the tracery directly above the central two lights in each group of four and in the upper transom. It is not obvious why the lower transom is so massive and plain. Money raised by Hull Corporation from the duty on wool exports 'for the work of the church' in 1361–2 might well have been for completing the choir or its fittings.

Along the S side are a series of stone-faced vestries built by *Scott* in 1873 to replace former chantry chapels (*see* interior). The Broadley chapel adjoining the transept is of medieval brick restored by *Scott*. The choir vestry E of the S porch of the nave was added in 1932. On the N side, just E of the transept, a blocked brick archway marks the site of another chantry chapel.

The impressive central **tower** is of three stages, the lowest early C14. The tall upper storeys are of stone and early C16 with two Perp windows to each side. Money was left from the 1490s to 1520s for building the tower. The clock acquired in 1772 was given four dials in 1840.

The long **nave** is of eight bays and of stone. Bequests of *c.* 1390 probably mark the beginning of the nave rebuilding, and in 1395 money was left to pay for the two easternmost windows in the N and S aisles. The tracery of the aisle windows is the same throughout and identical to that of the E window at Skirlaugh (East Riding) of *c.* 1400. As in the

---

*The architectural description owes much to the comments of Christopher Wilson.

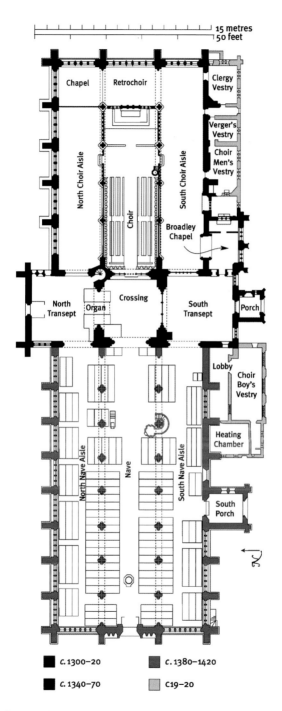

28. Holy Trinity, plan

choir the clerestory has two windows to each bay with battlements and pinnacles above.

The **w front**, with a grandeur that has few parallels in English medieval parish churches, makes a fitting climax to this outstanding building. The great Perp w window of nine lights is flanked by large seven-light windows to the aisles, and in the centre a doorway with an elaborate ogee gable and three large canopied niches to left and right. The parapet has blank quatrefoils and pinnacles and in the centre a niche with figure of Christ by *John Birnie Philip*, 1863.

The church, which was almost certainly finished when it was consecrated in 1426, is usually entered through the battlemented s porch. Note the blocked double doorway inside the porch, on the E side, that would have led to the Trinity or mariners' chapel.

Interior

Go first to the w doorway from where, looking E, the scale and unity of the interior can best be appreciated. The height and elegance of the piers, of a similar slim section throughout, and the 'great array of aisle and clerestory windows' make, in Pevsner's words 'the chancel and nave come close to the English late-medieval ideal of the glass-house'. The impression of lightness is somewhat hampered by the heavy woodwork of the early Victorian pews and the screens and organ case of the crossing tower.

The engaged piers of the **transept** arches and the large crossing piers with simple roll moulded capitals provide evidence of the earliest work. The NE pier has a nice ogee doorway that led to the former rood loft. The crossing ceiling has lierne vaulting of c. 1870 by *Scott*, painted by *C.A. Dreyer* of Hull.

The **choir** piers come very close to the standard Perpendicular four-shafts-and-four-hollows type but instead of hollows there are sunk chamfers. Christopher Wilson has shown that exactly the same section was used in the piers of the Franciscan church (Greyfriars), Newgate, London (dem.), begun in 1306 for Edward I's queen, Margaret of France by the royal master mason *Walter of Hereford*. The complex arcade mouldings die into imposts above the capitals in a very sophisticated way. The capitals have a shallow band of finely carved foliage, and the label stops are, most unusually, complete figures. These are mostly female or angels, including some playing musical instruments.

In the **nave** the piers echo those of the choir and the shafts are separated by the standard Perpendicular 'hollow chamfer' (i.e. concave) mouldings. Unusually in the Perp period, but no doubt in order to harmonize with the choir, the capitals are sculptured. Alongside foliage are figures including a mermaid, bat-like monsters, eagles and leopards which may allude to the arms of Michael de la Pole, almost certainly one of the patrons of the nave. Again as in the choir, the label stops have musician angels. *Thomas Binks* of Hull painted the wooden ceiling in 1845; it was redecorated to the same design in 1972–3.

29. Holy Trinity, choir, c. 1340–70

Remains of three **chantry chapels** can be seen on the s side of the church. John Leland recorded five chantry chapels *c.* 1540, four on the s side and one on the N. The blocked opening with panelled arch at the E end of the s choir aisle has been linked to the chantry founded by John Eland in 1533; the arms displayed are said to be his. The chapel entered from the s transept, now named after its Victorian benefactor Miss Broadley, was almost certainly the de la Pole chantry chapel, founded by John Rotenhering, merchant, in 1309 and endowed by William de la Pole in 1328 and Richard de la Pole in 1345.

The blocked archway to the E of the s door of the nave was probably the entrance to the mariners' chapel, of the Guild of Holy Trinity, the largest and wealthiest of the dozen medieval religious guilds associated with the church. The opening has mutilated carvings of the Holy Trinity and possibly a kneeling bishop, and near the base are crudely incised late C15 ships.

Furnishings

Topographically described from E to W.

Retrochoir. The superb rococo **altar table** of 1753. The square wooden panel carved with the vessels of the Holy Communion and cherubs' heads in clouds is a delightful piece. Nearby an C18 **painting** of the Good Samaritan. Is it by *Parmentier*? (*see* below)

Choir [29]. The fittings of the choir were designed by *G. G. Scott*. The **stalls** of 1876–8 include some C14 and C15 bench ends with poppyheads. Two have figures of St George and the dragon in relief and others have merchants' marks. Stone **reredos** and **screen** executed by *Simpson & Malone*, 1884. The **pulpit** was made by *James Elwell* of Beverley, 1888, were the oak **screens** fitted all around the choir, 1886–1900.

N choir aisle. The large **painting** of the Last Supper, 1711, by the French painter *James Parmentier*, sometime resident of Hull. Originally above the altar at the E end of the church it was removed to All Saints' church, Hessle, in 1831, where it was cut down, leaving only ten Apostles. The painting was returned to Holy Trinity *c.* 1870. **Transepts**. Restored C15 **screens** to the openings to the N nave aisle and the s choir aisle. The elaborate Perpendicular **screen** of four-light units to the crossing from the s transept is part of the rood screen originally in the choir arch, restored 1846.

Crossing tower. On the N side the **organ**, dating from 1711–12, remodelled in the C19 and C20.

Nave and aisles. The large oak **pews** carved by *George Peck* that overfill the nave and aisles belong to *Lockwood*'s restoration of the 1840s. They have poppyheads and some 200 medieval-style carvings of mythological figures, animals and birds. The pews are arranged lengthwise in the aisles and in the three eastern bays of the nave. Impressive Gothic stone **pulpit** with stone staircase curving round the pillar, 1846, by *Lockwood*. Large brass **lectern** of 1847 by *George Parker*, coppersmith,

30. Holy Trinity, nave s aisle, stained glass, by Walter Crane, 1896

of Hull. The **font** of coralloid marble of *c.* 1380 is exceptional. Very varied and very lively carving all over, with concave-sided crocketed gables rising from the underside up to the bowl, between each an angel with upfolded wings and leafage. It has sixteen sides with quatrefoils with fleurons, blank shields, a huntsman, a boar's head and a leopard's face. **Royal arms**, 1963, designed by *Francis Johnson* and carved by *Clifford Longley.*

Stained Glass

Retrochoir. E window 1919 by *Clayton & Bell*. **N choir aisle**. E window d.1882 by *John Hardman*. **s choir aisle**. E window 1925 by *James Ballantine*. s windows E to w. 1953, by *Harry J. Stammers* of York; 1919, designed and painted by a *Miss Hutchinson*, a niece of the donors; *c.* 1880 by *Clayton & Bell*. **Clergy vestry**. C15 mostly armorials with two C16–C17 Continental pieces. N **transept**. E windows d.1910–11 and w window 1924 by *John Hardman & Co*. s **transept**. s windows by *J. Silvester Sparrow*. The large window d.1893, with striking depiction of the Crucifixion. The w window is a mosaic of C19 pieces from former windows (including the great E window of 1833–5 by *Thomas Ward* and the great w window of 1862 by *John Hardman*) badly damaged in a Zeppelin raid 1915. E window 1909 designed by *Davis* and executed by *A.L. Ward*. **Broadley chapel**. Three windows 1921–2 designed by *E. Haworth Earle*, executed by *Samuel Harrison & Son* of Hull. s **nave aisle**. Two richly-coloured windows designed by *Walter Crane* [30], one a study for Psalm 148 'O Praise the Lord of Heaven', 1896 (executed by *Sparrow*), the other a Calvary scene, 1907 (executed by *Christmas*). Window over s entrance, 1952, by *Harry J. Stammers*. **Nave**. w window 1925 by *John Hardman & Co*.

Monuments

s **choir aisle**. The two earliest tombs in the church, both unidentified, have canopied niches; one without an effigy opens into the Broadley chapel. This chapel probably extended further E and therefore the second niche may have been open to it also. This ornate canopied niche, cusped and subcusped, with ogee gable has mid-C14 alabaster effigies. These may commemorate Richard de la Pole (d.1345), who asked to be buried in the church, and his wife Joan [31]. The other niche has an elaborate canopy clearly influenced by the Percy Tomb in Beverley Minster. It has a thickly crocketed arch, cusped and subcusped, with angels as cusps and figures in the cusping spandrels. Much of the carving was restored in 1863 including the twenty-four shields, on the two faces, the heraldry of which suggests that the tomb is to William de la Pole (d. 1366), son of Richard, above.

On the floor are a brass to Richard Byll, who died of the plague 1451, half-effigies of civilian and wife, and a slab with the worn incised figures of Thomas Dalton d.1591, and his two wives. The wall monuments include the bust of Thomas Whincop, lecturer at Holy Trinity and master of Charterhouse, d.1624, and good Georgian wall-tablets to William Maister, d.1716, possibly by *Robert Hartshorne*, William Skinner, d.1724, and John Huntington, d.1790, by *Edmund Foster*. The Hull sculptor *Thomas Earle*, d.1876, is commemorated by a monument he carved himself. Portrait medallion of William Thomson, Archbishop of York, 1891, in 'Petronite', a material manufactured at Hull.

N **choir aisle**. Here and elsewhere in the church are many good black Tournai marble ledger stones with deeply incised arms, C17–early C18. Such gravestones, probably partly cut, were imported in large numbers into Hull from the Netherlands. Two incised slabs with figures to Hugh Arminge, d.1606, and wife and John Ramsden, d.1637, and wife.

Monument to Thomas Ferres, benefactor of Trinity House, by *Thomas Earle*, 1859. Bust of Ferres and large figure of angel giving an exhausted man a drink. John Appleyard, also by *Earle*, 1860, with female figure. On the wall a cartouche to Giliad Goch, d.1700, and some nice late Georgian wall-tablets with the usual urns.

N **transept**. Excellent wall-tablet to Mark Kirkby, d.1718, and his daughter (mother of Richard Sykes, builder of Sledmere House) by *Robert Hartshorne*. Rev. Joseph Milner, d.1797, by *John Bacon jun.* with figure of Moses. Henry Maister, d.1812, by *John Earle*. Gothick framed sarcophagus. Portrait medallions to Dr John Alderson, d.1829, by *William Behnes* and John Parker, d.1841. John Gray, by *Thomas Earle*, 1860. Figure of angel holding drowned children.

s **transept**. Late c15 stone effigy of a woman, badly damaged. On the wall two cartouches with angels' heads and winged skull on draped background, Anthony Lambert d.1688 and Henry Maister d.1699. Bust of William Woolley d.1837 by *W.D. Keyworth sen.* George Lambert, organist, d.1838 by *John Earle*, with a carving of a church organ. John J. Matthewson, d.1863 by *W.H. Shaw*. Crudely carved scene of Moses striking the rock from which water flows. Matthewson was largely responsible for securing Hull's water supply in the mid c19.

Nave aisles. Nathaniel Maister, d.1783. Small medallion with seated female figure and urn. John Smith d.1875, erected 1980, and Rupert Alec-Smith, d.1983. Two Georgian-style tablets designed by *Ronald Sims* and carved by *Dick Reid*.

St Mary

Lowgate

The tower of St Mary is a prominent landmark on Lowgate, but few explore its surprisingly large and rewarding interior. Built on the Aton fee (the only land in the new town not acquired by Edward I), St Mary's, first mentioned in 1327 and described as 'new built' in 1333, was originally a chapel of ease of All Saints church, North Ferriby, 7.5 m. w. Although not formally separated from its mother-church, St Mary's was treated as independent by 1682.

The church was rebuilt from the 1390s, at least partly in brick, culminating in the construction of a w tower which is said to have collapsed in 1518, soon after completion, demolishing the w end. A new brick tower with stone buttresses and 'classical windows' was built in 1697. This and the rest of the church, encased in Roman cement in 1826, are now faced in ashlar, part of the extensive restoration by *Sir George Gilbert Scott*, 1861–3 [32]. Scott, a cousin of the vicar John Scott, added a further aisle on the s side with new porch and large vestry. Existing N and s aisles were set back at the w end exposing the base of the tower, through which he pierced a stone-vaulted walkway. This allowed Lowgate to be widened without demolishing the tower, as had been proposed.

Exterior

The church can best be seen on the N side from the open area in front of the Crown Court. Of six bays with no structural division between the nave and chancel, the building is an unusual shape. The three E bays form the chancel and the three w bays the nave. Aisles, one to the N, two to the s, run the full length of the building, with a clerestory above. The w tower was heightened by some 30 ft (9 metres) in the 1860s, when it was given its present windows. Elsewhere Scott either restored existing windows or introduced ones to the original design. Bilson suggested that the great seven-light E window had similarities to the aisle windows at the w end of Beverley Minster and that the clerestory of twelve three-light windows with two to each bay was evidently inspired by that at nearby Holy Trinity. The aisle windows, three-light on the N and three- and two-light on the s, are late C14 in style.

32. St Mary, Lowgate, tower reconstructed by Sir G.G. Scott, 1861–3

33. St Mary, interior, late c14–early c15; rood screen by Temple Moore, 1912

Interior

A great forest of pillars greets the visitor entering from the s porch and looking across two aisles to the chancel. The southernmost aisle is that added by Scott in the 1860s; his piers are reasonable copies of those of the original N and s arcades. The division between chancel and nave is marked by a break in the clerestory string course and a change in the arch mouldings and piers. The three E arches, late c14, forming the chancel are two-centred with carved heads as label stops and the piers have four attached shafts with fillets and the simplest of capitals; between the shafts mouldings rise uninterrupted into the arch. The responds either side of the E window end on angel corbels.

The three w arches of the nave, early-to-mid c15, are four-centred and the piers have the same section of four shafts and four hollows as Holy Trinity nave. The shallow capitals are also similar to those at Holy Trinity, here carved with faces, foliage, flowers, beasts and what might be the leopard's head from the arms of the de la Poles. Angels, many playing instruments, are the label stops. Signs that the present church had been extended at least one bay further can be seen at the w end where there is the truncated springing of another arch.

Fittings

Little survives in the church from before the mid-Victorian restoration other than an Elizabethan **altar table**. In the main vestry is a small section of Perp **screenwork** and the room is panelled with the greater part of a large three-decker **pulpit** of 1777–8 by *Hammond & Riddell*, joiners, and the front of a **reading desk** of 1816–17. In the small clergy vestry is a C15 **panel**, with tracery and the royal arms of France, discovered on the site of the de la Poles' manor house. Other C17 panelling came from No. 62 High Street, Hull.

There is a good range of Victorian and Edwardian fittings, the latter indicative of the transformation of the church into one of the centres of Anglo-Catholicism in Hull. The rather ornate spiky Gothic stone **reredos**, said to be based on panelling in the chapter house at Howden, was designed by *Scott*, 1863. The gilding and colouring were done in 1870 when the painting of the Last Supper was placed in the centre panels. *Scott* probably designed the elaborate carved wood **pulpit** and the rather ordinary Gothic **font** by the local mason *Thomas Frith*, both of 1863. The **screens** N and S of the chancel are by *Temple Moore*, 1908–9, as is the very fine Perp **rood screen** of 1912 [33], with cross and figures above by *Gilbert Boulton* of Cheltenham. It is a memorial to Edward VII whose head is carved under the central arch. The Gothic organ case is by *Moore*, 1904, and the N **chapel** with **reredos** with paintings by *H. V. Milner*, 1908.

Stained Glass

Four shields of C15 glass in the E **window**, including the arms of de la Pole quartering Wingfield, borne by the Earls of Suffolk after 1389. The E window is the largest of the fourteen windows by *Clayton & Bell* installed 1866–c. 1900. This excellent series form one scheme: the N aisle has Old Testament subjects, the E end and S aisle scenes from the life of Christ, the W end scenes from the life of the Virgin. The N clerestory windows installed 1919 depict the prophets.

Monuments

As the church was favoured by merchant families there are many memorials, but there were more. Most of the floor slabs were removed at the Victorian restoration and afterwards some were restored to the church. Others were destroyed or now pave the churchyard. Inside the church at the E end of the N aisle is an important early example of a **brass** with the figures incised rather than cut out. It commemorates Alderman John Haryson, 'scherman' (shearman) or woollen draper, d.1525 and two wives and children. In the chancel two **floor slabs** rescued from the churchyard in 1940: Alderman Thomas Swan, d.1630. Inlaid white composition incised with figures of husband and wife and children, worn smooth. Robert Hildyard, d.1683. Black marble ledger

34. St Mary, monument to Alderman William Dobson, d.1666

slab with coat of arms deeply incised. Of the **wall memorials** the earliest and best is above the N door, to Alderman William Dobson, d.1666 [34]. Frontal bust set in a classical arch, flanked by putti with cartouches of arms, skulls, swags and drops carved with fruit and flowers. Interesting decorative wrought ironwork below. Two excellent cartouches with cherubs' heads etc., to Jonathan Beilby, d.1711, and Philip Wilkinson, d.1716. Simpler wall-tablets commemorate Benjamin Blaydes, d.1771, builder of Blaydes House (*see* Walk 1, p. 95), Joseph Pease, d.1778, Dutch-born entrepreneur and Sir Samuel Standidge d.1801, the promoter of the whaling industry. Rev. John Barker, d.1816. Elegant wall tablet with sarcophagus surmounted by urn, books and chalice. Attributed to *John Earle*. Rev. John Scott, d.1834, by *James Loft*. Portrait medallion. John Bannister, d.1840. Portrait medallion with face covered. On floor at E end of S aisle, a medieval-style incised slab with figure of Rev. John Scott, d.1865, depicted in cassock, surplice, gown and stole. **War memorial**, 1921, in N chapel, brightly coloured panels designed by *Temple Moore & Moore*, i.e. *Leslie Moore*, decoration by *Charles Head. Leslie Moore* also designed the **churchyard cross**, 1921.

St Mary's Court at the SE corner of the churchyard was built as the vicarage 1868–9 by *Scott*. Gothic in red brick with blue brick bands and a stone oriel window. Adjoining on the N is the former **parish room** of 1878 also said to be by *Scott*.

Guildhall

Lowgate and Alfred Gelder Street

An initiative of Sir Alfred Gelder when Lord Mayor. Initially the idea was to extend *Cuthbert Brodrick*'s Town Hall (*see* topic box, p. 54) to replace the early C19 courts and provide a larger council chamber and much-needed additional office space. The site was provided by the purchase and demolition of the Kingston gas works, and a competition for the design held in 1903 was won by *Edwin Cooper*, of *Russell, Cooper, Davis & Mallows*. Then only thirty, this was his first major commission, and like many of his major civic buildings was in the style of English Baroque of the early C18.

Building work began in 1905 and the Law Courts were completed three years later. When the next stage, comprising offices and the Council Chamber, was nearing completion in 1911 Cooper managed to persuade the council to demolish Brodrick's Town Hall and replace it with a new Guildhall. This was built 1913–16.

35. Guildhall and Law Courts, Alfred Gelder Street, figure of Maritime Prowess by Albert H. Hodge

Cuthbert Brodrick's Town Hall

Won in competition in 1861 and built 1862–5, *Brodrick*'s Town Hall [36] was Venetian in character, rather fussy and lacking the monumentality and civic grandeur of his Leeds Town Hall. It had two tiers of large semi-circular-headed windows throughout, separated by columns on the main front and pilasters on the sides. The projecting central entrance bay was topped by a tall tower surmounted by a large stone dome. The exterior was highly ornamented, and inside Brodrick lavished decoration on the entrance hall and staircase, mayor's reception room and council chamber. The grand imperial staircase was 'composed of red Mansfield stone steps, Caen stone perforated balustrades and Sicilian marble hand rails'; above was an 'elegant arcade, formed by clustered pillars of Mansfield stone, decorated to represent rouge royal, the bases Egyptian green and Aberdeen granite'. Pilasters with 'painted arabesque ornaments of the light and chaste style of Louis XVI' decorated the reception room. The domed cupola from the top of the tower of Brodrick's building can be seen in Pearson Park (*see* Walk 6, p. 148) and other salvaged stones form a war memorial at Brantingham (10 m. w).

36. Town Hall, Lowgate, by Cuthbert Brodrick, 1862–5; lithograph by Goddard & Son

37. Guildhall and Law Courts, Alfred Gelder Street, by Edwin Cooper, 1905–16; sculpture by Albert H. Hodge

Exterior

Architecturally it is a building of two parts, the Law Courts and council offices with their main façade to Alfred Gelder Street, and the ceremonial Guildhall fronting Lowgate. What impresses most is the elevation to Alfred Gelder Street [37]. This is thirty-five bays long, chiefly of Ancaster stone and as Pevsner commented 'would look convincing in an Italian city where they did their *stile Vittorio Emmanuele* like that'. But this can only be viewed obliquely along the street. How much better it would have been set along one side of an open square.

The massive three-bay centre block, the principal entrance to the Law Courts, has a giant recessed arch on Composite columns with the seated figure of 'Law' on the projecting prow of a boat over the doorway. The carving is by *Albert H. Hodge,* a Scottish sculptor who worked elsewhere with Cooper. The centre block is flanked by fifteen-bay colonnades of giant Composite columns of Darley Dale stone above a rusticated first storey. The colonnades terminate against large rusticated end pavilions which are topped with colossal groups of sculpture, also by *Hodge.* These, called the 'Daughters of Neptune', are what really draw attention to the building. At the w end is depicted 'Maritime Prowess' [35], a female figure standing at the prow of a boat drawn by seahorses, and at the E end 'Strength', Britannia in a chariot accompanied by lions.

The County, Sessions and Police Courts each have a separate entrance from the street with elaborate trophies, again by *Hodge,* in the

Hull's Victorian Sculptors – Earles and Keyworths

Two local families of sculptors, the Earles and the Keyworths, are responsible for most of the public and monumental sculpture to be seen in the city. *George Earle* (1748–1827), a York stonemason, moved to Hull in the 1770s. Here he married Mary, daughter of Jeremiah Hargrave, carver and architect. Their son *John Earle* (1779–1863) was a prolific stonemason, sculptor and architect, designing amongst other buildings the Pilot Offices and Ferres Hospital. It was John's son *Thomas Earle* (1810–76) who became a sculptor of more than local significance. For at least a dozen years from *c.* 1831 he was an assistant to Sir Francis Chantrey, and then set up his own studio in London. Earle received many commissions from Hull, including the statues of Queen Victoria [110] and Prince Albert in Pearson Park and Edward I in the Guildhall, and the Ferres and other memorials in Holy Trinity church.

Earle's main rivals in his home town were *William Day Keyworth sen.* (1817–96) and his son *William Day Keyworth jun.* (1843–1902). Keyworth sen. was the son of *Joseph Keyworth,* a Hull stonemason who had also worked for a time in Chantrey's studio. Trained by Henry Weekes, Chantrey's senior modeller, Keyworth sen. specialized in portrait busts of which a number can be seen in the Guildhall. His son was more talented and like Thomas Earle had a studio in London where he received major commissions including the monument to Sir Rowland Hill in Westminster Abbey. Back at Hull Keyworth jun. carved the decorative frieze on Brodrick's Town Hall and five statues inside the building including those of Michael de la Pole (Guildhall), Andrew Marvell (now outside Holy Trinity church) and William Wilberforce (outside Wilberforce House) [65].

38. Law Courts, Alfred Gelder Street, cast-iron gates to Police Court, 1905–8

round-headed archways, and handsome cast-iron gates [38]. Lots of high-quality detail. The windows to the first floor have open pediments, alternately segmental and triangular with winged cherubs' heads below. The same motif is repeated on alternate capitals of the colonnade and on the cast-iron rainwater heads along with the three crowns of Hull.

The treatment of the Guildhall is simpler and the contrast can be seen best along the side elevations to Alfred Gelder Street and Hanover Square, particularly the latter with its starkly unadorned openings. It probably reflects a change in style on Cooper's part, rather than just a wish to emphasize a different stage in the building. The high, symmetrically placed clock tower of three stages bears great similarities to that on Marylebone Town Hall, London, for which Cooper was chosen as architect in 1911. The middle stage has an open Corinthian arcade, and the recessed top stage is surmounted by four putti supporting a small time-ball.

The entrance or Lowgate elevation is of nine bays with an upper recessed portico of coupled Composite columns with pediment. The s elevation on Alfred Gelder Street has a similar but smaller portico.

Interior

The grand ceremonial entrance hall with its avenue of marble pillars and Victorian busts, chiefly by *W.D. Keyworth jun.*, is not as impressive as it should be, nor is the handsome marble staircase which is rather tucked away. As planned the staircase would have been reached from the broad passageway to what is now the side door from Alfred Gelder Street, which has a fine small octagonal entrance hall walled in marble with figures in full-sized niches. At the foot of the stairs is a statue of Edward I by *Thomas Earle* (*see* topic box p. 56).

The principal rooms are on the first floor. At the E end is the **Banqueting Room** running the full width of the Guildhall. Lit by large full-height round-headed windows to the N and S and roof-lights in the barrel-vaulted ceiling, it has dark panelling introduced in the 1920s and portraits of civic dignitaries. Unfortunately *Frank Brangwyn*'s scheme of the 1930s to cover the E and W walls, above the panelling, was reject-ed by the council.* Heraldic stained glass by *A.L.Wilkinson*, 1956–8, replacing windows destroyed by a bomb in 1941. The adjoining **Reception Room** is cube-shaped with a central glazed dome. The walls, partly covered by dark walnut panelling of the 1920s, are divided up by pairs of fluted Corinthian pilasters supporting a rich cornice. The lobby area to the W has murals of 1953 by a local artist, *Patricia Field*, at either end. Nearby is the **Civic Suite** comprising three rooms reserved for the use of the Lord Mayor and Lady Mayoress with fittings designed by *Edwin Cooper*. The rooms have oak panelling and chimneypieces in a 'Wrenaissance' style enriched with heavy swags carved with seaweed, rope, fruits and flowers. Some of the furniture is of *c.* 1950 by *Gordon Russell*.

The most ornate room is the **Council Chamber**, completed in 1911 [39]. It has a huge coffered dome in the centre resting on four coffered arches supported by grey marble columns with elaborate Composite capitals enhanced as on the exterior with cherubs' heads and crowns. Under three of the arches are murals by *Harry Watson* who like Cooper came from Scarborough. The lunette of the fourth arch has stained glass with the city's arms. Excellent woodwork throughout including the original benches, their ends decorated with suitable maritime themes, and over the four doorways is carved a series of ships.

The original entrance to the **Law Courts** from Alfred Gelder Street opens into another marble-lined octagonal lobby leading to a broad passage and a fine marble staircase. Here is a statue of Michael de la Pole by *Keyworth jun.* At least two of the larger **Court Rooms** (now disused) retain their original oak fittings and late C17-style plasterwork to the barrel-vaulted ceilings, trophied panels and royal arms. The rooms are lit by semicircular windows and a series of circular domed roof-lights.

---

*Brangwyn's cartoons for the murals are in the Ferens Art Gallery.

39. Guildhall, Council Chamber, by Edwin Cooper, 1911

Queen Victoria Square

40. Maritime Museum (Dock Office), Queen Victoria Square, by Christopher G. Wray, 1868–71

Queen Victoria Square at the heart of the city contains three major buildings, the Maritime Museum (Dock Office) [40], the City Hall and Ferens Art Gallery [46]. The square was laid out 1901–2 following the clearance of an area of close-built streets of shops, offices and public houses. In the centre is a fine bronze **statue** of Queen Victoria, 1903, by *H.C. Fehr* with supporting figures, more than life-size, on a plinth designed by *J.S. Gibson*.

Maritime Museum

Built 1868–71 for the Hull Dock Company, it was converted for the museum in 1975 after a century in use as a dock office. The third and last of the port's purpose-built dock offices, it replaced the Georgian building that still stands on Dock Office Row at the N end of High Street (*see* Walk 1, p. 96). A larger, more central building was needed by the mid 1860s because of the additional docks and great increase in shipping.

HULL MARITIME MUSEUM

The little-known *Christopher George Wray* won the competition to design the new office in 1866. One-time architect to the British government in Bengal, Wray designed a large hotel in Cairo but no other major building in England.

He skilfully utilized what was an awkward triangular site overlooking Queens Dock and Princes Dock. The long curved front to Queen's Gardens is of nine bays, with shorter straight frontages of seven bays to Queen Victoria Square and New Cross Street. They terminate in rounded corners, each of three bays, with tall domed drums above. The building, of two principal storeys with a lesser third storey and basement, is in the Venetian style with a wealth of sculptured decoration, much of it on a maritime theme. *John Underwood* of London was responsible for the principal sculptures [41] and provided models for the others, and *Thomas Frith* of Hull carved the exterior capitals, friezes and decorative panels. The facing stone is Ancaster, with the basement of the harder-wearing Bramley Fall stone and the sculptures of Portland stone.

Exterior. The pilasters and columns of the ground floor are of the Roman Ionic order with rusticated bands; those of the first floor are of the Corinthian order, and a Composite order is applied to the tall drums of the domes. The windows to the ground and first floor are round-headed and those to the second floor are circular and placed in the decorative frieze. The end bays on each front have a full-height arch supported by broad rusticated pilasters framing the windows. The entrance on the w front is emphasized by a slightly projecting portico with paired Ionic columns and, above, pairs of Corinthian columns topped by a triangular pediment incorporating figures representing the Humber, Commerce and Prosperity, with two sea gods above, one with a rudder, the other with a sextant, flanking an elaborate display of the arms of the Dock Company, Trinity House and the Corporation. On the E front the entrance is through a portico with an open pediment supported on single Ionic columns. Above on the entablature is another sculptured group with Neptune and his wife Amphitrite riding seahorses, with the adopted arms of the Hull Dock Company (really the late C18 royal arms) in the centre.

41. Maritime Museum, w front, sculpture by John Underwood, 1868–71

42. Maritime Museum, railings, designed by C.G. Wray, 1869

43. Maritime Museum, Court Room, putti holding arms of Antwerp and Dunkirk

Mermaids and mermen are in the spandrels of the windows in the end bays and over the corner windows; there are scallop shells over the ground-floor windows and dolphins appear everywhere. They are ridden by putti in the frieze and they support the clock and the cupolas on top of the corner domes. Dolphin heads also decorate the tridents that with the harpoons make up the excellent contemporary cast-iron railings that surround the building [42]. The lavish decoration contributed to the high cost, almost £90,000, far in excess of the £15,000 originally estimated.

Interior. Recessed steps flanked by niches lead from Queen Victoria Square into the impressive **entrance hall** filled by a grand imperial **staircase** of Portland stone with elaborate wrought-iron balustrading by the *Midland Architectural Metal Workers Co.* of Coventry. There is a hint of a sea creature in the foliage design of the balusters that is repeated in the band around the staircase hall. Again there are maritime references everywhere, from the starfish on the brackets supporting the upper landing to the intricate diamond-patterned plasterwork of the coved ceiling in the form of knotted rope to suggest a fishing net. The frieze is decorated with garlands containing the cipher of the Hull Dock Company.

On the **first-floor landing** over the doorways to the right and left are sculptured groups displaying a winged staff and tridents between pairs of seahorses. To the left a passageway, bordered like the landing and staircase hall with decorative tiles by *Maw & Co.*, leads to the most sumptuous room in the building, the **Court Room**. With a curving outer wall the room occupies two storeys of the E front and is 70 ft (21.3 metres) long, 29 ft (8.8 metres) wide and over 21 ft (6.4 metres) high. Tall half-columns of Scagliola imitating red marble with elaborate

Corinthian capitals divide up the walls, and the round-arched windows on the outer wall are flanked by Corinthian pilasters with circular windows above supported by well-fed putti holding shields [43]. The putti continue above the doors on the side walls. Their shields display the arms of the ports, chiefly of the Hanseatic League, that traded with Hull, and as Ivan Hall has commented, 'the brilliant figuring of the pine doors', here and elsewhere in the Dock Office, 'are clear reminders of Hull's pre-eminent place in the Baltic timber trade'.

The heavy moulded ceiling is divided into three sections, each with a central 'sunburner' of decorative pierced metalwork. Starfish, scallop shells, seaweed and pearls decorate the borders around the circular openings, and the ceiling ribs are elaborately patterned.

On the **ground floor** the chief room is the **Wharfage Room**, below the Court Room and with the same curved outer wall. Now occupied by the whaling display, it is difficult to appreciate the scale of the room, 100 ft (30.5 metres) long, and its elaborate internal decoration. Here merchants and ship-owners and their clerks, and ships' officers dealt with the Dock Company and the public entrance was directly from Queens Dock. Doric pilasters divide up the walls, the capitals decorated by an alternate pattern of scallop shells and dolphins' faces, and pairs of Doric pillars with the same decoration partially screen off the end bays. The ceiling is divided into seven panels with the ribs or beams radiating at an angle from the shorter inner to the longer outer wall. The end and centre panels have circular openings with decorative sunburners. The circular room at the N end was once open to the Wharfage Room, divided off by the pairs of Doric columns now incorporated in the wall. It was the superintendent's office, which is the best-preserved of the round rooms at the corners of the Dock Office.

City Hall

One of the aims of laying out Queen Victoria Square was to provide a setting for a much needed grand public hall for music, meetings and civic events. Rather than seek a suitable design through competition the council put its faith in the abilities of the City Architect, *Joseph H. Hirst*, and they were well repaid with an imposing Edwardian Baroque composition. Hirst's remit was to provide a large concert hall on the first floor with sixteen shops and a café below, partly to accommodate businesses displaced by demolition and partly to secure a regular income for the building. Work began in 1903, and in 1906 it was decided to extend the building w to incorporate an art gallery (Victoria Galleries, now the Mortimer Suite) with shops below. The City Hall was opened in 1909 and the art gallery in 1910. Badly damaged in the blitz in 1941, it was restored and reopened in 1950.

Exterior. Three storeys of ashlar with a copper-covered roof to the concert hall. The entrance (E) front is of seven wide bays with a Tuscan porte cochère with balcony. Then comes a recessed portico with two

44. City Hall, panel by Gilbert Seale

Composite columns, flanked by pairs of identical columns supporting a large open segmental pediment with a swagged cartouche of the city's arms. Above is a tall drum crowned by a copper-covered dome with a Tuscan cupola. The drum, composed of Ionic pilasters, has four projecting pedimented tabernacles each with a seated female figure representing the Arts by *Gilbert Seale*.

The N and S elevations above the shops are divided up by large plain pilasters, between which the prominent canopied windows are flanked by smaller Composite pilasters. Segmental pediments emphasize the side entrances with their double doorways. The original symmetrical elevations were altered for the addition of the art gallery. Here there are no windows and the façade above the shops is divided by Composite pilasters into twenty-six panels, each having a carved portrait of a 'great' artist, also by *Seale.* There is much carved decoration with figures just below the frieze flanking the second-storey windows along each side, and more detailed scenes along the E front and over the entrances to the Mortimer Suite [44].

Interior. The entrance from the porte cochère was designed to impress with a grand imperial staircase in contrasting marbles rising to the second floor [45]. Here the coved ceiling has ornate drops, angel corbels and a central dome and flanking sidelights with delicate Art Nouveau glazing. On the ground floor are statues of Dr John Alderson, 1831, by *Thomas Earle*, Daniel Sykes, 1833, by *James Loft* of Hull, and James Clay, 1875, and Anthony Bannister, 1879, both by *W.D. Keyworth jun.*

On the first floor is the large galleried concert hall with seating originally for 3,000. The theatre architect *Frank Matcham* was consulted on its design and it shows in the enriched coved ceiling, the great Diocletian windows and the marble columned arcades to the main floor and gallery. Behind the stage the seating rises into a full-height recess filled with a vast organ case which partly obscures a plaster

45. City Hall, staircase, by Joseph H. Hirst, 1903–9

classical-style frieze of figures in medieval dress. The main reception room (Victoria Bar) on the second floor, with coffered and glazed dome and tall Corinthian columns, opens out onto a balcony overlooking Queen Victoria Square, the scene of many civic celebrations.

At the w end of the building at the centre of the Mortimer Suite is the former sculpture gallery. A delightful circular domed room, with decorative plasterwork, divided up by Doric columns, between which rounded arches open to half-domed recesses and the entrances to the former picture galleries.

Ferens Art Gallery

Built on the site of the church of St John the Evangelist of 1791, which had been extended and remodelled by *Cuthbert Brodrick* in 1863. The church closed in 1917 and it was acquired by Thomas R. Ferens, who gave it to the town with £50,000 to build an art gallery on the site. *S.N. Cooke & E.C. Davies* of London were chosen as architects and the gallery was built 1926–7 [46]. A simple restrained classical cube of fine ashlar. The two-storey projecting entrance block has a recessed portico with two Corinthian columns *in antis*, a balustrade above and side bays with round-headed windows flanked by plain pilasters. Lower wings to left and right have blank ashlar walls decorated with swags.

46. Ferens Art Gallery, Queen Victoria Square, by S.N. Cooke & E.C. Davies, 1926–7

47. Ferens Art Gallery, central gallery, by Cooke & Davies, 1926–7

The original heavy carved bronze doors under a pedimented door-case give entry to an elegant, well-preserved interior which retains much of its refined Neoclassical detail. The seven original top-lit picture galleries (one now the shop) surround the central octagonal sculpture gallery. The last, with marble floor and walls, has columns supporting a balcony with a dome above [47]. There is a further picture gallery over the entrance hall.

The art gallery, which has an excellent wide-ranging permanent collection including many maritime paintings, greatly benefited from the major extension of 1990–1, part of the adjacent Princes Quay Shopping Centre development by *Hugh Martin & Partners* of Edinburgh. This added three larger galleries, a live arts space and a café with an open-air court overlooking the former dock.

Other buildings of note around the square: At the sw corner the ornate **Punch Hotel**, 1896, by *Smith, Brodrick & Lowther* [48]. Brick and much terracotta in an extravaganza of Gothic and Jacobean detail with tracery, shaped and stepped gables and good lettering. Burmantofts faience panels by *E. Caldwell Spruce*. N of the City Hall is **Queens House**, 1951–2, by *Kenneth Wakeford*, a large Neo-Georgian block with clock tower, bounded by Paragon Street, King Edward Street, Jameson Street and Chapel Street. The best of the immediate post-war develop-

48. Punch Hotel, Queen Victoria Square, by Smith, Brodrick & Lowther, 1896

ments. A plaque at the SE corner marks the position of the tower of the Prudential Building, 1903, by *Alfred Waterhouse*, destroyed in the Second World War. It was a grander version of its neighbour the **Yorkshire Bank**, *c.* 1901, by *B. S. Jacobs*, with an addition of 1916. Mainly terracotta with lots of Renaissance detail and a corner turret with a two-tier cupola. Finally, to the left of the Ferens Art Gallery is **Monument Buildings**, 1907–8, by *William Bell* of the North Eastern Railway Co., stone-fronted in a 'Dutch Renaissance' style.

Trinity House

Trinity House Lane

Trinity House [50] (no public access) comprises the most extensive, and architecturally significant, group of older secular buildings in Hull. It covers the site of the Whitefriars (Carmelite friary), dissolved 1539 and given to the institution by Thomas Ferres in 1621, its premises facing onto Trinity House Lane, Posterngate and Princes Dock Side. In addition Trinity House developed the buildings on the s side of Whitefriargate (*see* Walk 2, p. 102).

The Guild or Brotherhood of Masters and Pilots, Seamen of the Trinity House of Kingston upon Hull, started as a religious guild in 1369, became a guild of mariners in the mid C15, and received a royal charter in 1541. The board of Trinity House consists of six Assistants, ten Elder Brethren and two Wardens, chosen each year from the brethren, all 'master mariners'.

49. Trinity House,
main entrance, 1753

51. Trinity House, court room, exterior, by Joseph Page, 1773

A timber-framed and tiled guildhall, almshouses and a chapel were built 1465–72 on land leased from the Carmelites, probably near the junction of Trinity House Lane and Posterngate where the main buildings are now located. In the C17 and C18 Trinity House increasingly took control of shipping and navigation on the Humber and along the East Coast, and also undertook charitable work. The still-flourishing **Trinity House Navigation School** was established in 1787. The school occupies buildings of the 1840s and later within the older complex. These were largely reconstructed and enlarged unsympathetically in the mid C20 by *H. Andrew*.

The present buildings that make up **Trinity House** are grouped around a courtyard. The oldest part, possibly incorporating the medieval core, is on the w side. Here on the w front are four plain pilasters to the ground floor, evidently part of a late C17 single-storey façade. The other three sides of the courtyard were built as **almshouses** in 1753–9, probably by *Jeremiah Hargrave*. The main front on Trinity House Lane [50] is of nine bays with an impressive central three-bay pediment filled with a richly carved coat of arms and the reclining figures of Neptune and Britannia by *Hargrave*, 1758–9. Below is a wide doorway with Doric columns and a segmental pediment. The stonework is by *William Rushworth*. To the left around the corner the main building continues for seven bays along Posterngate. Originally of exposed brick, it was stuccoed in 1828. The windows to the street light the corridors, those of the former pensioners' rooms looking onto the inner courtyard.

To the right of the main front was a chapel by *Sir William Chambers* built 1772. Chambers had family connections with Hull, and was born

52. Trinity House, court room, interior, by Joseph Page, 1773

in Göteborg where his father was a broker dealing with Hull merchants and mariners. Chambers arranged for the portrait of George III to be painted for the court room by *Sir George Chalmers Bt.* in 1775–6. As a result Chalmers settled in Hull by 1778 and spent several years painting members of the merchant community. Chambers's chapel was demolished in 1844 when the present offices were built by *William Foale* with a three-bay stone façade to Trinity House Lane. Foale, who was architect and surveyor to Trinity House, also designed the seven-bay block on the right for the Inland Revenue Office, 1865.

Inside Trinity House the finest rooms are the **court room** and **council chamber** on the first floor of the w range. These were remodelled by *Joseph Page* in 1773 when he heightened the walls of the existing buildings. The **council chamber** was gutted by a fire in 1924 and the Adam-style ceiling is a replacement. The chimneypiece is early Victorian. The spacious **court room** is unaltered and has two elegant Venetian windows overlooking the courtyard [51]. These are Ionic inside and Doric outside. The windows to the rooms below are tripartite. The w side of the room has a segmental recess with three round-headed windows. Excellent doorcases by *Jeremiah Hargrave* and a fine marble chimney-

53. Trinity House, reading room, interior, by William Foale, 1843

piece with Ionic columns and brightly coloured Scagliola inlays. The best feature of the room is the coved ceiling with delicate stucco decoration in an early Adam or Wyatt style [52]. The painted decoration on the coving, of ships, tritons and foliage, was by a certain '*Florio, Italiano*' in 1845. The other rooms on the first floor, the lobby, the fascinating well-stocked museum with unusual fretwork-patterned ceiling, and the oval top-lit reading room [53], are of 1843 as is the main oak staircase, with its marbled walls, leading to the court and council rooms.

The **chapel** was built on a new site to the w of the older buildings in 1839–43 [54]. It was designed by *H.F. Lockwood* in a Greek Revival style and cost £3,500. A simple rectangle with stuccoed exterior. The E front facing Trinity House is of stone with a pediment and Corinthian pilasters. In front a statue of Oceanus, reclining, by *Thomas Earle*, 1831. Originally on top of the Trinity Almshouses, Posterngate (*see* Walk 2, p. 107). The public w front is more austere with a tall porch flanked by antae and a tripartite lunette window above. The Neoclassical **interior** is spectacular, particularly the ceiling. The centre square is ceiled by a boldly ribbed and coffered dome, to the E over the altar is an apse with coffered half-dome and to the w, over the gallery, a coffered barrel-vault. Corinthian columns and pilasters throughout, the ornate capitals displaying maritime motifs. The apse columns are of brown Ashford marble, white elsewhere with a multicoloured floor. The chapel is lit by lunettes to the N, S and W. W gallery on square pillars to accommodate the boys from the Navigation School. Staircase with delicate cast-iron balusters. The **pulpit** of *c.* 1840 is square, with bronze mountings. The handsome **altar table** was designed by *Chambers* as part of the furnishings for his 1772 chapel. A marble slab supported on the outspread wings of a great eagle. There are original oak **box pews. Stained glass**. E window 1841 by *M. Stangroom*, Raphael's Christ of the Transfiguration, isolated above a landscape. **Monuments**. Original plaster model of the memorial in Holy Trinity church to Thomas Ferres by *Thomas Earle*, 1857. In the entrance the resited **gravestone** of John Ward, Hull's greatest marine artist, who died of cholera in 1849.

54. Trinity House, chapel, by H.F. Lockwood, 1839–43; figure of Oceanus by Thomas Earle, 1831

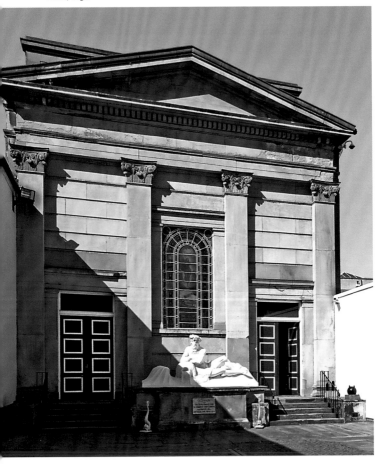

University of Hull

Cottingham Road

Architecturally the University of Hull has the lion's share of the best C20 buildings in the city, located on one of the most pleasing and well-maintained modern campuses in Britain [55].

The University was founded, as a University College, following a donation of £250,000 from Thomas R. Ferens, Managing Director of Reckitts, in 1925. He had already provided the site, and the city council gave a further £150,000 for the building work. The architect chosen was *William A. Forsyth* of *Forsyth & Maule* (later *Forsyth & Partners*), who had just designed a new teaching block at the Methodist Kingswood School, Bath, funded by, and named after, Ferens. Building work began in 1927 and the first full-time students arrived in October 1928. The University College became a full university in 1954.

Rather than design the University College as a single structure Forsyth chose to plan it as a series of detached blocks set in an extensive

55. University of Hull campus, Cottingham Road

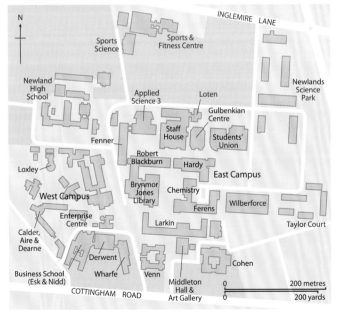

56. Venn Building, University of Hull, by William A. Forsyth, 1928

formal layout. The initial aim was for 1,500 students, but numbers rarely exceeded 200 before the Second World War, and only two buildings were completed, leaving between them a yawning gap where a great hall was intended. Following a rapid post-war expansion to nearly 800 students by the late 1940s and a target of 2,000 by the early 1960s, new buildings were added. Although conforming to Forsyth's original plan, and to his design, these were spread over the campus and the original formal layout gave way to 'a loosely-knit pattern of windswept open spaces punctuated by buildings and severed by service roads'.

In 1958 *Sir Leslie Martin* succeeded Forsyth & Partners as University architect, and his development plan skilfully unified and brought order to the disparate campus. Martin's objective was to arrange the new buildings 'in such a way that they created a new environment by forming a new forecourt, by forming new enclosed spaces, by organizing pedestrian routes through these and by removing cars to the periphery'. He created the heart of the present campus, and in addition to buildings to his own designs, he commissioned others by innovative young architects of the period including *Peter Moro, Peter Womersley*, the *Architects' Co-Partnership, Trevor Dannatt* and *Isi Metzstein* of *Gillespie, Kidd & Coia*. As consultant architect Martin had a few basic requirements, notably the use of brick and some conformity in elevation, but he had complete faith in his chosen architects and gave them a largely free hand.

An ambitious plan for 7,000 students by 1980, generous funding and the acquisition of additional land to the E of the main campus in 1967 enabled Martin to produce a development plan for a major extension that incorporated many of his ideas on spatial relationships. The new buildings were to be laid within a grid and linked by one single wide

57. Larkin Building, University of Hull, by Leslie Martin, 1965–7

pedestrian mall running N–S and two cross routes going E–W and linking into the original campus. Only the Wilberforce Building and the
present Students' Union were completed before funding was halted in
the mid 1970s, leaving an unsightly wasteland to the NE. *Robert Hughes*
of *Shepheard Epstein Hunter* took over from Martin in 1993 and his
development plan the following year focused on improving this area
with part of the site taken for the Newland Science Park.

In 2002 the University of Hull purchased the adjoining W campus
from the University of Lincoln. This was originally the site of
the Kingston upon Hull Municipal Training College, opened 1913.
From 1976 it was the headquarters of Hull College of Higher Education
and its successor institutions. The last of these, the University of
Humberside and Lincolnshire, became the University of Lincoln in
2001 when it relocated to that city. A master plan for the integration and
development of the two sites was prepared by *John McAslan & Partners*
in 2008.

East Campus. Looking N at the main entrance from Cottingham
Road one is faced by a contrasting scene. On the left and right are the
two original Neo-Early Georgian blocks by *Forsyth*, the **Venn** [56] and
Cohen Buildings, 1928, square plan, of dark red brick and with inner
courtyards; in the middle is the low, relatively small **Middleton Hall
and Art Gallery**, of brick also, but windowless and severely cubical.
These and the long range of the Larkin Building behind are by *Sir Leslie
Martin*, 1965–7. The interior of Middleton Hall is a cool classical space,
now used for public lectures, concerts and degree ceremonies but originally intended also as a theatre. It is surrounded by Martin's typically
broad corridors. (The Art Gallery has an excellent collection of C20
paintings and sculpture.) The **Larkin Building** [57] is three storeys,

58. Brynmor Jones Library, University of Hull, by Castle, Park, Dean, Hook, 1966–9

with even bands of windows, not at all assertive, and has wings at the ends projecting to the N. An archway through the building leads to the large central square.

Projecting into the square on the E side is **Chemistry**, 1955, a refined version of the original 1920s buildings (with plainer N extension of 1963) by *Forsyth & Partners*. At its SE corner *Shepheard Epstein Hunter* added the **Ferens Building**, 1994–6, of brick in a simplified interpretation of Forsyth's design with a glazed link to the Larkin Building. The W side of the square is dominated by the **Brynmor Jones Library** [58], a red brick block of 1957–9, still Neo-Early Georgian in spirit, by *Forsyth & Partners* with a major award-winning addition of 1966–9 by *Castle, Park, Dean, Hook*. This is the most prominent feature of the campus, eight storeys high over a two-storey basement, the top floor providing superb views across the city. The ground floor and the first floor project to the W; the second floor is considerably recessed; floors three to eight project again, but less. The motif of these upper floors is the boxed-out upper half of the window wall of each floor, the windows themselves as bands being canted inward. The building is air-conditioned and this window arrangement reduces the impact of the summer sun. The same architects also built a small N extension to the older building. It has to the N a row of six canted bays. Over the main entrance to the library and the entrance to the Education Centre at the s end of the 1950s building are sculptures by the Austrian artist *Willi Soukop*.

To the N the **Robert Blackburn Building**, by the *Architects' Co-Partnership*, 1965–7, is connected by a projecting left wing with the library and at its other end abuts against the older **Hardy Building**, 1959–63 by *Forsyth & Partners*. The Robert Blackburn Building, topped by an ungainly concrete 'control tower', runs parallel with the Larkin Building, and with strip windows, here emphasized by stone bands, shares something of its character.

The central walkway continues northwards through an archway and ends abruptly with the dark red brick **Staff House**, 1951–3 by *Forsyth & Partners*, still Neo-Early Georgian, which forms the E side of a square with the **Fenner Building** on the w and **Applied Science 3** on the N, both of the same build as the Robert Blackburn Building on the s, but lower, of darker brick and white bands. At the back of Applied Science 3 a lecture theatre projects, its surfaces of raw concrete. In the foyer is a **mural** by *Edward Bawden*, 1964.

To the E of Staff House is the stylish **Gulbenkian Centre** [59], 1969–70, by *Peter Moro & Partners* (partner in charge: *Michael Heard*). Octagon-shaped, the chamfered corners giving the building space in a rather cramped setting. Concrete and brick with a copper roof raised in the centre. Much of the interior is taken up by a teaching theatre, the

59. Gulbenkian Centre, University of Hull, by Peter Moro & Partners, 1969–70

first for a university drama department, and a pioneer audio-visual centre for training in television and radio acting. Moro, the most successful designer of truly adaptable theatres, produced a stage of moveable blocks and towers that can be made into any configuration, while the principal space is entirely spanned by counterweighted flies. This allowed complete flexibility for the stage and some of the seating, but Moro fixed the lighting grid as this would be hard to manoeuvre for each new show. The Gulbenkian is one of the most important buildings by the most interesting post-war theatre specialist. Opposite, the **Wolfson Building**, 1976, by the *Napper Collerton Partnership*, six storeys, brick with porthole windows. N of the Gulbenkian Centre the **Loten Building**, a well-proportioned nine-storey brick block with recessed balconies by *Castle Park*, 1962–4.

Now the 1967 eastern extension to the campus, where the buildings are all by *Napper Architects* of Newcastle, under a succession of names. First the **Wilberforce Building**, 1968–70, a large rectangular five-storey building that has a concrete frame, pre-cast concrete cladding and white marble aggregate facing, diverging from Martin's preferred brick. The s elevation with its four projecting wings is visually the most rewarding. An open first-floor concrete walkway links it N to the **Students' Union** (University House), 1975, a long four-storey range with the usual strip windows, brick to the ground floor, upper storeys faced with copper sheeting. Glass-fronted extension with curved glass roof on the w for new entrance, café and shop, 1996–7, and new external staircase 2007. To the SE **Taylor Court**, 1991–2, a Postmodern complex of five three-storey blocks around an L-shaped courtyard. Of brick with stone and timber detail, gabled roofs and projecting semicircular balconies above the entrances.

Finally, close to the NW boundary of the university site, the elegant **Sports and Fitness Centre**, by *Peter Womersley*, 1963–5, a straightforward square glazed block with close-set, very slender concrete verticals sloping inwards from the base. To the E a traditional brick and glass range, 1991 by the *Napper Collerton Partnership*, links the main hall with *Forsyth*'s 1950 changing rooms. Nearby the functional **Sports Science block**, 2004, by *Gammond Evans Crichton Ltd.*

West Campus. The most noteworthy buildings are the original four blocks of the Municipal Training College, 1909–13 by *Crouch, Butler & Savage* of Birmingham. Known as the **Nidd**, **Esk**, **Derwent** and **Wharf Buildings** they form a pleasing group in a Neo-Wren style with Baroque influences. The centre three bays of the two-storey brick **Derwent Building** project slightly with five-bay wings to either side. Distinctive quoins of alternate brick and stone to each corner. Central stone entrance with Doric columns *in antis* flanked by stone-mullioned canted bays with balcony above. Large mullioned-and-transomed windows to the first floor. The middle window is round-headed and set in a stone framework with pilasters and an open pediment; above is a cupola. The other blocks are in a similar style with a greater elaboration

60. Business School, University of Hull, by Crouch, Butler & Savage, 1909–13;
entrance by Farrell & Clark, 2005; sculpted heads by Joe Hillier, 2007

of the brick and stone chequer decoration. Two attractive Wrenaissance former staff **houses** front Cottingham Road. The Nidd and Esk Buildings on the w side have been joined to the Derwent Building by a large curved building, faced in brick and timber, with a steel and glass front to SE, 2005, by *Farrell & Clark*. It contains a tiered lecture theatre for the **Business School** [60], the main entrance for which is a two-storey glazed entrance to the SW, by the same architects, 2007. Here are two large sculpted heads by *Joe Hillier,* 2007.

To the N of the early buildings are four three-storey blocks, 1959–63, by *Andrew Rankine,* City Architect, brick, with brick and stone quoins echoing the original buildings. They have been adapted to new uses, one for the **Enterprise Centre** with a stylish angular International Modern entrance block by *Gammond Evans Crichton,* 2008. The same firm was responsible for the curved **Calder Building**, 2006, linking *Rankine*'s **Aire** and **Dearne Buildings**, and the **Anatomy Unit**, 2005, an angular timber-clad addition to the late 1960s octagonal **Loxley Building** by *A.R. Peadon,* City Architect.

On an adjoining site to the N is **Newland High School**, 1914, by *Joseph H. Hirst,* with an impressive thirty-six-bay Neo-Early Georgian s front.

Student accommodation. Much of the student accommodation is at Cottingham (*see* p. 194) and includes **Thwaite Hall**, Thwaite Street, built *c.* 1805 and altered in 1853 for the ship-owner Thomas Wilson.

Set in magnificent landscaped grounds, it has been a University hall of residence since 1928. There were major additions by *Forsyth & Partners* in 1938 and 1948–50. **Needler Hall** (formerly Northfields), Northgate, built soon after 1780, extended with a new block facing s by 1820. For the University *Trevor Dannatt* added a low brick range in 1962–4.

Further w along Northgate is **The Lawns**, a large site which includes **Ferens Hall**, a purpose-built Neo-Georgian hall of residence by *Forsyth & Partners*, 1956–7, and the major scheme designed by *Isi Metzstein* and *Andrew MacMillan* of *Gillespie, Kidd & Coia* and built 1963–7 [23]. This highly accomplished scheme, a contrast to the traditional halls of residence, was for twelve large blocks, each for 135 students in single and double rooms, the rooms grouped round five staircases. Only six blocks and the communal centre were completed. The blocks are all essentially identical: three storeys of buff brick, as canted and staggered as possible and placed so closely together that they seem to the eye to form one long undulating wall. In 1972 Pevsner commented: 'This is certainly not cosy architecture, nor even comfortable architecture; it is tough and uncomprising, as perhaps it should be.' The Lawns, which anticipated the kind of accommodation preferred at the new universities then beginning to be built, has stood the passage of time and although not exactly comfortable it fits well into its more mature landscape.

Walks

Walk 1. The Old Town: High Street 86

Walk 2. The Old Town: West of High Street 97

Walk 3. Waterfront 111

Walk 4. Queen's Gardens and the Northern Suburb 121

Walk 5. City Centre West and Park Street 132

Walk 6. Beverley Road, Pearson Park and Spring Bank 141

Walk 7. The Avenues, Newland and Newland Park 155

Walk 8. West: Anlaby Road and Hessle Road 162

Walk 9. East: Holderness Road and Garden Village 172

Walk 10. Sutton-on-Hull 181

61. High Street looking N from Scale Lane

Walk 1.

The Old Town: High Street

This is the first of two linked walks around the Old Town, the area of the medieval walled town. Much of the original street pattern remains providing delightful vistas along narrow lanes with the sense of enclosure heightened by the flat topography.*

62. Walks 1 & 2

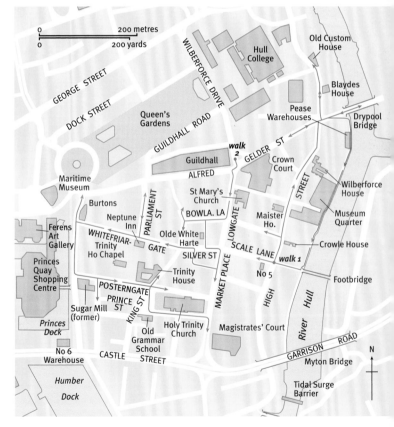

* Visitors to this fascinating area of Hull will notice that representations of many different fish have been enterprisingly incised or inlaid in metal into the pavements. These are by the artist *Gordon Young*, 1992.

High Street [61] is the place to start for it is where the town began in the mid C13. This narrow lane paved with stone setts winds N–S, following the line of the River Hull which lies immediately to the E. The street was the commercial heart of the town from its foundation until well into the C19. Here the merchants had their homes, those on the E side with warehouses behind fronting onto their private wharfs on the river, known at this point as the Old Harbour. The short lanes running E from the street to the river are called staiths, the local name for a landing place. These give access to a broad wooden walkway providing atmospheric views of the river and its setting.

The walk starts at the junction of High Street and Scale Lane. A glimpse s along High Street is all that is needed for here the older buildings have been cleared away, some destroyed in the Second World War and others demolished more recently. On the w side the brick **archways** in the boundary wall of the car park mark the position of the entrances to the narrow courtyards that were packed with houses and people in the late C18–C19. Just s of Scale Lane Staith on the E side of High Street, in the shadow of the monstrous 1960s **Oriel House**, is a mid-C17 brick warehouse. The staith leads to the exciting **swing bridge** by *McDowell & Benedetti*, under construction in 2010. The sleek curved footbridge will rotate 90 degrees at the w end and provides a link to the planned development on the E bank of which the **Premier Inn** tower by *Chetwood Associates*, 2009, is the first phase.

A short way up **Scale Lane** is No. 5 [63], Hull's only surviving timber-framed building. Probably C15, the narrow gabled front to the street is jettied on first and second floors. The side elevation is of medieval–C17 brick stretching back to fill an original burgage plot. Next, the **Manchester Arms**, a well-preserved Jacobean revival façade by *Brodrick, Lowther & Walker*, 1898, with oriel windows. Opposite stands **Burnett Avenue**, offices of the 1880s, in a Flemish Renaissance style with pilasters and a shaped gable topped with a scrolled pediment.

Now back on **High Street**, on the E side Nos. 44–46, **Danish Buildings**, demonstrate well the infilling of the long plots between the street and the river. First a block of 1858 with neat Italianate façade of brick and stone dressings by *William Botterill*, then a small courtyard behind with a five-bay, two-storey mid-C18 brick house, **Bayles House**, with pedimented doorcase and fine staircase, and finally a warehouse range. Next along High Street is **Bond 31** (Nos. 42–43), a pair of tall former warehouses dated 1828, with an arch opening to a narrow alley lined with warehouses. Here one gets a real sense of what the area would have been like in the C19.

A similar arrangement at No. 41, **Crowle House**, a mid-C19 front with behind, at right angles to the street and hidden down a narrow passage, the unexpected remnant of the house built by the merchant George Crowle in 1664. The original layout is unknown. What remains is a striking tower-like frontispiece of brick and stone with Artisan Mannerist details. The centre bay projects slightly with 'jewelled'

63. No. 5 Scale Lane, jettied timber framed building, probably C15

Corinthian pilasters to the ground and first storeys. The flanking bays have blank classical arches with stone capitals, key blocks and moulded spandrels. Decorative plaques with the initials of George Crowle and wife and the date. It is clearly the work of the same bricklayer-architect as the nearby Wilberforce House (*see* p. 92 and topic box, p. 90).

Opposite, **Ye Olde Black Boy**, early C18 with unspoilt 1920s pub interior, then set back is the other entrance to **Burnett Avenue** (*see* Scale Lane above) demonstrating how late C19 commercial buildings were developed on the maze of yards and alleyways on the w side of High Street. Next door **Dunwell's Forge**, No. 153, has a three-storey mid-C18 brick front but inside some medieval timber-framing and was once jettied. Dunwell was a shipsmith.

Across the road No. 40 (**Humberside Police Authority Headquarters**), formerly the Pacific Club by *B.S. Jacobs*, dated 1899, but built 1900–1. Jacobean Revival of red brick with a wealth of buff terracotta details, ornate doorcase and an oriel and other mullioned windows. The Pacific was set up as a meeting place and exchange for the port's many grain and oil-seed merchants. A large trading hall added at the rear in 1909 has been demolished. Look down **Bishop Lane Staith**, where amongst the former C19 warehouses on the n side is an initialled datestone of 1655, a fragment from another C17 merchant's house.

Back to High Street and make a short detour up the narrow **Bishop Lane**, named after property held here by the Archbishop of York in the C14. At the corner Nos. 1–2, two tall late C18 houses with basements, and further up a restored mid-C18 terrace of three-storey, four-bay houses (Nos. 10–13). **The Avenue** on the n side of the lane, with pilasters and

William Catlyn and Artisan Mannerism

Three buildings in Hull, Wilberforce House, Crowle House and the Olde White Harte, as well a further half-dozen in the East Riding and North Lincolnshire, are in a distinctive local version of a style that was termed 'Artisan Mannerism' by Sir John Summerson to refer to the free use of classical detail by bricklayers, masons and others.

The Hull buildings, which exhibit the influence of the Netherlands in their decorative brickwork and ornamented pilasters, can be attributed to *William Catlyn*, bricklayer-architect, son of a Warden of Hull Bricklayers' Company. Catlyn was working for the 1st Lord Burlington at Londesborough, East Riding, in 1661, and two years later was con-tracted to rebuild part of the Charterhouse at Hull. That same year an almshouse was built at Worlaby, North Lincolnshire for John, Lord Belasyse, then Governor of Hull, almost identical in detail to Wilberforce House. In 1667 Catlyn took an apprentice from Worlaby and by the 1670s he 'had great undertakings' in Lincolnshire which included Brigg Grammar School. Back at Hull in the 1670s–80s he built a chapel at the Charterhouse, 'beautified' the Guildhall and oversaw the building of the Market Cross. Catlyn bequeathed his 'Book of Architecture of Ancient Rome' to the library of Holy Trinity church, Hull.

terracotta decoration, is another example of a turn-of-the-century Old Town development utilizing an existing pattern of alleyways. Its other front, dated 1900 and decorated with terracotta swags, is on the w side of **High Street** opposite a good range of former warehouses well restored for student accommodation. Nos. 37–38 are a handsome early C19 pair of four storeys, retaining their central loading doors and bars to ground-floor windows; No. 37 has metal tie-plates dated 1829.

Slightly set back on the w side of High Street is **Maister House** (National Trust) built 1744–5 for Henry Maister, a wealthy merchant. *Lord Burlington* was consulted about the design, which is attributed to *Joseph Page* who was responsible for the stuccowork. Victorian bays were replaced at the restoration by *Francis Johnson* for the Georgian Society for East Yorkshire in 1968. The exterior is austere, a five-bay, three-storey brick façade only relieved by a pedimented Ionic stone doorcase, but inside is a magnificent staircase that Richard Garnier has attributed to *William Kent* [8]. The view up the stairwell through three storeys to the roof lantern is spectacular. The stone staircase with an elaborate wrought-iron balustrade by *Robert Bakewell* rises round three sides of the square hall to the first-floor landing. The walls are decorat-ed with stucco panels, brackets for busts, festoons of shells and swags of drapery suspended from lion masks. A niche contains a statue of Ceres by *Sir Henry Cheere, c.* 1754. Above is a square gallery with ironwork

64. Wilberforce House, High Street, staircase plasterwork, attributed to Giuseppe Cortese, *c.* 1760

balustrade reached by a separate staircase. The soffit of the gallery is supported on moulded brackets which divide it into coffered squares, each containing a large decorative rose. Above the gallery a coved ceiling with ornate stuccowork rises to an octagonal opening and the glazed roof lantern. Good doorways throughout and a first-floor room with a modest Rococo ceiling and fine chimneypiece of *c.* 1760 with pretty overmantel.

After the plain exterior of Maister House comes **Phoenix Chambers**, No. 161, another late C19 red brick and terracotta creation by *B.S. Jacobs*. Then back across the road No. 36, the imposing former **Corn Exchange**, 1856, by *Bellamy & Hardy* of Lincoln. (Their names are on the fine iron gates cast by *Joseph Wilson* of Hull.) Massive Italianate stone front, three storeys, three bays. High portal with two fluted Corinthian columns flanking the entrance arch. Large bearded mask to the keystone and agricultural motifs carved on the spandrels. Tripartite windows, but big semicircular windows to the top storey. It is now part of the **Hull and East Riding Museum** (Archaeology), one of the group of buildings that make up the so-called **Museums Quarter** entered a little further N along High Street through gates that open onto Chapel Lane Staith and an attractive formal garden. The three worn Portland stone **statues** by *W.D. Keyworth jun.*, 1883, of Minerva and the recumbent Art and Science, were originally on the Royal Institution, Albion Street, demolished after bomb damage in the Second World War. Set back along the river is the **Streetlife Museum** (Transport), 1989 and later, by *Ian Colquhoun*, City Architect, a long glass-fronted arcaded building given a distinctive character by the series of rectangular hipped mini-roofs on top. Fronting onto High Street and incorporated into this cultural quarter is **WISE** (University of Hull Wilberforce Institute for the study of Slavery and Emancipation) housed in Oriel Chambers, 1879 by *W. Botterill & Son*, with extension by *Hull Property Design Practice*, 2005.

Set back behind a C17 rusticated brick wall is **Wilberforce House Museum** (slavery and emancipation). In the 1680s the official residence of the Governor and Deputy Governor of Hull. It was owned by the Wilberforce family from 1730 to 1832, and opened as a museum in 1906. In the forecourt is a **statue** by *W.D. Keyworth jun.*, 1884, of William Wilberforce who was born here in 1759 [65]. The house was built 'new from the ground' *c.* 1660 by Hugh Lister (d. 1664), a merchant who spent time in Holland and France as a young man. Dutch influence is present in the elaborate Artisan Mannerist brick façade, undoubtedly by the same hand as Crowle House (*see* above), dated 1664, and Worlaby Hospital in North Lincolnshire, dated 1663. All three are attributed to *William Catlyn*, a Hull bricklayer (*see* topic box, p. 90).

The w front, rusticated throughout, is of nine bays and two storeys, with a central one-bay three-storey porch projection. The porch has elaborate indented Corinthian pilasters decorated with rectangular and diamond-shaped stone jewels. This detail is repeated on the lesser pilasters at first-floor level between pairs of windows. Sash windows except for a reconstructed casement on the first floor. The N elevation has two blocked brick mullioned windows. The first section of the N wing was added to the rear *c.* 1730, the s wing *c.* 1755–60.

Inside, some C17 features survive including the brick-arched fireplace in the former **kitchen** which is floored with small yellow bricks or 'clinkers' imported from Holland, as were the Delft tiles found elsewhere in the house. The so-called **Banqueting Room**, the principal first-floor room, has original C17 panelling divided by short Ionic pilasters and an imposing chimneypiece with clustered columns and the Lister family arms. Impressive **staircase hall** of *c.* 1760 with Venetian window and a rich Rococo stucco ceiling. The plasterwork, similar to work at Fairfax House, York, may be by *Giuseppe Cortese* [64]. The **Drawing Room** to the left of the entrance is mainly of *c.* 1760 with a pretty Rococo ceiling, also possibly by *Cortese*. Tall Ionic pilasters flank the entrance and the chimney-breast. The overmantel is original but the late C18 chimneypiece came from the Globe Hotel that stood opposite. The **Georgian Room** behind, originally the merchant's counting house or office, has panelling, cornices, decorative carved door frames and overmantel of *c.* 1740 from the demolished No. 21 High Street. At the rear is a courtyard, then a **walled garden** on the site of a warehouse, and then the River Hull. Here would have been the merchant's staith.

Adjoining N are the **Georgian Houses**, Nos. 23–24 High Street, part of Wilberforce House Museum. Built 1756–7 by James Hamilton, tar merchant, this pair of three-storey, three-bay houses has an unusual central Ionic double doorcase beneath a single triangular pediment. Few original features inside following restoration in 1956–7 after bomb damage, except matching dog-leg staircases lit by grand Venetian windows.

65. Wilberforce House, High Street, probably by William Catlyn, *c.* 1660; statue of Wilberforce by W.D. Keyworth jun., 1884

Just to the N the Dutch-born merchant Joseph Pease established Hull's first bank in 1754. His house, No. 18, was demolished after the war but part of the walling, rebuilt, survives, behind which are the **Pease Warehouses**, well restored in 1981 (now flats) [66]. A thirteen-bay, four-storey range of brick and pantile with former loading bays under brick arches dated 1745 to the N and 1760 to the S. The warehouses are best seen by turning right at the junction of High Street and Alfred Gelder Street and going onto **Drypool Bridge**. This electrically operated Scherzer rolling lift bridge, opened in 1961, replaced a swing bridge of 1888.

66. Pease Warehouses on the River Hull, 1745 and 1760, block on right rebuilt 1980s

Looking s from the bridge the Pease Warehouses are on the right and
the impressive former **Clarence Flour Mill** of the Hull-born miller,
Joseph Rank, on the left. The mill, tragically awaiting demolition at
time of writing, was rebuilt after war damage in 1952 by *Gelder &
Kitchen* incorporating part of a silo of 1891 by *W.A. Gelder*. It has similarities to The Baltic, Gateshead, by the same firm. To the s of the mill,
accessible by a footpath along the E side of the river, is the stone-walled
entrance to the Victoria Dock by *John B. Hartley*, 1850 (*see* Walk 3, p. 117)
Further s the prominent red brick structure, with rusticated stone
arched openings and decorative panels, was built as the **Trinity House
Buoy Shed**, 1901, by *David Christie*.

Back across Drypool Bridge to the N side of **Alfred Gelder Street**.
The **White Hart pub** by *Freeman, Son & Gaskell*, 1904, half-timbered
with first-floor gallery, has a rewarding interior with semicircular
Burmantofts tiled bar. The three-storey, five-bay Georgian house with
hipped slate roof, set back to the left of the White Hart, is No. 105 on
Salthouse Lane where its main front can be seen. Built *c.* 1780, it was a
branch of the Bank of England 1828–50 and a Sailors' Home 1860–1969.

Return to the junction with **High Street** and go N along what is pop-
ularly called 'Little' High Street, which was left isolated when Alfred
Gelder Street was cut through *c.* 1900. On the E side the handsome
Blaydes House (University of Hull Centre for the Study of Maritime
History), rebuilt *c.* 1750 for Benjamin Blaydes [67], merchant and ship-

68. Former Dock Office, Dock Office Row, *c.* 1820

builder. He built the *Bethia* in 1782 that was later the *HMS Bounty* of mutiny fame. The house, which appears to incorporate part of an earlier building, is attributed to *Joseph Page*. Of three storeys, five bays with parapet and quoins to the ground floor, it has a wide Doric porch under a triangular pediment. The marble floored entrance hall leads to a splendid staircase with an ornate Corinthian Venetian window. There is a near-complete suite of panelled rooms with marble chimneypieces. At the top of the house stairs lead to the roof where there was a belvedere or lookout for watching the movement of ships on the Humber. The remnant of the lookout with a small window can be seen in between the chimneystacks when the house is viewed from the s.

The N boundary of the medieval walled town has now been reached, marked by the lane to the w known as **North Walls** which runs to the s of **Hull College** (*see* Walk 4, p. 122). To the N is the former **Dock Office**, Dock Office Row, built *c.* 1820 [68], with hipped roof and cupola on slender Doric columns. Originally of five bays, the centre three bays projecting slightly with pediment over, it was extended three bays to the s in 1840. The building is flanked by dry docks. That to the s was owned by the Blaydes family and that to the N was the entrance to Queens Dock, opened 1778 (*see* topic box, p. 14).

There are two noteworthy buildings further N. A late C18 house, **No. 3 Dock Office Row**, and **New Northbridge House**, Charlotte Street, 1870 by *R.G. Smith*, a five-storey, nine-bay former warehouse with mansard roofs to outer bays.

Those wishing to return to the s end of High Street can do so by walking back to the Alfred Gelder Street junction and turning left to Drypool Bridge where a footpath at the sw corner gives access to the walkway alongside the river.

Walk 2 (*see* plan, p. 87)

The Old Town: West of High Street

This walk traces the city's commercial quarter with an array of late c19–early c20 banks, shops, and offices. We begin in front of the **Guildhall** (*see* p. 53) at the junction of **Lowgate** and Alfred Gelder Street near the **statue** of Charles Wilson, first Lord Nunburnholme, *c.* 1910 by *Derwent Wood*. To the N the **City Hotel** by *W.S. Walker* of *Brodrick, Lowther & Walker*, 1905, a four-storey brick and stone façade with lots of good detail, mullioned windows, segmental and triangular pediments to doorways and a corner turret with copper dome. Adjoining to the right, **Maritime Buildings**, *c.* 1910, also by *Walker*, an eight-bay, three-storey office block somewhat in the style of Norman Shaw's New Zealand Chambers (London, 1871–3), of brick and stone with recessed bay windows with applied open pediments.

The view sw is dominated by the former **General Post Office** [69], monumental Edwardian imperial of 1908–9 by *W. Potts* of *H.M. Office of Works*. Built on the site of Suffolk Palace, the de la Poles' medieval manor house. Three storeys, of Portland stone in sharp contrast to the mellow Ancaster stone of the Guildhall opposite. The nine-bay

69. Former General Post Office, Lowgate, by W. Potts, 1908–9

elevation to Lowgate has broad end pavilions with segmental pediments supported on paired Ionic pilasters flanking the recessed central seven bays, rusticated to the ground floor, with round-arched openings with massive keystones carved with human heads, and above an Ionic colonnade. A similar elevation to Alfred Gelder Street with a five-bay colonnade. The archway and the five-bay block to the right are a later extension.

To the N of **St Mary's church** (*see* p. 48), and with it forming a small piazza, is the **Crown Court** [70], 1988–90 by *Building Design Partnership* (lead architect: *Sidney H. Tasker*) of Preston. Prominently sited, this large Postmodern building complements its surroundings. The silvered dome on the great central lantern and the lesser dome on the rounded three-storey corner tower echo those on the Maritime Museum and City Hall. It is of brick, in contrast to its neighbours, with stone details. Neoclassical references throughout. Inside, a grand circular marble staircase leads to a first-floor landing from which the main court rooms radiate.

Continue along **Lowgate** past St Mary's church. On the w side **Ocean Chambers** (Nos. 54–55), 1900–1 by *W.S. Walker* [71], is one of the best with a strong stone façade, asymmetrical, with Baroque touches, shallow canted bays divided by squat Ionic columns, Mannerist gables and a heavy rusticated entrance. Next the former **Exchange** (No. 50), 1866 by *William Botterill* for the Hull Exchange Co., praised after its opening as 'one of the chief ornaments of the town'. Italianate, of three storeys with rusticated stone ground floor and white stock brick with Harehill stone dressings above. The arched entrance to the rounded corner is ornamented with the head of Neptune, and on the parapet a colossal figure of Britannia by *W.D. Keyworth jun*. Converted to Juvenile and Domestic Courts in 1980 by *Fisher, Hollingsworth & Partners* and used as such until 2002.

Now a diversion along **Bowlalley Lane**. On the N side **Cogan House**, 1876–8, red brick, Romanesque, by *Smith & Brodrick* (and the location of their office) has an elaborate decorative stone doorcase with twin openings. One of these leads to **Exchange Alley** lined with yet more Victorian offices. On the s side of Bowlalley Lane **Samman House** (Hull Chamber of Commerce and Shipping) has a good council chamber of 1919 by *B.S. Jacobs* and *T. Snowden*, with stained glass. s window 1921, the four E windows by *Pope & Parr*, Nottingham, 1951–4, illustrating the industries of Hull. Next **Victoria Chambers**, 1889, by *T.B. Thompson*, with stone-faced oriel windows, then the Italianate **Imperial Chambers** (now Courts Bar), 1876–8 by *W.H. Kitching*, on the corner of the curiously named **Land of Green Ginger**. Opposite the **George Hotel**, late C18 with mid-C19 stuccoed façade, and No. 7, 1890s by *Brodrick, Lowther & Walker*, of red brick with carved brickwork detail to pediment and segmental pedimented doorcase. There is a tall narrow late C18 building with charming Georgian **shopfront** at the N end of Land of Green Ginger. On its w an alleyway leads to a group of early C20 offices including **Kingston Chambers**, handsome Neo-Georgian, and **Crown Chambers** with Art Nouveau doorcase. To the E is **Manor Street**, No. 1

70. Crown Court, Lowgate, by Building Design Partnership, 1988–90

early C19, No. 2, 1870 by *William Botterill*, an elaborate Italianate façade of yellow brick with decorative stone details to door and windows, the latter with delightful cast-iron window guards. Then comes the intrusive and unsightly tower block of **Essex House** by *Wilson Mason & Partners*, 1976.

Back down **Bowlalley Lane** and just before Samman House turn down the passage on the right leading to the hidden **Olde White Harte**, another individual Artisan Mannerist façade of the 1660s built at a right angle to the street (cf. **Crowle House**, High Street). It was the residence of the deputy governor of Hull in the late C17. Painted brick, two storeys, seven bays with moulded string course and heavy modillioned eaves cornice. The three-storey central bay, flanked by pilasters, has an open pediment. The windows have wide brick surrounds and those in the centre brick pediments, triangular to first floor and segmental to attic. Restored 1881 by *Smith & Brodrick*. Inside, a good late C17 staircase and a panelled room with decorative frieze and ornate carved chimneypiece. This room is the so-called 'plotting chamber', the scene of a meeting to plan the overthrow of the Catholic governor in 1688.

71. Ocean Chambers, Lowgate, by W.S. Walker, 1900–1

Continue s along the passage which brings us to **Silver Street**. Directly opposite, Nos. 4–6, a neat nine-bay, three-storey block with round-arched windows to upper floors. Built as shops and offices in 1848 by *Cuthbert Brodrick*. The date with the name of the master and arms of Charterhouse, developers of the site, are displayed. Turn left and go to the junction with **Lowgate** and its southern continuation, **Market Place**. On the N corner in Lowgate **The Mint** (formerly the Midland Bank), 1869–70 by *William Botterill*, three storeys, Ancaster stone, Italianate with tiers of pilasters and round-arched windows. On the s corner the former **Lloyds Bank** by *John Bilson*, the brick and stone range on Market Place of 1902, the three bays with entrance of Portland stone on Silver Street of 1912 and the corner block of the late 1920s. Opposite on the corner of Lowgate and Scale Lane, No. 41 (formerly the **National Provincial Bank**), 1900 by *Brodrick, Lowther & Walker*. Quite an Arts and Crafts feel with its excellent stonework, decorative panels, steep gables, hipped roof, dormers, and other late C17 details. Going s

72. Hepworth's Arcade, Lowgate, by Gelder & Kitchen, 1894–5

on the E side of **Market Place**, No. 4 (**Old Custom House**) proclaims just below the cornice, 'Post & Telegraph Office'. It was built as such in 1877 by *J. Williams*. Italianate, Spinkwell stone façade, four storeys with entrance canopy supported by giant consoles. On the W side of Market Place, Nos. 62–63 are two-thirds of what was evidently a six-bay, four-storey stuccoed block of the 1840s with finely detailed Victorian shopfronts. Now return to **Silver Street** via **Hepworth's Arcade**, 1894–5 by *Gelder & Kitchen* [72], for the Leeds tailor, Joseph Hepworth.

73. Parliament Street, 1790s

The L-shaped arcade originally contained twenty-six shops; Marks &
Spencer opened their first Hull shop here in 1899. The elaborate four-
bay façade to Market Place has pairs of curved C17-style wooden bays to
the first and second floors with stone gable with swan-neck pediments
above. The Silver Street façade is in much the same style but of seven
bays. The delightful interior is of two storeys, the first-floor windows
divided by fluted pilasters and half-columns with a glazed barrel-vaulted roof on pierced cast-iron arches and a ribbed octagonal glazed dome
at the junction.

Exit the arcade into **Silver Street** and look across the road to Nos.
22–23, built for the Exchange and Discount Bank in 1886, a neat stone-
fronted four-storey Italian palazzo with rusticated ground floor and
Corinthian pilasters flanking first and second floors. No. 21, **Suffolk
House**, five bays, five storeys, yellow brick with stone details, panels
with swags, probably also of the 1880s. Then the **Royal Bank of
Scotland offices** (formerly National Westminster Bank), 1907 by *Dunn
& Watson*, London. Large seven-by-five-bay block of Portland stone,
three storeys with heavy moulded rustication to ground floor, segmen-
tal hoods to first-floor windows and carved lions' heads to parapet and
chimneystacks. Opposite the former Barclays Bank (now **William
Wilberforce bar**), 1897 by *W.W. Gwyther*. Classical of dark brown
Ancaster stone, three storeys with main seven-bay façade to Trinity
House Lane.

Whitefriargate, pedestrianized in 1975, begins at this point. A busy
street, where there is plenty of good architecture above the shopfronts
on either side. The S side is largely Late Georgian with a uniform

appearance created by Trinity House, the owner of almost all of the block of land bounded by Whitefriargate to the N, Princes Dock Side to the W, Posterngate to the S, and Trinity House Lane to the E. This was the site of the medieval Carmelite friary.

Begin at the corner of Trinity House Lane with Nos. 1–9, on the S side of **Whitefriargate**, a vast three-storey, twenty-nine-bay range of 1829–30 by *Charles Mountain jun*. In the middle is a handsome eleven-bay block designed for Smith's Bank. The five-bay centre with Ionic pilasters carries a pediment with a Rococo cartouche flanked by two sea gods and other maritime references by *Thomas Earle*. An archway to the right leads to the stuccoed **Conservancy Buildings**, built as a Post Office 1843. The chief glory of the Trinity House development is the next block, Nos. 11–14 Whitefriargate (**Boots** and adjoining property). This was built as the Neptune Inn, 1794–5 by *George Pycock*. It has what Pevsner called a 'swagger façade', of seven bays with a central archway and an over-arched Venetian window above. Bays one and seven each have a tripartite window with tripartite lunette over set in a blank arch topped by a pediment. The other bays have round-arched first-floor windows with Adam-style panels over. On the parapet above the centre bay is a panel with vines surrounding the arms of Trinity House. Inside, the former banqueting or assembly room, 52 ft (15.9 metres) by 24 ft (7.3 metres) and 22 ft (6.7 metres) high on the first floor has fine restrained wall decoration and a pretty tripartite plaster ceiling. The Neptune Inn, never a great financial success, was the Custom House from 1815 to 1913. Further W Nos. 24–28 form another unified composition of 1826–7 attributed to *Charles Mountain jun*. Eight bays, three storeys and attics, with giant pilasters and mostly tripartite windows to first floor.

Opposite the former Neptune Inn is **Parliament Street** [73], the most complete Georgian street in Hull. Built to link Whitefriargate with Quay Street and the new dock (Queens Dock) it required an Act of Parliament, passed in 1795. The land was sold off by auction in August 1796 in twenty-eight lots as laid out by *Charles Mountain sen.* and *Thomas Riddell*, who presumably designed the uniform elevations. Most of the development took place 1797–1803 and eighteen of the original three-bay, three-storey houses survive with their façades virtually intact. Of brick with a narrow stone sill band to the ground-floor windows and a wider sill band to the first floor. Pedimented doorcases with half-columns and a mixture of Doric, Ionic and Composite capitals. It was described in *The Builder* in 1861 as a 'snug street … full of attorneys, notaries, registrars, accountants, and law stationers'. The W side is interrupted by part of the former **Police Station**, Edwardian Baroque, 1902–4 by *Joseph H. Hirst*. Brick and stone, asymmetrical with large doorway with semicircular balcony over and blocked Ionic columns and window surrounds to first floor. The main elevation was to Alfred Gelder Street. Opposite the N end of Parliament Street, on the corner of **Quay Street** and **Alfred Gelder Street**, the handsome Neo-Georgian **Town Hall Chambers**, 1902 by *Llewellyn Kitchen* of *Gelder & Kitchen*.

Back down Parliament Street to **Whitefriargate**. The N side has a great range of late C19 and C20 commercial façades commencing at the corner of Land of Green Ginger with No. 67 (**Britannia**), built 1886 for the Colonial and United States Mortgage Co. Ltd, designed by *Robert Clamp* and *W.A. Gelder* in an ornate French Renaissance style with tiers of rusticated pilasters and dormers with scrolled and segmental pediments. To the W, Nos. 63–66 has a classic *Moderne*-style stuccoed front of 1934 by *A.L. Farman* (for British Home Stores) with suntrap windows. It was extended one bay to the left in the same style in 1956–7. Nos. 57–60, also of the 1930s in a more classical style with tall Tuscan pilasters above the shopfront. No. 55, **HSBC Bank**, 1878–9, by *Lockwood & Mawson*, another stone-fronted palazzo with giant fluted Corinthian pilasters. The ground-floor windows have massive sculptured heads for the keystones. Good interior. Nos. 46–48, originally **Martin's Bank**, 1904 by *Walsh & Nicholas* of Halifax. An eclectic stone façade with a touch of Art Nouveau in the floral decoration to the cornice above the shopfront and in the elongated keystones, under triangular and segmental pediments, on the first floor; the second floor more Baroque with squat Ionic columns. Nos. 40–43, **Marks & Spencers**, 1931, and extended 1938, by *Jones & Rigby* of Manchester and Southport. A bold Greek Revival stone façade. First and second floors recessed behind six giant fluted columns. On the parapet are stylized waves and a ship's prow. A great contrast to the ornate Renaissance façade of No. 39 (originally a pub) by *Robert Clamp*, 1884, to the left and the rather weak Postmodern details of Nos. 37–38, a late 1980s brick front with all the usual building-block elements. The street ends with a typical large **Burtons** store of 1935 by *Harry Wilson*, the company architect. Black polished marble, jazzy friezes, tall window openings with Art Deco pilasters and balconies.

At the W end of Whitefriargate stood the medieval **Beverley Gate**, the principal landward entry into Hull, demolished *c.* 1776 [4]. Initially a timber structure of *c.* 1330, rebuilt in brick in the later C14. The gate was similar to the surviving North Bar at Beverley (*see* p. 229): two storeys high with a central passageway flanked by projecting angle buttresses. Above was a steeple. The northern half was excavated in 1988 and is well displayed in an amphitheatre constructed 1989–90. Here is a substantial piece of the mid-C14–C15 **town wall**, brick on chalk foundations. It is some twenty courses high; the total height of the wall would have been *c.* 20 ft (6 metres). The line of the wall and the positions of interval towers and gateways are marked out in dark red brickwork in the pavement along the side of Princes Dock and The Marina.

At the end of Whitefriargate turn right. At the beginning of Alfred Gelder Street, on the S side, is the delightful Old English façade of the **Empress Hotel** converted from a warehouse in 1903 by *Joseph H. Hirst*. The charming decorative detail of the exterior with its two-storey oriel window was matched once by a superb Arts and Crafts interior. To the N can be seen the imposing **Queen's Court**, a vast apartment block

74. Princes Quay Shopping Centre, by Hugh Martin & Partners, 1988–91

alongside Queen's Gardens incorporating the BBC regional headquarters, 2003–4 by *DLA Architecture*. The nine-storey glass and cream brick-panelled building, with its long s front interrupted by projecting and recessed balconies and two full-height glazed staircase towers, makes the most of its setting. To the w is the **Maritime Museum**, described in the section on Queen Victoria Square (*see* p. 61).

From the w end of Whitefriargate turn s into **Princes Dock Street**. The w side is dominated by the **Princes Quay Shopping Centre** [74] by *Hugh Martin & Partners*, built 1988–91, which fills most of Princes (originally Junction) Dock. It is to be greatly regretted that the whole dock was not retained as open water but the vast building is visually successful and exciting when seen from the s or E across the water, especially when illuminated at night. On four levels, built on stilts over part of the dock. The multi-angled structure is clad in solar-controlled green and blue glass and ivory-coloured aluminium panelling. The roof is held up by an exposed structure of posts and cables with the intention of echoing the masts and rigging of ships.

Now the buildings on Princes Dock Street. The first three are part of the Trinity House estate. First the five-bay red brick **Colonial Chambers** (McCoys bar), 1846 by *William Foale*, still Georgian. Then the former **Ferres Almshouses** of 1822 by *John Earle*. Two storeys, five wide bays with pediment over the central three bays which slightly project. Sill and first-floor bands, tripartite sash windows to ground floor. Alongside is the **gateway** to the courtyard of Trinity House, built 1842 by *William Foale*, three bays, stuccoed, round-arched with two unfluted Ionic columns *in antis*. The rooms on either side of the arch comprised the Victoria Almshouses.

Left into **Posterngate**, a narrow lane that led to one of the lesser gates in the town wall. **The Sugar Mill** on the sw corner is an imaginative and sympathetic conversion of three C19 brick warehouses. The first fronts Princes Dock, dated 1831 with the initials of Joseph Pease in the gable; four storeys, three bays with central loading doors. It has a six-bay elevation to Posterngate where it adjoins a bonded warehouse,

1876, by *William Botterill* for a wine merchant. An imposing façade, five bays, four storeys and basement with central loading doors. Rusticated stone quoins and stone-framed pediment with lunette in tympanum. The third warehouse, similar to the last but without the stone details, fronts **Dagger Lane**. **The Mission**, the chapel-like building on the Dagger Lane corner was built 1926–7 as the Mariners' Church of the Good Shepherd (by *B.S. Jacobs* and *Thomas Snowden*), part of the adjoining Seamen's Rest. Down Dagger Lane on the corner of Prince Street (*see* below) which curves towards Holy Trinity church, is **Minerva Freemasons' Lodge** of 1802. Remodelled externally in 1978, it retains inside the original 'temple' room with coved ceiling and round-arched recesses. Back to **Posterngate** to the N side and the Trinity House estate. The two former **Mercantile Marine Offices**, 1868 and 1874, are by *William Foale*, Italianate of dark red brick with blue brick and stone details. Next, set back, the thirteen-bay **Carmelite House**, 1826, designed by *Charles Mountain jun.* as Trinity Almshouses for twenty-three seamen and wives. Converted to offices 1956–7. Stuccoed with the end bays flanked by giant Doric pilasters. The rest is plain, but originally the centre had a large Doric portico (removed 1936), with a statue of Oceanus on top. The statue is now in front of Trinity House Chapel (*see* p. 76).

Directly opposite, No. 6 Posterngate proudly proclaims across a first-floor band 'Parochial Offices for Holy Trinity and St Mary A.D. 1864'. Designed by *William Botterill*, of polychrome brick with stone details, Italianate with round-arched windows to both floors and pointed-arched hoodmoulds. On the N side the street ends with the stuccoed s range of **Trinity House** (*see* p. 71); the initials 'TW' on the boldly lettered C19 street sign stand for Trinity Ward. Right into **King Street** and the open space now known as **Trinity Square** at the W end of **Holy Trinity church** (*see* p. 39), once the scene of a lively open market, now paved, pedestrianized and fitted with seats and railings and a **statue** of Andrew Marvell by *W.D. Keyworth jun.*, 1887. King Street was laid out *c.* 1771 by *Joseph Page*. Only the W side remains with an eleven-bay, three-storey block with handsome pedimented central bay. Open archway to ground floor with Venetian window above. The arch leads to **Prince Street**, a most delightful curving three-storey terrace, part of the same 1770s development [9].

To the NE on Trinity Lane Corner is **The Kingston** pub with a striking mid-Victorian façade, stuccoed of three storeys. Next door on **North Church Side** is the splendid Edwardian **Market Hall**, 1902–4 by *Joseph H. Hirst* [75]. The five-bay s front is of stone with broad brick bands and parapet, and high copper-domed campanile attached. The arcade to the ground floor was originally open, with a large room built as a corn exchange with concert venue above. The large windows are mullioned and transomed with wrought-iron balconies. The four-

75. Market Hall, North Church Side, by Joseph H. Hirst, 1902–4

76. Old Grammar School (Hull Museums), South Church Side, 1583–5

storey entrance bay round the corner in **Trinity House Lane** has a
steep-pitched brick gable with decorative ankers (metal ties), that give
it a Low Countries feel, and a wide Baroque arched entrance with window above.

Now to the s end of **King Street** and the mid-to-late C19 **Merchants
Warehouse** (now flats), brick, four storeys, five bays with rounded corner and an impressive eleven-bay elevation to Robinson Row, the end
four bays 1895 by *W.A. Gelder*. Opposite is the **Old Grammar School**
(Hull Museums), an important early brick building of 1583–5 [76]. Built
originally to accommodate the old-established grammar school on the
ground floor and Hull Merchants' Company above. The merchants
gave up their hall in 1706, which then became the town's first assembly
room, but the grammar school remained here until 1878. The building
was restored in the 1880s by *Smith & Brodrick*. It is of two storeys and
four bays in English bond with four-light brick mullioned-and-transomed windows. The merchant's mark, date and initials of William
Gee, a major benefactor, are on panels on the ground floor with the
town arms and date above. The inside retains original four-centred
arched stone doorways and fluted columns to each side of what was the
main schoolroom. The columns were introduced by *John Catlyn jun.*,

77. King William III, Market Place, by Peter Scheemakers, erected 1734

THIS STATUE
was Erected in the Year
MDCCXXXIV
To the Memory of
KING WILLIAM The Third
OUR GREAT DELIVERER

master 1664–76, who also painted a curious series of emblematical panels that survive in the Old Grammar School and elsewhere. Catlyn was brother of the bricklayer-architect William Catlyn, and himself a former bricklayer. Attached to the w end of the Grammar School, part of the former **Fish Street Congregational School**, 1871 by *Samuel Musgrave* of Hull, with Romanesque doorway.

Now for **South Church Side** which is dominated by yet more large former commercial buildings. First the red brick former **woollen warehouse**, 1880s, with pink sandstone doorcase with broken segmental pediment. Then the four-storey former **offices and warehouse** of the leading iron merchants King & Co. Cream brick with stone details, built in two stages. The original seven-bay block on the left of 1877 is by *William Botterill*, with the five-bay block in a similar style to the right added by *Smith & Brodrick*, 1890. The walk ends in the **Market Place** at the e end of Holy Trinity church, once the principal shopping street of Hull. To the n of the church Nos. 51–52, converted into a cinema, the Gaiety Picture House, *c.* 1912 by *B.S. Jacobs*. He designed the neat Italianate façade with rusticated stone ground floor and wide-arched entrance. The e side of the street is dominated by the vast **King William House** and multi-storey car park, 1974–7 by *Elsworth Sykes Partnership*, whose dark glass façade provides interesting reflections of Holy Trinity church. To the s is the **Magistrates' Court** by *Austin-Smith:Lord* built 2000–1 on part of the site of the Dominican Friary. Finally in the middle of the street stands the superb gilded equestrian **statue** of King William III by *Peter Scheemakers*, erected in 1734 [77]. The statue had been rejected by Bristol in favour of one by Rysbrack. In front of the statue is Hull's celebrated Edwardian **public lavatories**, of 1902 by *W.H. Lucas*, the City Engineer. A rare survival, little-altered with transparent cisterns and fine Art Nouveau tile and faience work supplied by the *Leeds Fireclay Co.* at Burmantofts, Leeds. The shield on the coping comes from the *Accrington Brick & Tile Company* and the ornamental terracotta ventilating bricks from *J.C. Edwards* of Ruabon.

Walk 3.

Waterfront

This walk through the waterfront area to the s of the busy s orbital road explores the city's exciting maritime heritage and its relationship to the Humber estuary.

Start on **Castle Street** at the NE corner of the former **Humber Dock**, since 1983 the lively Hull Marina, filled with yachts, clippers, cruisers and other craft. Opened in 1809, the 7-acre (2.8-ha) dock, designed by *John Rennie* with assistance from *William Chapman*, was the first of the port's docks to open directly to the Humber. A lock on the N side, now infilled, led to Princes Dock, opened 1829, and with this the Old Town was encircled by water. The lock was to the w of **No. 6 Warehouse**, converted to offices and now isolated on the N side of Castle Street. Built 1846 by *John B. Hartley*, engineer to Hull Dock Company 1842–58, and *Edward Welsh*, it was dwarfed by Hartley's massive five-storey, eighteen-bay No. 7 Warehouse which stood on the other side of the lock until its much lamented demolition in 1971.

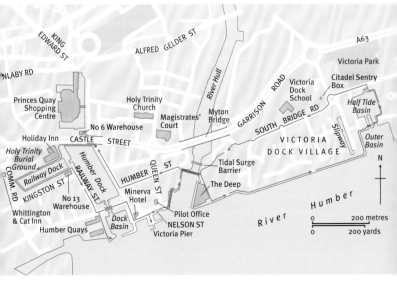

We now walk along the N side of Humber Dock, passing the **Spurn Lightship** (Hull Museums), built 1927, and turn left down the w side of the dock past the **Holiday Inn**, 1987, by *Abbey Hanson Rowe Partnership*. Before the modern Dutch-style lifting footbridge turn right along the N side of **Railway Dock** opened 1846. The 3-acre (1.2 ha) dock, designed by *John B. Hartley* as an extension of Humber Dock, closed in 1968 and reopened as part of Hull Marina in 1983. At the w end **sculpture** by *Stuart Bastick*, 1991. To the N is the former **Holy Trinity Burial Ground** opened 1783, closed 1861, a green oasis with plenty of trees, early lamp standards and many interesting gravestones. To the w on Commercial Road the **Whittington and Cat Inn**, *c.* 1907 by *Freeman, Son & Gaskell*, an extravagant brick and stone Flemish Renaissance façade with parapets, pilasters and shaped pediments. To the s on Commercial Road at the junction with **Kingston Road** are the dark red brick former offices, 1872, designed by *W.K. Reeves* for Thomas Wilson, Sons & Co., the largest private steamship company in the world in the late C19.

Continue E along the s side of the dock where the 1980s houses of **Kingston Wharf** with sloping gabled roofs and warehouse-like fronts are quite sympathetic to their surroundings but still a poor substitute for the long range of monumental warehouses that once stood here. One warehouse at the E end, **No. 13**, was retained and restored. Of red brick, seven storeys and nine bays, designed by *Edward Welsh* and built *c.* 1857; three rows of cast-iron columns divide the interior.

To the E of the warehouse, on the w side of **Humber Dock** [79], turntables and railway tracks can be seen set in the roadway. The brick wall to the w and back along the s side of Kingston Street is all that remains of the vast North Eastern Railway **goods station**. Built 1858 onwards it replaced the original terminus of the Hull & Selby Railway, 1840. Continue s down Humber Dock past **Freedom Quay**, a big apart-

79. Looking N from the dock basin across Humber Dock (Hull Marina), by John Rennie and William Chapman, 1809

80. Former Pilot Office, Queen Street, by John Earle jun., 1819–20

ment block by *Shepheard Epstein Hunter*, 2007–8, to **Humber Quays** (formerly Island Wharf), an attractive paved area alongside the impressive dock basin with its high stone walls opening onto the Humber.

A **sculpture** of a migrant family group by *Neil Hadlock*, 2001, records that it was here and at the nearby Steamship Wharf, formerly in the dock basin, that most of the 2.2 million transmigrants who passed through Hull in the years 1836–1914 landed. The migrants, the majority travelling on Wilson Line ships, came from Scandinavia, Germany and Russia and were on their way chiefly to the United States and Canada, via train to Liverpool or Glasgow. The two distinctive office blocks by *DLA Architecture*. **One Humber Quays**, 2005, an elegant design of glass and steel and **Two Humber Quays**, 2007, faced in Derbyshire sandstone and glass with a full-height open central atrium.

(To the w of Humber Quays is the entrance to **Albert Dock**, the first of the three docks to be built parallel to the estuary to the w of the Old Town. Covering 23 acres (9.3 ha), it was opened in 1869, with an extension, **William Wright Dock**, of 5 acres (2.0 ha) in 1880. Albert Dock closed to commercial shipping in 1972 but reopened as the fish dock in

1975. It is now largely disused. There is a dry dock for ship repairs at the w end of William Wright Dock, which adjoins the remains of the infilled **St Andrew's Dock**, opened 1883. Extended in 1897 and covering some 20 acres (8.1 ha), St Andrew's was the principal fish dock until it was closed in 1975. A public footpath, part of the Transpennine Way, accessed at the entrance to Albert Dock near the junction of Wellington Street West and Manor House Street, with superb views of the Humber and Humber Bridge, affords an opportunity to see remains of these later docks.)

From Humber Quays turn right and cross the **Wellington Street swing bridge** over the lock. Here are more railway lines, six large black cast-iron bollards lettered *Haigh Foundry Wigan* and dated 1846, and the contemporary **lock-keeper's cottage**, of stuccoed brick with hipped slate roof, originally the dock office. Having reached the E side of the dock one is now on land reclaimed from the River Humber using material excavated in the dock's construction 1803–9. The whole area s of Humber Street (formerly the southern boundary of the Old Town) to the river was laid out with new streets by 1813; Pier Street and an extension of Queen Street running N–S, and Nelson Street and Wellington Street running E–W. Much of this area is awaiting redevelopment in 2010.

On the corner of **Humber Place** and Wellington Street, Nos. 5–6 are a neat three-storey pair of the late 1840s, brick with a broad first-floor band and bold window and door surrounds, that to the right with pretty cast-iron balconies. Turn s along **Minerva Terrace** which ends with the **Minerva Hotel**, 1828–9, brick and slate, three storeys built on a triangular site with a satisfying rounded end with curved window openings. Further s the **Minerva Pier** overlooking the dock basin and river, to the rear the three-storey **Marine View**, with full-height canted bays and hipped slate roof, built as a customs watch house, 1909 by *William Bell*.

Now to the E side of the Minerva Hotel where we enter **Nelson Street**, a pleasant paved area with its rows of trees, Humber views and diverse mix of buildings including the 1930s **public lavatories**, famed for the well-kept tiled interior. From the early development of this area, which has some good original street signs, are the stuccoed building on the corner of Pier Street, with rusticated and pedimented façade and broad Regency doorcase at one end, and the handsome former **Pilot Office** [80] on the corner with Queen Street, at the other. The latter was built 1819–20 as the headquarters of the Humber Pilot Service, by *John Earle jun.*, of brick and painted stone with first- and second-floor bands. Recessed Doric portico to the E front. In the centre of the N side of the street the prominent eight-bay, two-storey building, of brick with stone surrounds to doors and windows, is dated 1880 and has the initials of the Manchester, Sheffield & Lincolnshire Railway Co. on the shaped pediment. From 1848 the company ran the Humber ferry, linking Hull with North Lincolnshire railways at New Holland, from the **Victoria Pier** on the s side of Nelson Street. The mid-C19 pier, as the principal public viewpoint for the Humber estuary, has long been a

81. Tidal Surge Barrier, River Hull, by Shankland Cox Associates, 1980

popular promenading place. The pontoon landing-stage was removed when the ferry closed on the opening of the Humber Bridge in 1981 but the 1930s **ticket office** survives, now a café.

Further E are **statues** of the leading medieval Hull merchant William de la Pole by *W.D. Keyworth jun.* 1870 and a tall bronze figure by *Steinunn Thorarinsdottir*, 2006, symbolizing the bond between Hull and Iceland. The latter overlooks the entrance to the River Hull with **The Deep** (*see* below) dominating the opposite bank.

Go N along the path on the W side of the River Hull with an early C19 **warehouse** on the left. The path bends round a derelict mud-filled dry dock, built 1843–4, before reaching the Millennium Bridge, a lifting footbridge, by which one crosses the river. To the N is the impressive **Tidal Surge Barrier** of 1980 [81]. Designed by *Oliver Cox* of *Shankland Cox Associates*, the elegant arch which frames the entrance to the river from the Humber estuary is over 120 ft (37 metres) high. The tall concrete

82. The Deep aquarium, by Terry Farrell & Partners, 1998–2002

towers, with their glazed staircases that are illuminated at night, support a 202-tonne barrier which is lowered to prevent flooding upstream when high tidal surges are forecast.

Once over the bridge turn right for **The Deep** aquarium, a landmark design by *Terry Farrell & Partners*, built 1998–2002 [82]. Triangular in plan, its distinctive angular form, said to represent a cliff-like slice of sedimentary rock rearing up from the ground, has been likened to a ship, an iceberg or even a shark as it rises dramatically over the estuary. Clad in aluminium and coloured glass panels its appearance changes with the qualities of light and reflections from the surrounding water. The observation point at the prow of the building gives stunning views over the city and across and along the Humber. The building is wrapped around a huge display tank, 10 metres deep, containing 2,850,000 litres of water and displaying some 3,500 fish, including 40 sharks. The aquarium's design and its displays were the responsibility of *John Czaky*. The Deep stands on land reclaimed from the Humber in the 1850s. Martin Samuelson, who established a yard here building iron ships 1857–64, is recalled by the area's name, Sammy's Point.

From The Deep we go E along the excellent promenade opened in 1992 that forms part of the sea defences built on the Humber foreshore to the s of the Victoria Dock housing estate. **Victoria Dock** (initially East Dock) was built 1846–50 by *John B. Hartley* with one entrance from the River Hull and another, through reclaimed land, from the Humber. The dock, the centre of Hull's extensive timber importing trade, was extended to the E in 1863 to cover some 25 acres (10 ha). It closed in 1970, was infilled soon after and the dock estate to the s developed with housing by Hull City Council and Bellway Urban Renewals 1989–96. The layout and overall design of the **Victoria Dock Village** has been well thought out, but it is let down by the detailing of the doors and windows which have the usual thin uPVC frames and reflective glazing.

Some 650 yds E along the promenade is the entrance to the **slipway**, now a water-filled feature, designed for hauling ships ashore for repair without need of a dry dock. At the N end of the slipway is the **winding house**, built 1866, which contained a coal-fired steam engine and winching mechanism. A little further on is the **Outer Basin** of the entrance to Victoria Dock. Turn N and cross the **flap-gate** with the cavernous 3-acre

Hull Castle and the Citadel

The fortifying of the E side of the River Hull was proposed by Henry VIII on his visit to Hull in 1541, as part of his scheme for defences along the s and E coasts of England in the face of threats of invasion from France and the Holy Roman Empire.

The new defences constructed 1542–3 by *John Rogers*, the king's master mason, consisted of three forts or blockhouses linked by a brick wall, 980 yds (830 metres) long and 5.5 yds (5 metres) thick. The large central fort, which became known as Hull Castle, was rectangular with a three-storey keep, and the smaller N and S blockhouses were trefoil-shaped. All had pointed segmental bastions unlike the rounded bastions of the earlier forts on the s coast.

The castle and s blockhouse were incorporated into the Citadel [83], a great triangular fort built 1681–90 by *Sir Bernard de Gomme* and *Martin Beckman* of the Board of Ordnance. Covering some 30 acres, it had substantial clay ramparts and brick gateways. At each corner there were projecting bastions, and the whole was surrounded by a wide moat. It ceased being used by the military in 1848 and the buildings were cleared away in 1863–4. A stone echaugette (sentry box) from the Citadel has been re-erected on its original site near Victoria Dock School.

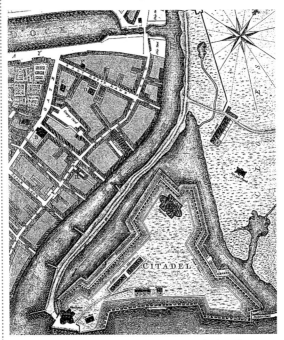

83. Citadel from plan of Hull, by J. Bryant, engraved Robert Thew, 1784

84. ARC building, Queen Street, by Niall McLaughlin Architects, 2006

(1.2-ha) **Half Tide Basin** with its great stone walls to the N.

(From the Victoria Dock Outer Basin the promenade continues further E and a public footpath can be followed crossing the entrance to **Alexandra Dock**, still active, built 1880–5 to designs by *James Abernethy* for the Hull & Barnsley Railway as an outlet for the South Yorkshire coalfield. After extension in 1899 it covered almost 54 acres (21.9 ha). The footpath continues to **King George V Dock**, 1914, terminus for the PO North Sea Ferries and **Queen Elizabeth Dock**, 1969. In the distance, and visible for many miles when illuminated at night, is the vast BP chemical works at **Saltend** which had its origins in a wooden jetty built 1914 with a rail link to King George Dock. First used for pumping oil ashore by Shell and Esso.)

Walk along the E side of the Half Tide Basin to the N end where a **swing bridge** goes over the former entrance to the main **Victoria Dock** which lay to the N and is now covered in part by the public park. Now W along South Bridge Road to the N of the housing estate. At the roundabout the **winding house** to the slipway is on the S and a re-erected small circular **echaugette** (sentry box) from the late C17 **Citadel** (*see* topic box, p. 118) to the NW. The position of the SE corner of the Citadel, demolished in 1864, is marked on the ground. The walk, now roughly following the line of the S side of the Citadel, continues along South Bridge Road until the road turns S. Here take the footpath that runs N of the car parks at The Deep to the Millennium Bridge.

Cross the bridge and turn right and then immediately left along Humber Street, which follows the line of the medieval town wall, with the estuary to the S. To the NW of the junction with **Queen Street**, s of Castle Street stands, at the time of writing (2010), the innovative **ARC** building by *Niall McLaughlin Architects*, 2006 [84], designed to be relocatable to different sites. Triangular-shaped and tent-like, with its great sloping roof of curved aluminium panels and forest of thirty-eight tall poles carrying small wind turbines and photovoltaic panels, it has won numerous awards for its originality and 'green' credentials.

Now s along Queen Street, past the much-altered former **Victoria Rooms**, 1837, on the w corner with Humber Street. Also on the w side, on the corner of Wellington Street, the four-storey grey brick **Wellington House**, 1850, the most substantial building surviving in the city by *Cuthbert Brodrick*. Tripartite stone-detailed windows to the rounded corner, flanked by pilasters with banded rustication. Opposite the **Oberon Hotel**, a neat mid-C19 seven-bay façade, brick with stone bands and window surrounds.

Retracing our steps we turn left into **Humber Street** where one finds a great concentration of purpose-built fruit and vegetable warehouses currently awaiting redevelopment. On the N side a number of mid-C18 buildings and late C19–early C20 fruit warehouses, with tiled names at entrances to former narrow yards or 'squares'. On the s side the best of the warehouses, No. 73, at the w end, 1950s with good lettering and delicate wrought-iron balcony.

On reaching **Humber Dock** (The Marina) turn right along the E side of the dock where the line of the medieval town wall is marked on the walkway in darker brick. Older buildings to the N include **Hesslegate Buildings**, 1884, with oriel windows and shaped gables, and the **Green Bricks** pub (formerly the Humber Dock Tavern), named after the green glazed bricks added 1907 with decorative panels by *Leeds Fireclay Co. Ltd.* The walk ends at a **sculpture** by *Kate Hartford*, 1988, to the s of Castle Street.

Walk 4.

Queen's Gardens and the Northern Suburb

We begin by exploring **Queen's Gardens**, the large public park that occupies the greater part of the infilled Queens Dock (1778–1930) which in 1935 was laid out with a wide tree-lined pedestrian boulevard flanked by ornamental gardens and with the **Wilberforce Monument** at the E end. This is an immense Doric column, 90 ft (27.5 metres) high, of 1834 by *John Clark* of Leeds, topped by a statue of William Wilberforce, originally erected just s of the Maritime Museum.

The gardens in the present form are as redesigned by *Frederick Gibberd*, who was appointed in the early 1950s to develop them as the city's civic and cultural centre. They were set below the level of the surrounding road to give a sense of the former dock, and sculptural panels, commissioned 1958–9, were placed on the walls. A large concrete panel at the E end is by *Robert Adams* and a series of carved stone panels along the N wall by *Kenneth Carter*, then a lecturer at Hull College of Art. *Gibberd* also oversaw the plans of the four-storey **Central Police Station** by *Lazenby & Priestman*, 1956–7, with its panels of sea-green slate divided by ribs of Portland stone, on the N side of the gardens.

85. Walk 4

86. Hull College, by Frederick Gibberd, 1960–2, from across Queen's Gardens

The main nine-storey block of **Hull College** (originally College of Technology) by *Gibberd* (architect in charge: *A.E. Kelsey*, associate architect: *J.B. Forrest*) was planned in the early 1950s but not built until 1960–2 [86]. Workshops to the rear by *Gibberd* were built 1952–6. Although described by Pevsner as 'run-of-the-mill', the main building stands well at the head of Queen's Gardens and its Festival of Britain style, with its symmetry and broken skyline, has an agreeable simplicity lacking in many more recent buildings in the city. The long bands of windows are interrupted on the fourth floor by a **decorative panel** [87] of cast concrete finished with synthetic resin by *William Mitchell*, who worked with Gibberd at Harlow New Town and Liverpool R.C. Cathedral. It depicts nautical and mathematical instruments.

The four-storey **Wilberforce Building** (originally College of Commerce) on the N side was completed 1968 and the **School of Art and Design** on the S side, 1974, both by *Gibberd*. More recent additions to the college have included the striking **Horncastle Media and Performing Arts Centre** with its great curved glass wall, and the glass-fronted **Chesters Learning Resource Centre**, enlivened by the massive 'parallel bars' fixed to the exterior, both 2004 by *DLA Architecture*.

On the s side of Queen's Gardens, on **Guildhall Road**, are two mid-to-late C19 former dockside **warehouses** and the **City Treasury**, 1989, of brown brick with blue brick bands in a quasi-warehouse style. On the corner of Guildhall Road and Lowgate is a delightful red brick office-cum-warehouse of 1881 by *Joseph Tiffen*. Originally three storeys, with arched and porthole windows and pretty terracotta tiles. In 1908 *Brodrick, Lowther & Walker* added the top two storeys and corner turret with conical slate roof and nice weathervane of a sailing vessel.

To the N of Queen's Gardens can be found the remnants of the Georgian 'Northern Suburb' for merchants and professionals which developed after the opening of the dock in 1778. New streets were laid out on the Dock Company estate, beginning with Dock Street and the much grander George Street, and on the adjoining small estates of the Baker, Pryme, Sykes and other families. There was no overall plan and the development was piecemeal and patchy.

Beginning at the Wilberforce Monument, at the head of Queen's Gardens, walk N along Wilberforce Drive then left into **George Street**, the eastern section of which was initially called Charlotte Street. On the N side two handsome houses built *c.* 1782, Nos. 83 and 85, are attributed to *Charles Mountain sen.* who was architect of the imposing eleven-bay block for J.R. Pease which adjoined the E. No. 83 [88] is of two storeys with basement, five bays with the centre three bays projecting under a pediment. Steps up to a central Corinthian portico. No. 85 is similar but

87. Hull College, concrete and resin panel, by William Mitchell, *c.* 1960

88. No. 83 George Street, attributed to Charles Mountain sen., *c.* 1782

of three storeys and basement. These are all that remain of an impressive terrace of fifteen houses, damaged in the blitz and demolished by 1972. Part of the site is filled by the former Nautical College, 1974 (now **Derek Crothall Building**, University of Lincoln), by *A.R. Peadon*, City Architect. A tall glass block partially on stilts. On the s side of George Street, going w towards the town centre, there are other late C18 houses, including Nos. 90–94. George Street backs on to **Dock Street** where a few late C18 properties remain on the N side including Nos. 9–12, a three-storey range built *c.* 1792. The first and last houses are pedimented.

89. Albion Street, terrace, 1794–6

90. Central Library, Albion Street, by J.S. Gibson, 1900–1

Back on the s side of **George Street** there are several good later buildings including No. 36, an elaborate mid-Victorian stuccoed front, four
storeys and basement. This contrasts with the Art Deco façade of Nos.
30–34, **Halifax House**. Opposite, a large 1880s stuccoed building in an
Italianate style, **The Goose**, flanked by humbler Georgian survivals.
Back on the s side the corner building is **The Dram Shop**, 1894 by *Smith
& Brodrick*, an excellent Victorian Gothic pub façade. Hoodmould
stops with a great variety of carved beasts.

Right into **Bond Street**, which is dominated by the ugly high slab of
Kingston House, by *Fry, Drew & Partners*, 1965–7. It runs N to **Albion
Street** [89] where some of the former character of the late C18 Northern
Suburb can still be seen. Until the Second World War this was the show
street of Hull, with elegant Georgian terraces and two superb classical
buildings, *H.F. Lockwood*'s Albion Chapel (1841–2) and *Cuthbert
Brodrick*'s Royal Institution (1853–4). The site of the latter is a car park
but opposite, on the N side, a fine range survives (Nos. 17–30), built
1794–6. Although the effect is that of a unified terrace the houses were
built by more than one developer and there are noticeable differences.
Some are of two bays, others of three. They are all of three storeys and
basement, and the doorcases have Doric columns, pediments and fan-
lights. No. 17 has an Ionic doorcase of *c.* 1820 to Percy Street. At the E end
of the terrace are the former **School Board Offices**, 1898 by *John Bilson*,
brick with Baroque stone details. Continue along Albion Street to the w
end. The five-bay house on the N side, with a dignified ashlar façade and
porch of pairs of Doric columns with balcony above, was built *c.* 1846
for Dr James Alderson and is attributed to *H.F. Lockwood*. Next the
Central Library, 1900–1 [90], pleasing Edwardian Baroque by *J.S.*

Gibson of London. Of red brick and Ancaster stone, the central bay is of ashlar and projects with recessed entrance porch, large round-arched window and pedimented gable. On the right an octagonal corner tower of brick with stone bands; the upper part of stone projecting above the roof has Ionic columns with semicircular pediments and is surmounted by a dome. Extension of 1959–62, by *Andrew Rankine*. Return along Albion Street to the junction with **Percy Street**, which runs N. The E side was developed 1795–7 but No. 2, by *Appleton Bennison*, is *c.* 1820. Cream brick with stuccoed bands and windows with stone architraves. Turn left along **Baker Street**, which has an attractive street sign. On the N side a good cream brick terrace built 1810–24 by *Appleton Bennison*. Three-bay, three-storey houses with sill bands and simple round-arched Regency doorcases. One has been Victorianized. To the W the buildings are red brick and Late Victorian–Edwardian including the former **Hull and Sculcoates Dispensary** of 1886 by *Botterill & Bilson* with shaped and pedimented gable and pilasters. Unsightly modern front at ground-floor level. The block next door, with shaped end gables, is dated 1879 and 1910 and was built as **offices** for the British Gas Light Co. At the end of the street, on the S side, *David Harvey*'s 1930 extension to the **Central Library**. Right into Prospect Street, past the former **Presbyterian church**, 1960 by *Gelder & Kitchen*, then first right brings us to **Wright Street** which, like Baker Street, was only partially built up by 1850. On the N side Nos. 6–11 built *c.* 1803–24, the usual three-storey, three-bay houses, some with Doric doorcases. Turn right at the junction with Percy Street, then left down Baker Street and right into **Union Street**, where there is a modest late C18 former **stable block**, five bays with pedimented entrances to each end. The opposite side of the street is filled by the main façade of the Late Victorian **School Board Offices** (*see* above, Albion Street).

Turn left into **Jarratt Street** (the eastern continuation of Albion Street). On the S side **St Charles Borromeo R.C. church**. Built 1828–9 by *John Earle jun.*, altered by *J.J. Scoles* in 1834–5, and again by *Smith & Brodrick* in 1894–6. The stuccoed five-bay front with rusticated quoins is largely of the 1830s. The centre three bays project with a pediment and have the arms of St Charles Borromeo in the tympanum. The Corinthian portico, added in the 1890s, is flanked by niches with statues of St Margaret Clitherow and St Charles Borromeo.

The exterior does not prepare one for the dramatic and opulent Baroque **interior** [91]. The **gallery** at the N end with its slender cast-iron columns and decorative ironwork and the windows placed high up in the side walls are survivals of Earle's more restrained 'Grecian' design. Scoles was evidently responsible for lining the church with the pairs of pilasters and a decorative cornice with Borromeo's arms between the windows and for creating the stunning **sanctuary**. This is a great Southern Baroque set piece with the **high altar** flanked by pairs of tall fluted Ionic half-columns supporting an elaborate sculpted and

91. St Charles Borromeo, Jarratt Street, interior, by J.J. Scoles, 1834–5 and Smith & Brodrick, 1894–6

92. Hull History Centre, by Pringle Richards Sharratt, 2009

painted representation of the Holy Trinity. All this is evidently of the 1830s, but it was made even more striking in the 1890s when a large dome with lantern was introduced to light the sanctuary and every surface painted with scenes and figures by *Henry Immenkamp*, a German artist then resident in Hull. At the same time were added rows of figures of saints and martyrs each side of the sanctuary and a Lady Chapel with its own half-dome. In the main body of the church the centre of the previously flat ceiling was arched and arcades on paired Ionic columns were opened out to reach the new narrow aisles. All elaborately coloured and decorated throughout. In the basement are burial vaults and rooms originally used for a school.

E of the church is the N range of the former **Hull Brewery**, 1867–9 by *William Sissons*. Red brick with stone details to windows. Fourteen bays, three storeys; the centre six bays were raised to five storeys in 1908. The top floor of the centre block has continuous glazing and on the roof is a hexagonal domed cupola. Behind are similar buildings around a central courtyard. Successful conversion to residential and commercial use. On the opposite side of Jarratt Street is **Kingston Square**, laid out by John Jarratt in 1801. The centre, well-maintained with luxuriant trees and bushes, is delightful but the surrounding buildings, except perhaps the theatre, are not those of a grand Georgian square. On the w side, incorporated into a nondescript early C21 block of flats is the stone façade of **Hull Medical School**, 1833 by *Henry R. Abraham*. A Greek Revival composition, quite modest in scale but well detailed. A wide central bay flanked by pilasters supporting an entablature and pediment with Egyptian-style doorcase. To the N are three good three-bay houses, early-to-mid C19, and the rather over-decorated Victorian **Kingston Theatre Hotel**. This was formerly the home and salon of Madame Clapham, Hull's celebrated dressmaker whose clients included Queen Maud of Norway. On the N side of the square is **John Street**, chiefly unremarkable mid-C19 terraced houses, but towards the w end No. 16, *c.* 1870, has triple barge-boarded gables, a Lombardic frieze and a striking Gothic doorcase with gabled buttresses. At the E end stands the former **Christ Church Schools**, 1847 by *Cuthbert Brodrick*, converted to flats in 1994. Cream brick with stone details. Perp doorway with large Dec window above. On the E side of Kingston Square is the **New Theatre**, built 1830–4 as the Assembly Rooms by *Charles Mountain jun.* Stuccoed brick. Five-bay front with a three-bay giant portico of detached unfluted Ionic columns, originally with pediment. To **Jarratt Street** eleven bays with a portico of attached columns, also originally with a pediment. It was converted to the New Theatre in 1939 by *R. Cromie & W.B. Wheatley.*

Jarratt Street ends with a largely unspoilt terrace on the s side, Nos. 1–9, built 1803–6. Mainly two-bay houses, three storeys and basement, with steps up to half-columned and pedimented doorcases. The corner property, No. 12 **Grimston Street**, has a full-height bow. The vista E along Albion Street and Jarratt Street nicely terminates in the short unified terrace of Nos. 21–25 **Worship Street**, 1806. Eight-bay, three-storey brick range with hipped roof; the centre four bays project slightly with a shallow pediment. The symmetry is spoilt on the left by the ground-floor pub façade of the **Old English Gentleman**. Further N on Worship Street is the former **Central Fire Station**, 1927 by *Joseph H. Hirst* and opposite the stylish **Hull History Centre**, 2009, by *Pringle Richards Sharratt* [26, 92]. A long two-storey building with an elegant wide glazed arcade running full-height along the s side formed by twenty-four curved laminated timber beams covered with three-layer inflated ETFE (Ethylene Tetrafluoroethylene, a transparent polymer) cushions. This superb resource centre contains a local studies library, search room and education spaces on the ground floor with the archives of the city and the University of Hull stored above.

Outlier

Charterhouse Hospital [93], Charterhouse Lane, N of Freetown Way. A surprising and delightful complex of C17 and C18 buildings in an area of local authority housing and decayed industry. The hospital or almshouse lies on the N side of the street, the master's house on the s.

William de la Pole founded a hospital here in 1354. This 'Maison Dieu', for twenty-six poor men and women in equal numbers, was incorporated into the Carthusian priory founded by Michael de la Pole, Earl of Suffolk, in 1379. Five years later the hospital was separated from the priory and established anew. The priory was dissolved in 1539 and soon after Hull Corporation took over the patronage of the hospital,

93. Charterhouse Hospital, Charterhouse Lane, attributed to Joseph Hargrave, 1778–80

called God's House or Charterhouse. The poet Andrew Marvell lived there when his father was master 1624–40. The hospital buildings were razed to the ground in 1643 prior to the first siege of Hull during the Civil Wars. Both hospital and master's house were rebuilt on the same site 1649–50, possibly by *John Catlyn sen.* His son *William Catlyn* was responsible for the new block of rooms erected on the N side of the lane in 1663 and an adjacent chapel built 1673. These buildings on the N side were demolished and the hospital rebuilt in its present form in 1778–80, probably by *Joseph Hargrave.* It is a handsome two-storey building of red brick and a hipped slate roof consisting of a seven-bay central block with projecting two-bay wings. The centre three bays project slightly and are surmounted by a pediment and open Ionic cupola. The entrance has a semicircular domed porch on Doric columns.

Inside, rows of small rooms flank central corridors on both floors with stone staircases at the junction with the side wings. In the middle of the N side of the central range is the **chapel** [94] with a superb, largely unaltered Georgian interior, lit by tall round-headed windows to E and W and by a central dome. **Box pews** for the almspeople are ranged on the s wall either side of the entrance. Grander pews for the master and officers flank the **pulpit** which is an exceptional piece by *Hargrave.* It is semicircular with a sounding-board, and is reached by steps from the vestry behind. The pulpit, the raised bracket which supports it and the frieze behind have elaborately carved swags, drops and other decoration. The **altar** is raised on three steps and enclosed by **communion rails** with heavy turned balusters. Four chandeliers designed by *Francis*

94. Charterhouse House, chapel with pulpit by Joseph Hargrave, 1778–80

Johnson who restored the chapel in 1981. The plaster **ceiling** is divided into three panels with decorative raised bands. **Monuments**. The earliest is a ledger stone with incised coat of arms dated 1768. The various wall tablets, mostly to masters, include a nicely lettered oval inscription of 1786 to Rev. John Clarke. One in the style of a Greek sarcophagus to Rev. George M. Carrick d.1849 by *W.D. Keyworth sen.* and three with portrait medallions: Rev. Thomas Dykes d.1847, grandfather of the hymn writer J.B. Dykes, William T. Dibb d.1886, a benefactor, and Rev. Henry W. Kemp, d.1888.

Behind the chapel are a number of later accommodation blocks including **Bourne Wing** of 1804. On the opposite side of Charterhouse Lane is the **Master's House** with an unexpectedly large walled garden. The house was severely bomb-damaged in 1941, but although gutted most of the walls up to the eaves survived and were incorporated in the restoration by *Horth & Andrews*, 1954–6. The ten-bay two-storey range overlooking the garden is essentially the hospital building of 1649–50. It has an original shaped gable at the w end and before the war the four bays at this end still retained their brick mullioned-and-transomed windows on the ground floor. The rear wing at the E end was rebuilt *c.* 1780 as the Master's House fronting Charterhouse Lane. As restored in the 1950s the neat brick and pantile building is of five bays with an C18 plaque bearing arms of Michael de la Pole over the central entrance.

Former **Charterhouse Lane School**, E of Charterhouse. 1881, by *William Botterill* for Hull School Board. Gothic, with pointed windows, turrets and towers.

Walk 5.

City Centre West and Park Street

The walk covers an area that suffered much destruction during the Second World War and subsequent redevelopment. We begin NW of **Queen Victoria Square** (*see* p. 60), at the junction of **King Edward Street** and **Jameson Street** which is dominated by the curved façade of the former Co-operative store (now **BHS**) with its huge mosaic mural by *Alan Boyson* of Wolverhampton, 1963, depicting three ships in tribute to the Hull fishing fleet [96]. Continue N along **King Edward Street** where, on the E side, a few early C20 buildings survive to show how dramatic the street looked when first developed. Nos. 46–50, the Baroque corner building of *c.* 1905, has an ornate copper dome with curly volutes and round windows. Nos. 58–60 are of the same date and style. In between is the Flemish Renaissance **Ariel Chambers**, *c.* 1920, probably by *T.B. Atkinson,* red brick with much white faience. Then the domed five-bay Baroque stone front of the **Methodist Central Hall**, 1902, by *Gelder & Kitchen*, and No. 66, faience, and No. 70, brick and terracotta, dated 1919 and 1923, still Edwardian Baroque. King Edward

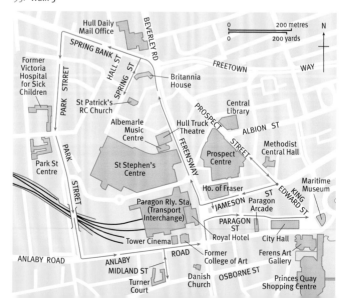

96. BHS store, Jameson Street, with mosaic by Alan Boyson, 1963

Street becomes **Prospect Street**, on the w side of which is the **Prospect Shopping Centre**, 1976, by *J. Seymour Harris Partnership*, an unworthy successor to *George Pycock*'s General Infirmary of 1784 which it replaced.

Now back to the junction and turn right into **Jameson Street**, the s side of which is dominated by the early 1950s **Queens House** (*see* Queen Victoria Square, p. 69). Further w, on the same side, three striking early C20 buildings. First **King Albert Chambers**, designed 1915 but completed 1923, by *T.B. Atkinson*, a rich Flemish Renaissance façade in brick and white faience with Belgian hand-painted tiled panels in the entrance. Next the quieter **White House Hotel**, 1909, by *Gelder & Kitchen*, brick and terracotta, banded on the attic storey with circular windows and fancy gable. Finally, on the corner of South Street, the **Masters Bar** (formerly Waverley Hotel), 1903, by *Peter Gaskell*, with florid free Baroque façades of brick and terracotta.

97. House of Fraser (Hammonds), Paragon Square, by T.P. Bennett & Son, 1950

Now to the w end of Jameson Street. On the s side **Festival House**, 1951, by *C. Cowles-Voysey* and *John Brandon-Jones*, a restrained Neo-Georgian office block, and on the N side the much more original **House of Fraser** (formerly Hammonds), 1950, by *T.P. Bennett & Son* [97], its angular shape and alternate layers of glass and white walling with classical references resulting in an interesting combination of 1930s and Festival of Britain styles. It is a building that should be preserved from redevelopment. In **Paragon Square** to the s are the **South African War Memorial** of 1907 by the *Leeds Marble Works* and First World War **Cenotaph** by *T. Harold Hughes*, erected 1924.

We have now reached **Ferensway**, on the w side of which is the **Royal Hotel** (formerly the Royal Station Hotel), by *G.T. Andrews*, completed in 1849. Italianate, of ashlar, the main E front was originally of three storeys and nine bays. The five central bays are recessed with Doric pilasters forming an open arcade to the ground floor and attached Ionic columns to the first floor. Heightened and extended 1903–5 by *William Bell*. The interior was reconstructed following a serious fire in 1990. Adjoining is the main entrance to **Paragon Station**, an extension of 1903–4 by *William Bell* for the North Eastern Railway to the original station building of the 1840s, which survives facing Anlaby Road (*see* below). Bell's work includes the stunning platform roof of five spans and the former **booking hall** which retains a good glazed brick and tile interior with central wooden ticket office. **Kiosk** with charming Art Nouveau detail. A canopy was added to the front of the station as part of the changes for the **Transport Interchange** by *Wilkinson Eyre*, opened 2007.

98. Paragon Station, original station buildings by G.T. Andrews, 1846–8

99. Albemarle Music Centre, Ferensway, by Holder Mathias Architects, 2007

The area immediately N of the station has recently been transformed by the 40-acre multi-use **St Stephens** development (named after St Stephen's Square and the Anglican church by *H.F. Lockwood*, 1845, that stood near there until the mid 1950s). The overall scheme was designed by *Foster & Partners*. At its heart is the **Shopping Centre**, 2007, by *Holder Mathias Architects*. Major features of the design are a 46-ft (14-metre)-wide undulating glazed roof over a covered street, thrusting prow-like over the entrance, and an adjacent hotel tower block. The eye-catching **Albemarle Music Centre** [99], N of the shopping centre, with its vivid lavender-blue cone and glazed spiral stair tower, is also by *Holder Mathias*. At the end of the block **Hull Truck Theatre**, 2009 by *Wright & Wright* [100]. Dark brick with full-height glazing to the two-storey foyer. Inside is what matters. The impressive main theatre, which seats 440, has a wide stage reaching into a curving auditorium, creating a sense of intimacy. Opposite and further N is what survives of Ferensway as the original developers intended it to look. Opened in 1931, the street was planned as a great Neo-Georgian boulevard. The first building, completed that year, was at the N end of the street: **Crown House** by *Scarlett & Ashworth*, an elegant well-detailed Neo-Georgian office block of brick with stone dressings. A further half-dozen similar buildings soon followed. The same firm designed **Ferensway House**, 1933, opposite, and **Ferensway Chambers** and **Brook Chambers**, 1934 [18], all with additions of the 1950s.

100. Hull Truck Theatre, Ferensway, by Wright & Wright, 2009

A left turn at the end of Ferensway, past **Britannia House**, a dreary early 1970s office block, takes one to **Spring Bank**, which has its origins in a narrow lane running along the side of the open Spring Ditch that brought fresh water into Hull from Spring Head to the w. The once tree-lined street was developed from *c.* 1820. Beginning on the s side, a detour down the first street off to the left, **Spring Street**, leads to the redundant R.C. church, **St Patrick**, 1903–4 by *Brodrick, Lowther & Walker*. Romanesque in dull red brick with stone round-arched entrance, rose window, and domed corner turret. Return to **Spring Bank** and turn left, passing the stuccoed corner block with decorative pilasters, perhaps of the 1840s. The mid-C19 **Spring Bank Tavern** stands on the corner of **Hall Street**, which has a **fire station** of *c.* 1887 on the left with delightful carved heads of horses and firemen. Back on Spring Bank Nos. 53 and 55, with steps up to front doors and wrought-iron railings, are part of the three-storey **Belgrave Terrace**, *c.* 1840. No. 63 is the sombre Tudor-style **Institute for The Deaf**, 1925–6, by *F.J. Horth & H. Andrew*. Then set back with front gardens is **Minerva Terrace**, Nos. 71–81, built *c.* 1853 for Trinity House, probably by *William Foale*. On the N side of Spring Bank more terraces of a similar date.

Back on the s side turn down **Park Street** with two large Victorian public buildings, both on the w side. First the former **Victoria Hospital for Sick Children**, 1890, by *Samuel Musgrave* and *W.H. Bingley*, red brick and stone in a rather exotic Gothic that contrasts with the refinement of the large gabled 1920s extension on the left. Then the **Park Street Centre** of Hull College, cream brick with stone dressings. The five-bay block to the left with three-bay pediment was built *c.* 1856 as a private school. To this were added the centre three bays and the matching five-bay block to the right by *William Botterill* in 1869, when it became an orphanage. The pediment over the centre contains a sculptured group by *W.D. Keyworth jun.* of Charity with orphan children, maritime emblems and the arms of Sir Titus Salt, the major benefactor. In 1898 it opened as Hull Municipal Technical School with alterations and additions by *Botterill, Son & Bilson (John Bilson).* Also on this side of the street a number of mid-C19 villas.

The southern end of Park Street crosses the railway, with good views to the left of the five-span roof of the **station**, and on the right a refined Art Deco **signal box**, 1938, and a dreary 1930s **masonic hall** enlivened by an Egyptian-style doorway. At the end turn left onto Anlaby Road, the s side of which is dominated by 1960s tower blocks. On the N side **The Lair**, a long single-storey yellow brick building with hipped slate roof, was the Immigrant Waiting Room or reception hall by *Thomas Prosser*, 1871, enlarged 1881 by *William Bell.* Here East and Central Europeans en route to North America were accommodated while waiting for trains to Liverpool. It stands near the **station** of 1846–8 by *G.T. Andrews*, built for the York & North Midland Railway [98]. A dignified Italian Renaissance ashlar-faced composition comprising a central booking hall, of two storeys and five bays with eleven-bay single-storey wings linked to three-bay two-storey end pavilions. Opposite, running s from Anlaby Road, is **Midland Street** (named after the railway). On the right, on the corner with **St Luke's Street** is **Turner Court** (Model Dwellings), 1862 by *H.M. Eyton* [101] for the Society for Improving the Condition of the Labouring Classes, their only project outside London.

101. Turner Court (Model Dwellings), Midland Street, by H.M. Eyton, 1862

102. Former College of Art, Anlaby Road, by E.A. Rickards, 1904

A large two- and three-storey building of grey brick with red brick and stone dressings arranged around a courtyard. Opposite, the **Age Concern Healthy Living Centre**, 2002, by *Gammond Evans Crichton Ltd*, and round the corner in **Osborne Street** the Northern Renaissance façade of **Owbridge's Factory**, 1895, incorporated into a housing scheme 1992–3. The factory made cough mixture. Further E on the corner of Ferensway **St Nicolai Danish Lutheran church**, 1955, by *Wheatley & Houldsworth* with detached open bell-tower.

Back at the E end of **Anlaby Road** some important survivals from the Edwardian period. First the former **Tower Cinema**, 1914, by *H. Percival Binks* of Hull [17]. An ornately decorated classical front of green and cream faience with an allegorical female on the parapet. On the rounded corners two domes, replacements for the originals, decorated with mosaic. The corner entrances have scrolled pediments with swags and cartouches. The former **Regent Cinema** opposite, 1910 by *John M. Dossor*, was built in seven weeks and it shows. The towers are later additions. Back on the N side the best of the city's Edwardian buildings, the former **College of Art**, 1904 by *E.A. Rickards* [102], displaying on a small scale and a bad site the architect's flamboyance. Seven bays, three-storey gabled centre of banded brick and stone, with slightly projecting two-storey wings. The semicircular two-storey porch, supported on Tuscan columns, is topped by a wrought-iron balcony. Caryatids carved by *H.C. Fehr* embellish the first-floor window and the tympanum above has a mosaic portraying the triumph of the arts over ignorance by *Alfred Garth Jones*, executed by the *Bromsgrove Arts Guild*.

At the end of Anlaby Road on the corner of Ferensway, **Europa House**, 1974–5 by *John Brunton & Partners*, Bradford. A curved façade

103. Former Cecil Cinema, Carr Lane, by Gelder & Kitchen, 1955

in eleven alternating bands of black and gold reflecting glass. To the SE the imposing former **Cecil Cinema** [103], rebuilt 1955 by *Gelder & Kitchen*, typical of the period. When built it had the largest screen in the country and could seat 2,052. Opposite is the lively **Regent House** by *John M. Dossor c.* 1904. Brick with rendered first floor, open pedimented gables and at the corner a pretty turret. The adjoining block on Ferensway, **Ferensway House**, with its pleasing tiled name plaque, is 1930s but in keeping. Right into **Paragon Street**, where on the left side the classical columns on the front of the Edwardian Baroque **Seaton Buildings** by *Gelder & Kitchen* are echoed by those on the 1929 white faience façade of the former William Jackson's grocery shop (**Sainsburys**) by the same architects.

Further along, on the opposite side of Paragon Street, is **Paragon Arcade**, 1892, by *W.A. Gelder*. The short straight arcade running through to Carr Lane has a Venetian Gothic front with central pointed archway flanked by oriel windows. Interior with fine decorative cast-iron and glazed roof. Paragon Street takes us back to Queen Victoria Square.

Walk 6.

Beverley Road, Pearson Park and Spring Bank

Beverley Road, one of the most important of the radial routes leading into the city centre, began to develop from the s around 1820 with middle-class terraces and individual villas. A surprising number of the original buildings survive in what is now an untidy entry to Hull.

We begin near the city centre, at the junction of Spring Bank and Beverley Road. Called **Blundell's Corner**, after the paint manufacturers who were based here from the early C19, the site is now filled by the **Hull Daily Mail Office**, 1989 by *Kenneth W. Reed & Associates*. On the opposite side of **Beverley Road** No. 44 is an unusual stuccoed **cottage** of *c.* 1837, probably by *H.F. Lockwood* who was architect of Kingston College (now **Kingston Youth Centre**) to the N. The cottage, seemingly the college lodge, was originally single-storey. Gothic doorway but

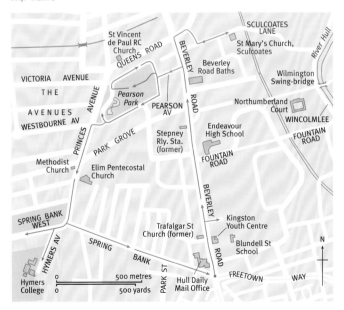

105. Trafalgar Street Baptist church, Beverley Road, by George Baines & Son, 1904–6

classical detail to the first-floor windows. The Gothic stone **gatepier** to the left is identical to the pair at the present entrance to the **Youth Centre**, which incorporates the remaining part of Lockwood's college, built 1836–7. Red brick, Tudor style with mullioned windows and corner turrets.

On the w side of Beverley Road is the former **Trafalgar Street Baptist church**, 1904–6 by *George Baines & Son*, London [105]. The style is their usual freely expressed Perp with hints of Art Nouveau. The building is faced in flint, unique in Hull, with red brick and sandstone dressings to quoins and openings. Tall tower topped by a curious arrangement of an open wooden bell-turret with small leaded spire. N of the chapel is **York Parade** (Nos. 53–65) of *c.* 1820, a much-altered terrace, originally of seven two-storey, two-bay houses set back with sizeable front gardens. Nos. 53–55, now one house, has a classical porch flanked by great semicircular bows with tripartite sash windows. No. 57 has an equally large two-storey bow. The yellow brick Gothic building that comes next, now a **Masonic Hall**, was originally Beverley Road Wesleyan chapel schoolroom, 1865 by *William Botterill*.

We now cross back to the E side of the street and turn right down **Strand Close** to see **Brunswick House**, 1890 and further E, set back, the former **Blundell Street School**, 1878, two excellent Board Schools respectively by *Botterill & Bilson* and *Botterill* (*see* topic box, p. 18). Back on Beverley Road Nos. 74–84 (**Granville Terrace**), built in the early 1860s, are attributed to *Samuel Musgrave*. These three-storey houses have richly carved woodwork to porches, bays and eaves cornice, a particular feature of mid-Victorian houses in Hull.

Opposite is **York Terrace** (Nos. 77–83), a group of four three-bay Grecian-style villas built 1832 to the designs of *David Thorp*. All had two-storey bays flanking Doric porches with cast-iron balconies and front gardens. Nos. 79 and 81 are the least altered. No. 89, a stuccoed two-bay house with Doric doorcase, is of the 1820s. No. 91, of the 1860s, has twisted columns to the bays, echoed in the attic windows of Nos. 94–98, opposite, of a similar date. The next stretch of Beverley Road has several solid terraces of three-storey mid-Victorian houses, with shops at ground-floor level, but only a few individual buildings of note. On the E side the former **Swan Hotel** (boarded up at the time of writing) has the usual fine brick and terracotta work and decorative faience panels typical of Hull's splendid Late Victorian pubs. To the right is the brick and stone façade of the **National Picture Theatre**, 1914, by *Runton & Barry*, burnt out in the blitz, the only building to survive in Hull in its bombed state and worthy of retention as a memorial. The entrance flanked by pairs of Ionic pilasters leads to the ruins of a foyer.

Then across Fountain Road is **Endeavour High School**, 2002–3, designed by *Bond Bryan Partnership*, Sheffield, in conjunction with *HBG Construction Ltd*, Batley. L-shaped, the main W wing, red brick and reconstituted stone with blue rendering to the curved ends, is of three storeys, the centre bay flanked by towers echoing elements of the Victorian workhouse that it replaced. Alongside is the former **Northern Library** of 1895 by *H.A. Cheers* of Twickenham, a late Gothic building of brick with stone details. Fussy, lots of gables, a squat castellated tower with pyramidal roof, and mullioned-and-transomed windows. No. 190, on the corner of Pendrill Street, was originally **Hull Savings Bank**, built 1901, probably by *Gelder & Kitchen*. On the W side of the road the former **Stepney Railway Station**, 1852–3 by *William Botterill*, then architect to the York & North Midland Railway. Red brick with grey brick corner pilasters and white-painted round-arched ashlar surrounds to windows and doorways. **Glad Tidings Hall** on the corner of Cave

106. Bull Inn, Beverley Road

Street, a simple stuccoed classical building with a pedimented gable, was built by the New Connexion Methodists in 1849. Then another pub, the **Rose Hotel** by *G.H. Mumby*, 1911, red brick, faience to ground floor, good lettering and rounded corner with onion dome. Opposite is the far more ornate **Bull Inn**, 1903–4 by *Freeman, Son & Gaskell*. Brick with stone and terracotta detail, faience panels and a handsome figure of a bull [106]. The shaped gables echo those of the nearby **Stepney Primary School**, 1886 [14], one of the best remaining of *Botterill & Bilson*'s Board Schools in a Queen Anne style. Then comes the copper domed Edwardian **Beverley Road Baths**, 1905 by *Joseph H. Hirst* [107]. The entrance hall has exceptional Art Nouveau tiling by the *Campbell Tile Co.*, and tiling also to the baths, corridors and individual cubicles. Bronze portrait plaque by *E. Caldwell Spruce*, 1905, in the entrance.

At this point the grander housing recommences. On the W side Nos. 263–269 are four identical three-bay grey brick villas. They are of the early 1870s as is the larger and more elaborate **Claremont House**, adjoining, with shaped gables and a corner turret. Similar features are exhibited by the building N of Pearson Avenue which incorporates Dorchester House, built 1861–2 by *Bellamy & Hardy* for John Bryson. Of painted brick with stone dressings, the house has a profusion of shaped gables and corner turrets topped by slate-covered spires. Bryson also developed the houses on the N side of **Pearson Avenue**, which leads into Pearson Park; Nos. 10–18 were built *c.* 1865 to the designs of *William Kerby*. Shaped gables again.

107. Beverley Road Baths, by Joseph H. Hirst, 1905

Before exploring Pearson Park, the more adventurous might wish to continue N along Beverley Road to the junction with Queen's Road and turn E along **Sculcoates Lane** to see **St Mary, Sculcoates**, by *Temple Moore* 1915–16. An unappealing exterior of red, handmade Lincolnshire bricks and Ancaster stone details conceals an aisled interior of fine proportions and the austere beauty of Moore's late work at its best. St Mary's is a replacement for a church of 1760–3 which stood some distance to the E, the Tuscan columns of which were reused in the N chapel. The church was incomplete in 1916 and was finished off by *Leslie Moore*, 1925–6, with the W bay of the nave but not the W tower Temple Moore had intended. Tall, wide, very plain arches in the nave but with a peculiar flat label, unique in Moore's output. Chancel as high as the nave but slightly narrower and divided from it by an arch. Clerestory to the nave and chancel, but most of the chancel N wall is occupied by two tiers of pairs of round arches, giving the asymmetrical effect Moore often enjoyed. **Fittings.** The **font** began life as a Georgian wine cooler from Hotham House, Beverley [108]. The panelled **pulpit** is of *c.* 1760.

In the N chapel an **altar** with wooden Jacobean panels. **Woodwork** in s chapel by *Robert Thompson* of Kilburn, 1933. Several **wall tablets** from the former church including one to Jane Delamotte d.1761, with an inscription totally in Byrom shorthand, and others by *John Earle* and *Thomas Earle*.

The C18 St Mary's, which replaced a medieval church, stood on the corner of **Air Street** until its demolition *c.* 1916. Its tower survived until the 1960s. The churchyard with some **memorials** remains.

Now back to **Pearson Park**, Hull's first public park, occupying a 27-acre site given in 1860 by Zachariah Pearson, a Nonconformist ship-owner. Pearson's intention was to provide the 'working classes' with 'a place which they might call their own, for the purpose of health and recreation'. The park, opened in 1862, was designed by *James Niven*, curator of Hull Botanic Garden. It is still well maintained, with plenty of trees and shrubs, a small serpentine lake, and a Victorian-style **conservatory**.

The principal entrance to the park is the cast-iron **triumphal arch**, by *Young & Pool* of Hull, 1863 [109], which stands at the end of **Pearson**

108. St Mary, Sculcoates, Sculcoates Lane, Georgian font (wine cooler)

109. Pearson Park, triumphal entrance arch, by Young & Pool, 1863

Avenue. Inspiration for the design may have come from Robert Adam's gateway to Syon House, London. On either side of the main arch are pedestrian entrances with pairs of gate pillars with dolphin finials formerly topped with lamps. All the gates have been removed. Close by is **East Lodge** (boarded up at the time of writing) of 1860–1, by *R.G. Smith*, yellow and blue brick with decorative bargeboards.

Cross the park to the NW corner. Within the park there are **statues** of Queen Victoria, 1863 [110], young and seated, and her consort Prince Albert, standing, 1868, both by the local sculptor *Thomas Earle*. There is also a marble **plaque** with the head of Zachariah Pearson carved in relief by *W.D. Keyworth jun.*, mounted on a plinth of Cleveland ironstone.

110. Pearson Park, Queen Victoria, by Thomas Earle, 1863

Several features have been removed from the park over the years, but there is still an ornate cast-iron **drinking fountain**, installed in 1864. The stone **cupola** is from *Cuthbert Brodrick*'s town hall of 1862, and was brought here when it was demolished in 1912.

Zachariah Pearson retained 10 acres of land surrounding Pearson Park on which to build 'villa residences'. The site was far enough away from the industrial parts of the city to avoid the noise and smells, but not too far to travel to work, and the proximity to such a public space does not seem to have been a deterrent to the professionals and industrialists who made their homes around the perimeter of the park. Development had barely begun when Pearson went bankrupt in 1862, and the plots were filled piecemeal over a long period. The result is a great mixture of architectural styles. Starting at the NW corner No. 43 (**Studley House**), a handsome double-fronted cream brick villa of 1867, shows the skills of Hull's craftsmen in its ornate woodwork, especially in the canted bays and the frieze of the broad Corinthian porch. It was built for a timber merchant. The pair next door, Nos. 44–45, have full-height corner pilasters with acanthus capitals. Nos. 48–49, a semi-detached pair in red brick designed by *Smith & Brodrick*, 1894, are plainer than their neighbours although there is a good deep coved cornice. **Albert House** (No. 50) [111] comes next, one of the first houses to be built in the park. The date is 1861–2 and the architect was *William Reeves*. An imposing cream brick house with rusticated quoins,

111. Albert House, No. 50 Pearson Park, by William Reeves, 1861–2

Corinthian doorcase and moulded architraves; the ugly fire escape is particularly intrusive. Nos. 52–53, designed by *Robert Clamp*, 1886, have half-timbering and pargetting, and tile-hung gables. Another early house comes next, **Avon Lodge** (No. 54), a neat Italian villa with an open pedimented gable. To the right of the rounded bay is a pretty ironwork veranda. It was built in 1862 for Joseph Fox Sharpe, Borough Engineer, who chose a West Bromwich architect, *G.B. Nicholls*. No. 55, double-fronted with a decorative frieze to the bays, is of 1871, by *F.W. Hagen*. Its more handsome neighbour, No. 56, of *c.* 1874, is of three storeys, built of yellow brick with stone details. The style is Italianate, with round-arched windows and a bold bracketed eaves cornice. The houses on the N side of the park end with a pair built 1865 by the Hull architect *William Botterill* who chose a Gothic style, with mullioned-and-transomed windows and decorative bargeboards. Several of the gables retain delicate metal finials. On the E side of the park there is little of note save for the **Pearson Park Hotel** which was designed *c.* 1892 by *F.S. Brodrick* for himself, in a simple Queen Anne style. It is typical of his work: red brick, partly rendered, with tile-hung gables, decorative chimneystacks and oriel window.

On the S side of the park the first houses worth mentioning are really Nos. 17–18 (**Kingston Villa**) of *c.* 1870, with an imposing double porch in the centre. **Keysell Villa** (No. 19), built 1862–3 to the designs of *William Reeves*, has a rustic timber porch. No. 20 (**Daulton House**), also by *Reeves*, is quite different, more like a small Italian villa with its three-storey tower and shallow hipped roof with overhanging eaves. Then comes another pair of semis, **Linden Villas** (Nos. 21–22), 1870 by *R.G. Smith*. The centre block is of three storeys, with two-storey wings with ground-floor bays topped by decorative cast-iron railings. Smith's design incorporates unusual brick pilasters with decorated capitals, which are not altogether successful. The rest of the houses are fairly undistinguished, although Nos. 29–30 have matching terracotta panels and the date 1891. Nos. 31–32, built 1892–3, have half-timbered gables with Venetian windows, and an attractive cast-iron gate. From 1956 until 1974 the top flat of No. 32 was the home of the poet Philip Larkin, and the setting provided the inspiration for *High Windows* (1967).

West Lodge stands at the Princes Avenue entrance to the park. It was reconstructed in the 1890s by *Smith & Brodrick*, and has a half-timbered gable with a large clock, decorative tile-hanging and chimneystacks with terracotta flower panels. Walk 7 (*see* p. 155), which explores the northern section of Princes Avenue and the associated development known as The Avenues, begins here.

Those continuing on Walk 6 should turn left onto Princes Avenue, the southern section of which has a handful of buildings worth seeing. On the w side, on the corner of Blenheim Street, is the brick tower with spire of *Gelder & Kitchen*'s Gothic **Wesleyan Methodist church** of 1905, the rest of which was demolished in 1995 and rebuilt the following year. Nos. 83–85 Princes Avenue, with its advertisement panels in white faience at first-floor level, was formerly a Jackson's grocery **shop**, built in 1905. Across the road **Elim Pentecostal Church** of 1898–9 by *W.H. Bingley*, built as the Fish Street Memorial Church (Congregational), lively Gothic of red brick with stone dressings and an octagonal tower. Back on the w side, on the corner of Thoresby Street, No. 63, originally a butcher's **shop**, retains its tiled sign; the interior has a decorative scheme that includes tile paintings of pastoral scenes, designed to look like framed pictures. Further s an Edwardian parade of nineteen purpose-built shops, three storeys with shaped gables.

At the end of Princes Avenue turn right into **Spring Bank West**. On the N side is **Hull General Cemetery**, laid out for the Hull General Cemetery Co. in 1847 by *John Shields* with Gothic lodges and chapels by *Cuthbert Brodrick*. There are Gothic **gatepiers** to Spring Bank West, but the lodges and chapels have long gone. Among the **memorials** one to Captain John Gravill who died 1865 aboard the steam whaler *Diana* which was frozen in the ice in the Davis Straits. Long inscription with oval carved relief above showing his trapped ship. N of the cemetery **Thoresby Street School**, 1902 by *John Bilson*, with its elegant tower.

On the opposite side of Spring Bank West is **Hymers Avenue** which leads to **Hymers College**, 1893 [112]. By *Botterill, Son & Bilson* (*John Bilson*). Exemplary buildings in a Free Jacobean style. Brick with stone bands and other details. The original building symmetrical with two

112. Hymers College, Hymers Avenue, by John Bilson, 1893

projecting wings filled in between on the ground floor. Central entrance porch with arched entrance, and above, a stone panel with arms and a segmental pediment. Mullioned-and-transomed windows throughout, those to the first floor with arched lights. Handsome clock tower with cupola. Later additions including science wing, 1908, and memorial hall, 1924, also by *Bilson* in a similar style. Recent buildings include the **Craft, Design and Technology block** by *Gelder & Kitchen*, 1988–9.

Back to the junction with Princes Avenue, and continue E along **Spring Bank**. On the s side the **Polar Bear**, rebuilt 1895 by *Freeman, Son & Gaskell*, and extended in 1922, has a magnificent *Burmantofts* ceramic-fronted bar. On the N side and the streets off are many sizeable mid-to-late Victorian terraced and semi-detached houses with rewarding details. Good examples of the 1870s include Nos. 226–228, ornate woodwork to porches and bays and ironwork balconies and Nos. 160–162, bargeboarded gables and tiled entrance surrounds. **Peel Street** and **Hutt Street** were built on the site of the Zoological Gardens (1840–62), which had a series of exotic buildings by *H.F. Lockwood*.

Back on the s side a few houses of the 1840s survive, much altered, including No. 109 which has Doric porch and a first-floor bow over a modern shopfront, and Nos. 93–99, (**Carlton Terrace**), some with railings and Doric doorcases.

The buildings on the final stretch of Spring Bank, which takes us back to Beverley Road, are dealt with in Walk 5 (*see* p. 137).

113. Northumberland Court (Municipal Hospitals), Northumberland Avenue, by Smith & Brodrick, 1884–6

Outlier

Northumberland Court [113], Northumberland Avenue, reached from Beverley Road via Fountain Road. A surprising building to find in this unpromising setting. Built as the Municipal Hospitals, 1884–6 by *Smith & Brodrick*, combining in one building several almshouse foundations originally located in the Old Town. A large complex including a chapel arranged around a spacious turfed quadrangle. The buildings are a mixture of brick walls, tile-hung bays, half-timbered gables and charming corner turrets. Tudor arched gateway with oriel window and a great tower of unexpected and welcome fancifulness.

114. Wilmington Swing Bridge, Wincolmlee, 1907, and grain silo, by Gelder &
Kitchen, 1915

Nearby are two former schools, **Northumberland Avenue Board
School**, 1897, by *Botterill & Bilson* and **Fountain House**, Fountain Road,
1904, by *Joseph H. Hirst*, both Neo-Georgian with the usual pretty turrets. Just to the E the Victoria Dock branch railway line was carried
across the River Hull by the enchanting iron arched **Wilmington Swing
Bridge**, 1907 [114], topped by a delightful wooden cabin. Nearby an
imposing brick silo of 1915 with another further N of 1912, both by
Gelder & Kitchen.

115. Park Avenue, fountain, 1870s

The Avenues, Newland and Newland Park

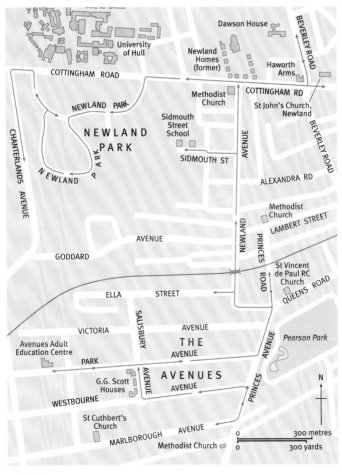

Map labels:

Dawson House

BEVERLEY ROAD

University of Hull

Newland Homes (former)

Haworth Arms

COTTINGHAM ROAD

COTTINGHAM RD

St John's Church, Newland

Methodist Church

NEWLAND PARK

Sidmouth Street School

NEWLAND PARK

SIDMOUTH ST

BEVERLEY ROAD

CHANTERLANDS AVENUE

NEWLAND PARK

AVENUE

ALEXANDRA RD

Methodist Church

LAMBERT STREET

NEWLAND

PRINCES

AVENUE

GODDARD

St Vincent de Paul RC Church

ROAD

QUEENS ROAD

ELLA STREET

VICTORIA

SALISBURY

AVENUE

THE

Avenues Adult Education Centre

PARK

Pearson Park

AVENUE

AVENUE

PRINCES AVENUE

G.G. Scott Houses

AVENUES

AVENUE

WESTBOURNE

St Cuthbert's Church

MARLBOROUGH AVENUE

Methodist Church

N

0   300 metres

0   300 yards

116. Walk 7

117. The Avenues, Salisbury Street, houses, by George Gilbert Scott jun., 1877–9

Leaving Pearson Park by the western exit (*see* Walk 6, p. 146) one enters **Princes Avenue**, a wide tree-lined boulevard 'opened' on 29 March 1875. This marked the beginning of the development known as **The Avenues** which was laid out by a local ship-owner and shipbuilder David Parkinson Garbutt. The long straight tree-lined streets that make up this enclave of middle-class housing (originally known as the Princess Bank or Westbourne Park estate) run off the northern section of Princes Avenue. The estate comprises Marlborough Avenue, Westbourne Avenue, Park Avenue and Victoria Avenue that run e–w, with two cross-ing streets, Richmond Street and Salisbury Street, intersecting at right angles. A prospectus issued in 1878, advertising building plots for sale, emphasized proximity to the tramway and railway stations, making it 'especially convenient for gentlemen engaged on business in the town', and the footpaths planted with trees, designed to 'afford pleasant shade and give a general park-like appearance to the Estate'. Much of housing here is standard late Victorian speculative terraces but there is plenty of good detail and a variety of styles. Former residents include Amy Johnson, Dorothy L. Sayers, Ian Carmichael and Anthony Minghella.

The first of the streets running off Princes Avenue is **Marlborough Avenue**. Towards the w end stands a simple brick hall church in a mod-est Georgian style, **St Cuthbert**, by *Douglas Potter* of *Gelder & Kitchen*, a 1956 replacement for a small Anglican mission church. Next comes the

grandest, **Westbourne Avenue**. Beginning at the junction with Princes Avenue, Nos. 2–4, 1878, were among the first houses to be built. Designed by *William Freeman*, they have much carved wood and stone detail, with large bays and Italianate windows. Nos. 34–40, 1904 by *John M. Dossor*, provide a good contrast, with their half-timbering, rendering and tile-hung gables. Also by *Dossor* is No. 92 (**Ebor Lodge**), on the corner of Salisbury Street, which shows the influence of the Arts and Crafts Movement with its deliberate asymmetry, tall tapering chimney and shaped gutter supports. It stands near one of the two remaining splendid cast-iron **fountains**, adorned with mermaids and herons. There were once six fountains on the estate, each forming a focal point at a main junction. On the w side of **Salisbury Street** and round the corner into Westbourne and Park Avenues are the most distinctive buildings on the estate, a group of eight houses in the Queen Anne style by *George Gilbert Scott jun.* [117]. They were built 1877–9, for Scott's cousin John S. Cooper, a Hull solicitor. Six detached houses in two designs and one large semi-detached pair. All have white-painted rendered panels framed by rubbed red brick with lots of stucco decoration, flat-tile roofs and tall stacks. Some have shaped gables. One (No. 109 **Park Avenue**), was rebuilt *c.* 2000. At the junction of Salisbury Street and Park Avenue is the other **fountain** [115]. At the w end of **Park Avenue**, on the N side, Nos. 204–212, *c.* 1900, stand out, red brick with yellow brick detail, with crenellations and corner towers. Also of interest is the **The Avenues Adult Education Centre**, by *William Botterill*, built in 1888 for Hull School Board as the Industrial School for Girls. At the eastern end, on the N side No. 78 (**Ivy Villa**), of the 1880s, with its Gothic windows, is by *George Thorpe*. Many of the houses at this end of Park Avenue have colourful tiled entrances.

Back on **Princes Avenue**, opposite Pearson Park, there are several lofty three-storey Victorian red and yellow brick terraces with a great assortment of carved heads as keystones. The last of the Avenues proper, **Victoria Avenue**, has plenty of attractive houses but nothing of particular merit. Then one reaches **Queen's Road** and the **Queen's Hotel**, built *c.* 1865, which once had its own bowling green. Nearby, on the corner of **Princes Road**, is *John M. Dossor*'s **parish hall** of 1902, built to serve *Temple Moore*'s Anglican church of 1896, St Augustine of Hippo, on Queen's Road, which was demolished in 1976. On the E side of Princes Road is some of Hull's earliest surviving cul-de-sac or 'court' housing, **Beech Grove**, dated 1884 and **Willow Grove**. Looking N, a bridge carrying the former Hull–Barnsley railway line, opened 1885, interupts the distant view of **Lambert Street Primitive Methodist Church**, 1894 by *T.B. Thompson* and *W.A. Gelder*.

E along Queen's Road, set back, No. 41, built 1899–1900 as St Augustine's vicarage by *Temple Moore*. Brown brick with red brick and painted ashlar dressings. A six-bay façade of tall narrow sash windows, twelve-pane to the ground floor, ten-pane to the first floor. Then **St Vincent de Paul R.C. church**, 1932 by *Jopling & Wright*, Romanesque Revival with a Byzantine feel to the tall campanile. Alongside is the former **St Vincent's Boys Home**, now flats, Arts and Crafts influenced, of grey and red brick with hipped slate roof. Five bays, the centre three projecting forward with large mullioned-and-transomed bays to the ground floor and basement, and a rendered central canted bay to the third and attic storeys. It was built 1908–9, and designed by *Arthur Lowther* who was probably also responsible for the adjacent **St Vincent's R.C. Primary School** of 1904.

W along Queen's Road brings us to **Newland Avenue**. The first road on the left, **Ella Street**, has on the S side several substantial Late Victorian houses with shaped gables. Behind, three 'squares' of houses of the late 1880s, designed for clerks and artisans. Further N some of the last courtyard housing to be built survives off **Sidmouth Street**, which runs W from Newland Avenue. This was built just before the First World War, and stands opposite an excellent **school** of 1911–12 by the City Architect, *Joseph H. Hirst*.

Newland Avenue leads into **Cottingham Road**. At the junction two contrasting places of worship. On the NW corner **Newland Methodist Church** (Wesleyan), 1927–8 by *Gelder & Kitchen*, octagonal with a great dome. The same firm designed the less traditional **Hull Community Church**, 2006, extended 2009, on the other corner. Opposite, on the N side of **Cottingham Road**, stands the complex formerly known as

118. St John Newland, Clough Road, by William Hutchinson, 1833, with chancel and vestry by Smith & Brodrick, 1893

Newland Homes, built 1895–1902 as the Port of Hull Society's Orphan Homes. By *W.H. Bingley*, in a style more reminiscent of the 1870s than the end of the C19. Solid grey brick houses, named after benefactors, are sited around a large open green with a school at the N end.

Further E, at the junction with **Beverley Road**, the half-timbered **Haworth Arms**, 1925 by *Llewellyn Kitchen*. This lies at the heart of **Newland**, a former hamlet in the parish of Cottingham where in the early C19 a number of Hull merchants erected country villas. These have been demolished but the Anglican church built in 1833, **St John (Newland)** [118], at the W end of **Clough Road**, and the memorials inside and in the churchyard, are a reminder of that era. Built of white brick by *William Hutchinson*, the church was originally a simple rectangular building with lancet windows. Chancel and vestry added 1893 by *Smith & Brodrick* when the windows on the S side were enlarged and given Perp tracery. Good C20 stained glass by *Burlison & Grylls*, *William Aikman*, *Harry J. Stammers* and others. Adjacent **vicarage**, a grey brick villa of 1862.

Two buildings further N need to be mentioned. On the W side of **Beverley Road** stands **Dawson House** (originally Endsleigh), an Italianate villa by *Smith & Brodrick*, 1876–7 for William Glossop, brewer. In 1901 it became the convent of the Sisters of Mercy (R.C.) who in 1905 established a teacher training college, later part of Humberside University, with a chapel and other buildings by *Edward Simpson*.

119. No. 137 Newland Park, by Blackmore Sykes, 1923

A mile or so NE, between Beverley Road and the River Hull, stands **Haworth Hall** or **Hull Bank House**, a substantial mid-C18 country house. Richard Burton (d.1765) was described as of 'Hull Bank' in 1741 but a 'great part' of the house was rebuilt for his successor Ralph Burton, *c.* 1765–8, almost certainly by *Thomas Atkinson* of York.

Back on **Cottingham Road,** walk w as far as the **University of Hull** (*see* p. 77), opposite which lies **Newland Park**, the most pleasing of Hull's late Victorian middle-class planned developments. The estate was laid out by *William Botterill* in 1877–8 with surprising originality. Instead of the grid-like plan of The Avenues here the street layout is in the form of a distorted figure of eight. The land was divided up for sale into some ninety large plots but the take-up was slow. Only five houses had been built by 1885, fourteen by 1905, but 115 by 1930. Many of the houses are therefore classic examples of early C20 suburbia.

Enter Newland Park via the entrance opposite Ferens Avenue. On the right Nos. 8–10 by *Wellsted, Dossor & Wellsted*, 1908, rendered with gables, have an Arts and Crafts feel, a contrast to Nos. 18–20, *c.* 1885, probably by *William Botterill*, a sizeable red brick pair with a slate roof and terracotta and stone details. The Arts and Crafts style is back with Nos. 22–24 by *Dossor*, 1906. On the opposite side No. 37, built 1922, is by the best local architectural practice working at this period, *Blackmore Sykes*; more rendering, mock timber-framing to the gable above a central porch, and distinctive shaped corner bays. Back on the right-hand side, Nos. 28–30 are by *Brodrick, Lowther & Walker*, 1906, a rather dull pair in red brick, not their most inspired work. Opposite, No. 41, by *J. McLardie McGeoch*, 1920–1, has an interesting curvy gable. The substantial house on the corner, No. 45, 1924–5, is another by *Blackmore Sykes*, half-timbered, with panels of herringbone brickwork set in the two-storey shaped corner bays. Across the road, also half-timbered, is No. 62 by *Blanchard, Wheatley & Houldsworth*. Turn left and follow the curve of the street to the next bend. On the right-hand side, on the corner plot, stands a neat rendered house with a hipped roof and tall stack (No. 90) by *Dudley Habron c.* 1928. No. 105, further along on the opposite side, was the home of Philip Larkin 1974–85, who described the four-bedroomed brick box with a prominent integral garage (altered beyond recognition since he lived there) as 'an utterly undistinguished little modern house'. On the opposite side of the street, as it bends N again, No. 108 by *Wheatley & Houldsworth*, 1926–7, is a picturesque faux medieval manor house, half-timbered with gables and tall diagonal stacks. No. 110, 1923–4 by *Blanchard, Wheatley & Houldsworth* also has mock timber-framing. Approaching the junction Nos. 124–126 are by *Habron & Robson*, 1910, rendered with two-storey bows. Opposite is one of the most distinctive houses in Newland Park, No. 137, 1923, another from the *Blackmore Sykes* stable [119]. Queen Anne, red brick with a hipped roof, made original by the addition of a two-storey porch with a shaped top in a blatantly Art Deco style. The corner plot of the loop, opposite, is filled by **West Garth** (No. 132), 1910 by *Wellsted, Dossor & Wellsted*, almost certainly the work of *John M. Dossor*. He utilized the fashionable 'butterfly plan', the revolutionary layout pioneered by E.S. Prior at The Barn, Exmouth, Devon in 1896, with wings set at an angle of 45 degrees, leading off a central hall. Diagonally opposite are Nos. 46–48, another competent pair by *Dossor*, 1907. Continue N towards Cottingham Road, passing on the left No. 159 Newland Park, rendered with buttresses and heavy timbers, by a little-known Hull architect *B.J.A. Smith*, 1925.

Turn left at the junction with Cottingham Road, then left into **Chanterlands Avenue**. On the w side **Northern Cemetery**, 1912, with chapel by *Joseph H. Hirst*.

West: Anlaby Road and Hessle Road

There are two main roads leading w from the city, Anlaby Road and Hessle Road, both of which began to be developed in the early C19. Much of the easternmost section of **Hessle Road** is taken up with a 1980s dual carriageway leaving little of interest other than the grey brick **Vauxhall Tavern**, *c.* 1814, and the elaborate faience, terracotta and half-timbered **Alexandra Hotel**, *c.* 1895, by *Smith, Brodrick & Lowther*. There is more to see at the beginning of **Anlaby Road**, but that is covered elsewhere (by Walk 5, p. 138).

This walk begins at **Hull Royal Infirmary** [121], which stands on the N side of Anlaby Road on the site of *Lockwood & Mawson's* **Workhouse** of 1851–2. The main fourteen-storey, thirty-two-bay tower block of concrete faced with mosaic panels, 1962–7, by *Yorke, Rosenberg & Mardall*, dominates the city skyline. At the rear are two large dark brick ranges of 1892 and 1912, the centre bays of the latter flanked by tall Italianate

120. Walk 8

121. Hull Royal Infirmary, Anlaby Road, by Yorke, Rosenberg & Mardall, 1962–7

towers. Much has been added to the site in recent years including the three-storey **Women & Children's Hospital**, 2003, by *Taylor Young Partnership*, a New Modernist white rectangular building. In front of the main tower is a **statue** of Dr John Alderson by *Westmacott jun.*, 1833.

Although most of the older buildings opposite the hospital, on the s side of Anlaby Road, have been replaced by local authority housing some C19 houses survive. No. 197, *c.* 1855, (now a shop) offers a glimpse of what has been lost. Adjoining to the right is a piece of walling with a pair of stuccoed pilasters; this is a fragment of **Hope House**, 1840, by *Charles Hutchinson*, built as a female penitentiary 'for the reclamation of fallen women'. Off to the left is **Linnaeus Street**, so-called because it led to the Hull Botanic Garden, laid out on a 6-acre site in 1812 and closed *c.* 1880. Tucked away on the E side of Linnaeus Street is the former **Western Jewish Synagogue**, 1902 by *B.S. Jacobs*. Romanesque, of red brick with terracotta details, much like a Nonconformist chapel, with a portico flanked by rather chunky two-storey canted bays.

122. No. 215 Anlaby Road, 1840s

Interior with original fittings including gallery. Back on **Anlaby Road**, No. 215 [122], a delightful stuccoed Greek Revival villa built in the early 1840s, probably by *George Jackson*, is a rare survival.

Further w, past the large roundabout and a scruffy mid-Victorian row that ends with the smarter **Eagle Inn**, one reaches **Coltman Street**, a long street with fine examples of early-to-mid-Victorian lower-middle-class housing fortunately saved by a rehabilitation scheme in the 1980s. The street was laid out *c.* 1840 and developed piecemeal over the next thirty years. Many of the original houses survive. Those of the 1840s–50s have simple classical detail, e.g. on the w side Nos. 179–186, a stuccoed terrace, and on the e side Nos. 37–38, all with doorcases with Doric columns *in antis*. On the w side again No. 168, *c.* 1854 by *Benjamin Musgrave*, red brick with a Doric doorcase recessed in a segmental arch; No. 114, also by *Musgrave*, is similar. Some of the later Victorian houses have elaborate woodwork. No. 50, on the e side, has a particularly exuberant carved doorcase and a bay window topped by an ornate wooden balcony. Back on the w side Nos. 138–141, nicely inscribed **Calvert Terrace**, have arched stone doorways with heads. The passageway has a pretty wooden fanlight. Finally on the e side an early pair, Nos. 100–101 [123], stuccoed with Doric columns, and No. 102 (**West Hull Liberal Club**), a small 1840s villa.

123. Nos. 100–101 Coltman Street, 1840s

Coltman Street runs through to **Hessle Road**. From here westwards Hessle Road is a lively shopping street beginning with the **Premier Store**, 1898, by *W.A. Gelder*. When just completed it was described in *The Builder* as 'a somewhat extravagant corner shop ... the most showy piece of shopbuilding in the town'. Flemish Renaissance gables, brick with stone bands and decorative frieze, squat Tuscan colonnade to second floor and an octagonal corner turret with cupola. As showy is the former **Primitive Methodist Chapel** opposite, by *William Freeman*, 1880–1. Romanesque with substantial buttressed towers with pyramidal roofs to left and right and a rose window. Continuing w along the N side of Hessle Road there is a good Art Deco **shopfront** to Nos. 164–168, built for Burton's in 1939. On the corner of Marmaduke Street the **Criterion**, a three-storey Victorian pub, built of grey brick with red brick detail, with a chequerboard band at eaves level, is one of the more distinctive buildings in the area. Hessle Road was the once the heart of the fishing community. The modest terraces in the surrounding streets where the trawlermen lived have all been swept away, but on the s side of the main road, at the junction with Boulevard, stands the Fishermen's Memorial, 1906, a **statue** by *Albert Leake*. It commemorates three local men who lost their lives in the 'Dogger Bank Incident' in 1904 when Russian gunboats mistakenly attacked a fleet of Hull trawlers. (In the distance, past Eton Street, is a French Renaissance **Yorkshire Bank**, 1901, by *J.R. Whitaker*, Leeds, of brick and terracotta decorated with splendid lions holding shields, and next door an impressive inter-war **shopfront**, white faience with upper colonnade, built for Crafts Ltd, drapers.)

Turn right up **Boulevard**, a wide, tree-lined street laid out in 1870 which leads back to Anlaby Road. There was an unfulfilled scheme to link it up with Princes Avenue and so provide a grand boulevard to the w of the town. The street has plenty of large late C19 terraced housing with good details but it did not fulfil its early promise. There are a number of public buildings. On the w side is *W.A. Gelder's* **Western Library**, 1894, of red brick with terracotta and stone details in a Northern Renaissance style. Ornate doorcase and good original interior. Further N comes **St Wilfrid's R.C. church**, 1954–6 by *Williams, Sleight & Co.* Brick with round-headed windows divided by slim buttresses. To the N the 1950s Arts and Crafts-style presbytery with metal leaded windows. Set back is the former **School for Fishermen** of 1914 by *Joseph H. Hirst*. Neo-Early Georgian, brick with stone details, fine ashlar entrance bay with segmental pediment. On the flat roof behind the high parapet the pupils practised signalling. On the E side the former **Hull and Sculcoates Dispensary** by *Hubert Boden*, 1909. Red brick with terracotta details, pilasters and ground-floor arcade.

At the junction with Gordon Street and Chomley Street is a **fountain** of 2008, resplendent with mermaids and herons. It is modelled on the Westbourne Avenue fountain (*see* Walk 7, p. 157). Boulevard Baptist Church, built 1903 on the sw corner of Boulevard and **Gordon Street**, has been demolished but the **Sunday School and Institute** of 1904, next door, survive. Further along Gordon Street is a **police station**, built 1885 and still in use. Continuing N along the w side of **Boulevard** we come to **St Matthew's Parish Hall**, 1904, brick with a half-timbered gable, possibly by *John M. Dossor* and a little further up the **vicarage**, a tall red brick house of 1878. The former Boulevard Higher Grade School, on the E side of Boulevard, 1895 by *Bilson*, a lofty building of red brick with stone bands, has been converted to flats (**Rosedale Mansions**). The choice of new windows is unfortunate. On the corner of Boulevard and Anlaby Road stands **St Matthew**, 1870 by *Adams & Kelly*, a robust building of cream brick with red brick dressings in an E.E. style. It cost £7,000. Big NE tower with broach spire, aisled nave with clerestory and apsidal chancel. Lancets (in the clerestory in groups of three) and plate tracery. Six-bay arcades with round stone piers, but brick arches. Elaborate carved capitals. **Stained glass.** E window 1900 by *Jones & Willis*. N and s aisle, two windows 1907 by *Arthur J. Dix*. w window with Christ in Majesty, 1922, by *John Hardman & Co.*

The view from the N end of Boulevard is obscured by the early 1960s concrete viaduct, known locally as the 'flyover', which takes a realigned Anlaby Road over the railway line. Before crossing to West Park, which lies the other side of the viaduct, it is worth taking a detour E along

124. KC Stadium, West Park, by Miller Partnership, 2002

Anlaby Road back as far as the Coltman Street junction. The houses on **Clyde Terrace** (Nos. 335–343 Anlaby Road) of the 1860s have especially ornate doorcases, in contrast to the more restrained Nos. 289–311 (**Canton Place**) which date from the 1840s, grey brick, two storeys and basement, with steps up to columned porches. On the N side of Anlaby Road, further E, are five extravagant cream brick houses of the 1870s. No. 252, Gothic with oriel window, bargeboards and an elaborate castellated doorway. Nos. 254–256, a semi-detached pair with shaped gables and exotically canopied stone bays and porches. Nos. 258–260, also with shaped gables, have decorated capitals to the doorcases and bays.

  West Park, a municipal park opened in 1885, occupies a block of land bordering Anlaby Road, N of the viaduct. The original layout was by *Joseph Fox Sharpe*, the Borough Engineer. Arts and Crafts-style **lodge** by *Joseph H. Hirst, c.* 1910. Adjoining the park is the spectacular **KC Stadium**, 2002, by *Miller Partnership* [124], with prominent external masts that give it a nautical flavour. In the shape of a great asymmetrical bowl, the football and rugby stadium accommodates 25,000, and includes a learning zone with library and classrooms. To the N, on the E side of Walton Street, is the site of Hull's annual October pleasure fair, one of the largest in Europe. Back on **Anlaby Road**, at the entrance to

125. Carnegie Library (Heritage Centre), Anlaby Road, by Joseph H. Hirst, 1905

West Park, is the former **Carnegie Library** of 1905 by *Joseph H. Hirst*, now the Carnegie Heritage Centre [125]. A delightful half-timbered building centred on a two-storey octagon with pyramidal roof, quite a contrast to the striking classical façade of the former **West Park Picture Palace**, 1914, directly opposite.

The walk ends here but 1 m. further w on Anlaby Road and Hessle Road are isolated groups of significant early c20 buildings:

Lee's Rest Houses [126], at the corner of Anlaby Road and Pickering Road, founded by a local doctor, Charles Lee (d.1912). A superb Early Georgian composition by *Henry T. Hare*, 1914–15. Sixteen large detached two-storey blocks, each originally with eight flats, of brick with hipped tiled roofs, neatly arranged around a spacious quadrangle of grass and gardens. In the centre a pretty pavilion. Arched and pedimented entrance to one side and a reading room with clock tower and cupola to the other. Set back on the opposite side of Anlaby Road are the **Trinity House Almshouses**, 1938–40 by *F. J. Horth & H. Andrew*, a series of more typical Neo-Georgian houses. Just w of Lee's Rest Houses, on the Hull boundary, is **Anlaby Park** [127], a private development from 1911 on the grounds of Spring Villa, a house built *c.* 1840 by John Hudson, a Hull merchant. Its former **lodge**, now No. 2 **The Greenway**, with decorative bargeboards and wooden veranda, survives. The layout and initial housing of the estate was by *Runton & Barry*, and here they developed the ideas used at the Garden Village a few years earlier (*see* Walk 9, p. 174). The estate has a regular street plan with a large central green. Fairly typical detached and semi-detached houses in a mixture of vernacular and Neo-Tudor styles, with half-timbered jettied gables, tile-hanging and rendering, line **Mead Walk**, **Spinney Walk**, **Coppice Side**, **The Greenway** and **Plantation Drive**. A suburban Arcadia. **The Roundway**

126. Lee's Rest Houses, Anlaby Road, by Henry T. Hare, 1914–15

and **Orchard Road** on the opposite side of Anlaby Park Road were developed by the City Land Syndicate, 1914–16, with lesser housing in a similar style, again to the designs of *Runton & Barry*.

Pickering Park, Hessle Road

The 50-acre **Pickering Park**, laid out 1909–11, was presented to the city by Christopher Pickering, a trawler owner, who also provided almshouses, museum, girls' home, Anglican church and vicarage all built on adjacent land along Hessle Road. Little survives of the original park layout and buildings except the large lake and a wall-mounted bronze **drinking fountain**, with portrait medallion, resited on the aviary. The lodge and handsome wrought-iron **gates** by *Joseph H. Hirst* are flanked by the charming **Pickering Almshouses**, 1909, also by *Hirst*

128. Pickering Almshouses, Hessle Road, by Joseph H. Hirst, 1909

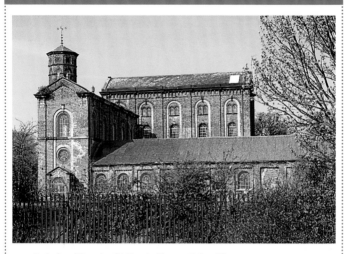

129. Springhead Pumping Station, by Thomas Dale, 1862–4

A Victorian waterworks pumping station on Springhead Avenue, off Willerby Road, 3 m. w of the city centre. A monumental Italianate L-shaped building of red brick with cream brick and stone dressings, built 1862–4, by *Thomas Dale*, Hull Corporation water engineer. s front of two storeys, five bays with pairs of round-arched windows divided by pilasters and a projecting central bay with pediment and octagonal lantern above. w front of three storeys, five bays. Spectacular interior, with a great open hall rising through two storeys containing a vast Cornish beam engine, 1876, supported on four massive Roman Doric cast-iron columns.

[128]. They were presented to the corporation primarily 'for the benefit of persons previously engaged in the fishing industry'. Two single-storey Tudor-style terraces, spacious and friendly looking. Brick and stone, in lively alternation. Mullioned windows, gables and little recessed loggias. Three more terraces in the same style were built a little further w in 1914 and 1952. In between is the former **Museum of Fisheries and Shipping**, built as a combined museum and reading room. Chapel-like, and less successful than the other buildings. Again by *Hirst*, 1912, but said to have been 'virtually designed' by Pickering himself. *John Bilson* was the architect of **Worsley House** (the former Pickering Home for Girls), and the **vicarage**, both 1914 and Neo-Early Georgian, and also **St Nicholas's church**, 1914–15, demolished 1968 and replaced with present building by *Elsworth Sykes*, 1969–70.

Walk 9.

East: Holderness Road and Garden Village

Holderness Road is the old turnpike road leading NE from the city to the plain of Holderness, the flat sweep of rich agricultural land that lies between the coast and the Humber estuary. The first stretch, E from **North Bridge**, rebuilt 1931, is known as **Witham**, a wasteland of workshops, car dealers' showrooms and service garages. Only a few buildings stand out including on the S side the **Annison Building**, *c.* 1900, originally livery stables, a prominent corner block. Stabling on the first floor, an extraordinary arrangement. Otherwise it is the pub façades that grab attention. **The Plimsoll Ship**, refronted 1874, has ornate woodwork with carved heads of kings on leafy backgrounds and the more prominent **Windmill Hotel**, *c.* 1870, remodelled 1902, has splendid multi-coloured faience to the ground floor. Between these two, on Malton Street, is a pleasing former **Board School**, Queen Anne style with stepped gables, by *Botterill & Bilson*, 1888.

130. Walk 9

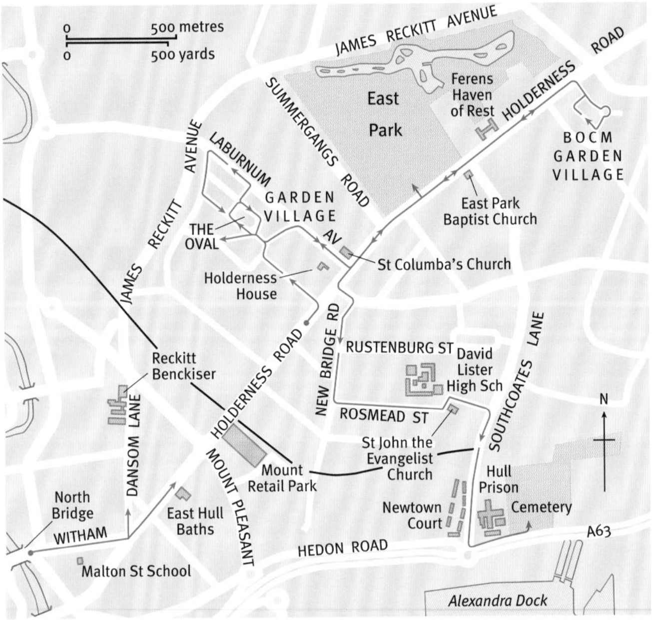

130. Walk 9

131. Holderness Road, East Hull Baths, by Joseph H. Hirst, 1897–8, with former James Reckitt Public Library, by W.A. Gelder, 1888–9, right

Opposite the Windmill Hotel is **Dansom Lane** where on the w side are the mutilated remains of *H.F. Lockwood*'s Gothic **British School**, 1838. Dansom Lane leads to the large factory complex of **Reckitt Benckiser**. Here Isaac Reckitt began his starch-making business in 1840; a hundred years later, as Reckitt & Colman, it had 7,000 employees. The oldest surviving building is the admirable Early Georgian **Francis Reckitt Institute**, 1917, by *G.B. Carvill* and *Frank N. Reckitt*. The latter had worked for Lutyens. A two-storey ashlar-faced range, *c.* 1923, links with the large Neo-Georgian **office block**, 1951–2, by *Yates, Cook & Darbyshire,* who also designed the adjacent **research centre**, 1951–6, five storeys, brick with full-height projecting rounded stairwells. War memorial **fountain** with figure, 1922, and James Reckitt **memorial** with bronze figure of woman and child, 1926, both by *William Aumonier*. The Reckitt family, and Thomas R. Ferens, Managing Director and later Chairman of the firm, were the chief benefactors of the city.

Holderness Road [131] proper begins at Dansom Lane, and a little way E on the s side is the former **James Reckitt Public Library**, 1888–9 by *W.A. Gelder*, Hull's first public library. Venetian Gothic to the ground floor, Tudor above with central three-storey tower and oriel window. Red brick with Ancaster and Howley Park stone detail. Next door is the more extravagant **East Hull Baths**, 1897–8 by *Joseph H. Hirst* then of the City Engineer's Department. Alternate brick and yellow terracotta bands, scrolled and broken terracotta pediments and a pretty wrought-iron balcony. Superb original tiles to the entrance hall.

It is now ½ m. before we reach any buildings of particular interest. Just beyond Jalland Street, on the side of Holderness Road, is a somewhat altered terrace of middle-class housing, **Chestnut Villas** (Nos. 365–71) of the 1880s, probably by *W.A. Gelder* who lived in No. 365. His friend and client Joseph Rank, founder of the milling firm, lived in No. 371. The film magnate J. Arthur Rank was born here. Opposite, No. 348 is a neat mid-Victorian villa with a prominent porch. Back on the N side, at the corner of Village Road stands a statue of James Stuart, local Liberal politician, by *William Aumonier*, 1924, placed here by Thomas R. Ferens who lived in the nearby **Holderness House**. Set back in wooded grounds, this grand Jacobean Revival mansion was built 1838 by *James Clephan* for B.M. and J.E. Jalland. Of grey brick with stone dressings, the house has shaped gables, mullioned-and-transomed bays and a tall porch tower.

It was on the estate attached to Holderness House that the **Garden Village** [132] was built 1907–13. This was developed by Sir James Reckitt chiefly for the workers in his factory on Dansom Lane (*see* above) and is really more of a garden suburb than a village. Reckitt was a Quaker, and in creating Garden Village he was following in the footsteps of fellow Quaker industrialists George Cadbury, who built Bournville for his workforce, and Joseph Rowntree, who developed New Earswick near York. The latter was begun in 1904, only three years before Reckitt announced his own determination to 'establish a Garden Village, with-

132. Garden Village, bird's-eye view, by Runton & Barry, from *Academy Architecture*, 1911

133. First-class housing, The Oval, Garden Village, by Runton & Barry, *c.* 1907–8

in a reasonable distance of our Works, so that those who are wishful might have the opportunity of living in a better house, with a garden, for the same rent that they now pay for a house in Hull – with the advantages of fresher air, and such Clubs, and out-door amusements, as are usually found in rural surroundings'. The same year, 1907, he purchased the Holderness House estate, on the N side of Holderness Road, and established the Garden Village Company, commissioning *Runton & Barry* to design the layout and buildings for the 'village' on the 130-acre site. The Garden Village was officially opened on 2 July 1908 and by the middle of 1913 over 500 houses had been completed.

Percy T. Runton (brother-in-law of Thomas R. Ferens's adopted son) and William E. Barry were competent provincial architects for whom Garden Village was a major commission. Their inspiration probably came from the work of Parker & Unwin at New Earswick, located less than 40 m. away. The Hull development lacks the originality of New Earswick, nor does it boast the picturesque mix of styles found at Port Sunlight, where the soap manufacturer W.H. Lever employed a range of architects for his model village. Yet by contrast to the stark brick terraces and squalid courtyards where many of the Reckitt's factory workers had previously lived, Garden Village must have seemed idyllic.

There are twelve tree-lined streets or avenues, an irregular mix of curves and straights lines; most are named after trees or shrubs, as at New Earswick. The roads, not designed for motor cars, are quite narrow (local bylaws had to be suspended to permit this), a space-saving exercise to allow as many houses as possible whilst adopting Parker & Unwin's model of a maximum of twelve per acre. The majority of the houses are semi-detached or in short terraces, and characteristically have small front gardens with longer ones behind. Privet hedges help to maintain the rural feel. There are also some groups of terraces at right angles to the road, such Nos. 25–47 **Lilac Avenue**, which have a footpath in front, an adaptation of the familiar courtyard plan favoured by speculative Hull builders in the c19.

The obvious starting place to explore Garden Village is the green space called **The Oval**. The key public buildings were sited here: the **Club House**, 1909, and the Village Hall, 1910. The former is a stuccoed building in a bland Wrenaissance style with a semicircular porch. A contrasting style was chosen for the Village Hall. The large brick and timber-framed building, used chiefly for church services and meetings, was demolished following war damage, and several undistinguished bungalows now occupy the site. s of the Club House, and separated from it by the houses of Lime Tree Avenue, is the former **Shopping Centre** [134], designed 'to assist in giving the Village some architectural interest'. It was built in 1909, the same year as the Club House, and is in a similar style, though more successful. The two-storey complex is set around three sides of a courtyard, and has a central arched entrance with pedimented gables and domed clock-turret colonnade with balcony above providing access to first-floor flats.

The polite architecture chosen for the Club House and Shopping Centre contrasts with the vernacular-influenced housing. Although 'not self conscious and aggressively and irritatingly artistic and arty and craft', as Reckitt's biographer put it, the influence of the Arts and Crafts movement, and especially the work of Voysey, is evident. The emphasis is on simple hipped roofs, low sweeping pitches, wide eaves and tall chimneys. Some of the houses have distinctive corner buttresses, and many have recessed porches. The dominant building materials are roughcast brickwork, sometimes with tile-hanging or mock timber-framing adorning the gables, and small plain clay tiles for the roofs, echoing the vernacular buildings of the Home Counties rather than paying homage to anything found locally. Five grades of house were built, all two-storey. Among the first (and best) houses to be erected were those on the NE side of **The Oval** [133]. These were of the 'first class', designed for supervisory staff, and had two sitting rooms, kitchen, scullery, W.C., and on the first floor, three or four bedrooms, a bathroom with lavatory and a separate W.C. The fourth- and fifth-class houses had downstairs a living room, a kitchen or scullery with bath, W.C. and upstairs two or three bedrooms. Most of

134. Shopping Centre, Garden Village, by Runton & Barry, 1909

the houses are now in private ownership, and the replacement of timber doors and casements with uPVC has spoilt the appearance of
many, in spite of the designation of Garden Village as Hull's first
Conservation Area, in 1970.

Around the Garden Village are three sets of almshouses, all half-timbered with prominent chimneystacks. The **Juliette Reckitt Haven of
Rest**, 1911, and the **Frederic Reckitt Homes of Rest**, 1912, both by
Runton & Barry, are towards either end of Laburnum Avenue. In 1924
the group known as the **Sir James Reckitt Village Haven** was built on
Village Road, to the designs of *F. Runton Waller*. Also on Village Road is
a half-timbered house, No. 71, built as the **Village Office** in 1908.

135. Khyber Pass, East Park, by E.A. Peak, *c.* 1887

Leaving Garden Village via **Laburnum Avenue** takes one past **St Columba**, which stands on the E side, at the junction with Holderness Road. This large brick church with shallow buttresses and round-headed lancet windows was built 1958–60. It was designed by *W. Milner & R.B. Craze* as a replacement for an incomplete church of 1926–9 by *E.E. Lofting & E. Priestley Cooper*, destroyed by bombing in 1943. Aisled nave, chancel and small NE spire. Excellent white-painted interior with large pillars to the tall nave arcades and a shallow arcade around the chancel. Nave and chancel in one. The lower half of the walls at the E end and the piers in the first bay of the nave are retained from the bombed church. The C19 stone **font** was formerly in St James, Hull. The mural **painting** on the altar wall is by *Robert Hendra & Geoffrey Harper*, 1960 who were also responsible for the **stained glass** in the W window and N chapel windows. Back on Holderness Road No. 435 (**Wood Grange**) is one of the more attractive houses in the area. Built in 1880 by *Henry E. Bown* of Harrogate for Frederic I. Reckitt. Red brick with a jettied half-timbered and tile-hung gable to the left and a corner turret with half-timbering and tiled pyramidal roof to the right.

A little further along Holderness Road is **East Park** opened in 1887 and designed by *Joseph Fox Sharpe*, Borough Engineer. The **lodge** at the entrance designed by *Joseph H. Hirst*, 1903. The park was extended eastwards to cover some 120 acres. The gates were replaced in 1964 by a brutalist concrete **gateway**, but a number of original features survive in the park, notably the **Khyber Pass**, a rocky canyon, designed by *E.A. Peak* [135]. A water chute by *Wicksteed*, installed in 1929, is still in use.

After East Park, continue E along the N side of Holderness Road to **Ferens Havens of Rest**, 1911, by *Runton & Barry* for Thomas R. Ferens. Twelve Tudor brick and stone almshouses around three sides of a green. Then the former **Astoria** cinema, white-painted classical with clean lines and refined simplicity, by *J. Adamson*, 1934.

On the S side, just before the junction with Ings Road and Maybury Road, is the **BOCM Garden Village**, laid out in 1921. A modest venture by the British Oil and Cake Mills, said to have been designed by *A.I. Windross*, estate agent, and Major *Edward Goddard*, timber merchant, evidently with advice from the architect *T.B. Thompson*. The 'village' consists of three short streets – **The Broadway**, **Seafield Avenue** and **Willows Avenue** – and the **Bowling Circle** around a small green. Some of the semi-detached and terraced houses are standard inter-war suburban; others bear similarity to those of Reckitt's Garden Village, which no doubt influenced this development.

The walk ends here, but there are other things to see on the S side of **Holderness Road** as one returns SW towards the city centre. An extravagant Edwardian Baroque stone-fronted **shop** with upper Ionic colonnade and corner turret on the corner of Southcoates Avenue was built for the grocer William Jackson, 1912, probably by *W.A. Gelder*. On the opposite corner the modest Free Gothic **East Park Baptist Church**, 1916 by *J. Illingworth*, Leeds, and next **The Mill** pub comprising a five-storey tower mill, *c.* 1820, with four sails and a former mill house. The last was the birthplace of Joseph Rank in 1854. Then two more pubs, **The Crown**, 1938 with distinctive Art Deco pilasters, and **The Bank**, a neat classical former savings bank, 1920, by *John Bilson*. Turn left down **Southcoates Lane** and first right along **New Bridge Road** as far as **Steynburg Street** and **Rustenburg Street**. Here are the earliest surviving council houses in Hull, built 1902–3 by *Joseph H. Hirst*, for families displaced on the building of Alfred Gelder Street. The houses, in pairs, or short terraces, have distinctive canted bays. Further along New Bridge Road on the left is **Rosmead Street** towards the end of which is **St John the Evangelist church**, 1924–5, by *Leslie T. Moore*. Partially destroyed by bombs in 1941, and rebuilt by Moore to the original plan, 1952. The spacious austere Gothic interior owes much to the work of the architect's father-in-law *Temple Moore*. The interior was skilfully adapted for combined use as a community building and place of worship by *Jonathan Hobson* of *Ingleby & Hobson*, 2007. Nearby is **David Lister High School**, 1964–6, by *Lyons, Israel & Ellis*, a large complex of one, two and three-storey white concrete blocks with even bands of windows (demolition planned).

From here return to Holderness Road or go to the end of Rosmead Street and turn right down Southcoates Lane to **Hedon Road**. Here at the junction are **Newtown Buildings**, three-storey inter-war flats to the W, and to the E of **Hull Prison**, 1865–70, designed by *David Thorp*, Borough Surveyor, and completed by his successor *R.G. Smith*. Described by a contemporary as being in 'Carpenters Gothic' style it has

136. Crematorium, Hedon Road Cemetery, probably by Joseph H. Hirst, 1899–1901

a prominent central ventilating tower with cell blocks radiating from it and the usual monumental gatehouse entrance, somewhat disfigured by a rather clumsy single-storey addition. Adjoining the prison on the E the 24-acre **Hedon Road Cemetery**, laid out 1873–4, has plenty of good memorials, a Gothic stone **lodge** and a disused early **crematorium** of 1899–1901 [136], probably by *Joseph H. Hirst*, with **columbarium**. Opposite, on the S side of Hedon Road, can be seen the tower of the 1880s **hydraulic engine house** on Alexandra Dock, one of the few remaining Victorian dock buildings in Hull.

Marfleet village, 1 m. further E, was taken into the borough of Hull in 1882. **St Giles's church**, Church Lane, 1883–4 by *J.T. Webster* of Hedon, Gothic, chancel, nave and bellcote. Early to mid-C19 wall-tablets and good stained glass window by *C.E. Kempe*, 1905. **Marfleet Primary School**, Marfleet Lane, 1892 by *John Bilson*.

Walk 10.

Sutton-on-Hull

Sutton lies 3 m. NE of the centre of Hull, and more than 1 m. from the river to which the latter part of the name refers. It was taken into the city in 1929 and is the only settlement within the boundaries to retain its village identity. A small agricultural community with a handful of gentry living in large houses in the surrounding countryside, Sutton developed from the mid C19, stimulated by the opening of a station on the new Hull to Hornsea railway line in 1864. The village has managed to retain its compact historic centre in spite of being surrounded by later C20 housing.

Begin at the parish church of **St James**, Church Street [138]. The tower and nave are of medieval brick, the chancel is of stone. Roughcast applied to the brickwork in 1793 to imitate stone was removed from the tower in the 1860s and from the s side of the nave in 1955. There was a chapel at Sutton in the mid C12 attached to St Peter's church, Wawne, but the present church dates from the mid C14 when it was made collegiate. A college with a master and five chaplains was founded in 1347 and the church consecrated in 1349 just as the Black Death was raging.

137. Walk 10

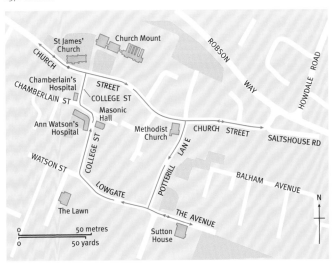

138. St James, Church Street, nave and chancel, mid-c14; tower c15

The founder of the college, Sir John de Sutton, rebuilt the nave at this time and the chancel was rebuilt by the rector. The w tower, which has stone quoins, came later in the c15 and the nave aisles were extended w to embrace it. The aisle and chancel windows are straight-headed. The five-light Dec E and Perp w window are of the 1866–7 restoration as are the windows immediately w of the N and s doorways and the vestry on the N side of the chancel. The organ chamber was added in 1883 by *F. S. Brodrick* of *Smith & Brodrick*, who removed the clerestory on the N side of the nave and added the new battlements and pinnacles to the tower in 1889. The s clerestory and aisle parapets were rebuilt in 1965 and the c18 s porch was removed in 1972.

Inside, the tower is supported on very big, diagonally placed and canted piers with Perp panelling. The rest of the interior is largely of the restoration of 1866–7 by *R. G. Smith*. He replaced the massive octagonal brick piers and arches with more slender octagonal stone piers and triple-chamfered arches. The roofs were raised, a new chancel arch inserted and the clerestory windows removed. Late c12 **font**, tub-shaped with a top band of very small nailhead. **Pulpit**. Gothic, of Caen stone carved by *Thomas Frith*, 1867. **Painting**. Small late c18 panel of

St James the Great signed *Parkin*. It was on the front of the pulpit, under the chancel arch, before the mid-c19 restoration. Very good Perp **screen** between tower and s aisle. **Choir stalls** of 1920, designed by *John Bilson*, and **woodwork** in vestry by *Robert Thompson*, 1969. **Stained glass**. Early c19 quarries in the head of some chancel windows. Nine mediocre windows of the 1870s–80s including E window, 1874, by *H. Hughes*, and s chancel window, 1881, by *Ward & Hughes*. The NE window of *c.* 1906 by *Kempe* is far superior. **Monuments**. In the chancel an effigy in armour on tomb-chest with shields in quatrefoils. Of high quality, it commemorates Sir John de Sutton d.1357 [139], but was set up when he rebuilt the church. Some good early-to-mid-c19 wall-tablets, including ones by *George Earle* and *W.D. Keyworth sen.*

w of the church, on the N side of **Church Street**, stands the former **primary school** of 1858 by *W.D. Keyworth sen.* in a Tudor Gothic style. E of the church is **Church Mount**, a speculative development of twelve tall, gabled villas in red brick, built 1865–70 for a Hull jeweller, Thomas Kirk, who intended to capitalize on the coming of the railway. They are quite urban in character. Long gardens to the rear, and in front a generous communal green bordered by trees, set behind iron railings. On the s side of the street **Belmont Villa** (No. 76) is a solid yellow brick Victorian villa with an elegant doorcase with fluted columns. Elsewhere in Church Street there are a number of c18 and early c19 brick farmhouses and cottages. Some were originally single-storey as indicated by changes in the brickwork or the presence of the former roof-line in the gable. This can be seen clearly on Nos. 82–84 Church Street, which was

139. St James, effigy of Sir John de Sutton d.1357

140. Sutton Methodist Church, Church Street, 1859

probably a single-storey, three-bay farmhouse with axial stack and baffle-entry plan. The most substantial is No. 98, a late C18 three-storey, four-bay farmhouse, gable end to the street. The finest building on the street is **Sutton Methodist Church** [140] (Wesleyan), a handsome brick building of 1859 but still in the Georgian tradition. Three-bay pedimented façade with stuccoed bands, arched window surrounds and a porch of pairs of Tuscan columns.

Church Street eventually becomes **Saltshouse Road**. No. 375 is of *c.* 1820, grey brick, hipped slate roof with Doric porch. Beyond are a handful of pleasing Late Victorian suburban villas. The most striking is No. 365 (**Addison House**), dated 1900, by *Freeman, Son & Gaskell*, in a Tudor style, with battlemented towers at either end, gargoyles, stone-mullioned windows and tile-hanging. The same architects were also responsible for No. 369, with its tile-hanging, mullioned windows and decorative chimneystack, No. 351 and possibly No. 347 (**Sutton Place**), a large house with half-timbering and an oriel window.

Return to Church Street and turn left down **Potterill Lane**, a pleasant backwater on the E side of which are three early C20 bungalows with overhanging eaves with decorative cast-iron brackets. At the end turn left into **Lowgate**. On the N side No. 4, which dates from the mid C19, is lodge-like, of yellow brick and slate. The larger **Cramond Lodge** nearby, set well back from the street, is early C19. Lowgate leads into **The Avenue**, on the s side of which is **Sutton House**, of the 1770s, built for a Hull merchant, Richard Howard. Major extensions in the C19 but the original s front remains. Three storeys, five bays, of painted brick with stone dressings. The centre three bays project slightly and are pedimented. The entrance portico has fluted Doric columns. Returning to **Lowgate**, No. 6 (**Jasmine Cottage**) on the N side is single-storey, of the mid C18. On the opposite side **Victoria Cottage** (Nos. 23–25), another single-storey cottage in white painted brick with a wide pantile roof, is remarkably unspoilt. It probably dates from the late C17, and is therefore a rarity in this part of Yorkshire. Three bays, with a gabled porch at the right end bay. Next come Nos. 27–29, of *c.* 1800, then **The Lawn** (No. 22), a white brick villa with Welsh slate roof with an attractive cast-iron belvedere, said to have been built in the 1860s.

Lowgate leads into **College Street**. Set back on the E side is a pair of large grey brick houses (**The Elms** and **Beech Lawn**) of the 1850s. Further N is the former Primitive Methodist chapel (now the **Masonic Hall**) of 1876 by *Joseph Wright*, overtly High Victorian with its polychrome brickwork and Italianate detail. Opposite is **Ann Watson's Hospital**, a 'College' originally designed to provide accommodation for the widows and daughters of Anglican clergy. The original two-storey grey brick block of 1816 has a N front of seven bays, of which the second and third, and fifth and sixth bays project slightly with a first-floor band. The addition to the S of 1864–5, with a rounded end linking it to the original block, was designed by *William Kerby*. Further along College Street is another almshouse complex, **Chamberlain's Hospital**, of 1804 [141]. The pleasing two-storey, five-bay brick façade has a centre bay that projects slightly and a pediment with an oval plaque. Good wooden cornice.

141. Chamberlain's Hospital, College Street, 1804

142. Sutton Grange, Saltshouse Road, *c.* 1815

Several Hull merchants built large houses around the village from the later C18. Most have been demolished, including East Mount, built 1812–14 for Thomas Priestman, and Tilworth Grange, built 1810–20 for Hugh Casson. Lambwath Hall, a late C18 house rebuilt in 1897, has also gone. Two grander houses survive. **Sutton Grange** on **Saltshouse Road** [142], E of the village, was built *c.* 1815 by George Alder, Hull merchant. Grey brick with stone dressings and hipped slate roof. The three-bay w front with Doric portico is framed by giant Doric pilasters. w of the village, on **Wawne Road**, is **Netherhall**, built *c.* 1810 by Henry Bedford, a Hull banker, a grey brick villa. It was altered and extended in 1873.

Excursions

Hessle and the Humber Bridge 188

Cottingham and West Hull Villages 194

East of Hull: Hedon and Burton Constable 203

Beverley 211

Hessle and the Humber Bridge

Hessle can be considered the mother parish of Hull, for Holy Trinity church was a mere chapel of ease to All Saints, Hessle, until 1661. Now a substantial part of the former parish (but not the town) lies within the city boundary. Until the late C18 Hessle was little more than a large agricultural village with a haven where shipbuilding took place and a ferry that crossed the Humber to Barton. Enclosure of the open fields in 1796 released land for building and wealthy Hull merchants erected country residences on the high ground to the w of the village. They were followed in the mid C19 by professionals, tradesmen and trawler owners with their villas and semis built on estates laid out near the newly opened railway station. Hessle has continued to develop as a dormitory town and had a population of around 15,000 in 2005.

143. Hessle

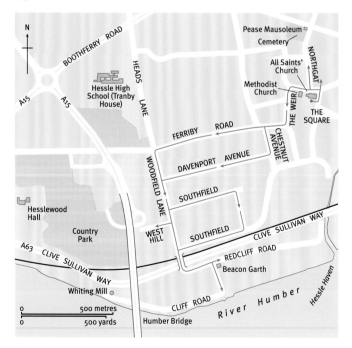

144. All Saints, C13–C15, major alterations by R.G. Smith, 1868–71

NW of **The Square**, a characterless open area created 1921–3, is the fine medieval parish church of **All Saints** [144]. There was a church here in the C11, and the present building is chiefly of the C13–C15, although substantial alterations took place in the C19. The N side of the brick chancel was rebuilt in stone, and the arcade heightened in 1841 by *C. Appleton*. A full restoration was undertaken by *Cuthbert Brodrick* in 1852–3 but the greatest changes took place in 1868–71 under the supervision of *R.G. Smith*. The chancel and its side chapels were taken down and rebuilt further to the E, the nave was lengthened by two bays to the E and the aisles rebuilt, almost trebling their original width. The area of the church was doubled.

Of the Norman church little remains except a collection of **fragments** built into the N wall of the chapel S of the chancel. The S and N doorways and three westernmost arcades of the nave are E.E. The arcades have round piers and moulded capitals with rare painted scrolls. The handsome N aisle windows with reticulated tracery are Dec, most of the other windows are Perp, including the five-light E window. Perp also are the clerestory and the W tower with its graceful recessed spire. At the same time the aisles were extended to embrace the tower. The W ends of these extensions show the original width of the nave aisles. The S porch was built 1874, the E.E. chancel arch heightened 1896 and the vestry added at the W end by *Brodrick, Lowther & Walker* in 1901–2.

Of **furnishings and fittings** the **reredos** of Caen stone with mosaic panels by *Salviati*, and the floor **tiles** by *Maw & Co.* are of 1870. Except for medieval fragments in a window in the s chapel and the Legard arms, probably C18, in the s clerestory most of the **stained glass** is Victorian. The e window, w window and the five s aisle windows by *Hardman*, 1870s, and an excellent n aisle window by *Morris & Co.*, 1899. Other windows by *Percy Bacon & Bros*, 1909, and *L.C. Evetts*, 1971. **Royal arms** of 1725 and a rare modern **hatchment** in n chapel, 1983, with arms of Rupert Alec-Smith, Lord Lieutenant of Humberside and founder of the Georgian Society for East Yorkshire. **Monuments** include a brass inscription to Ann wife of Sir Henry Percy, 1511, and various early-to-mid-C19 wall tablets, classical and Gothic, by *E.H. Baily*, *Thomas Denman* of London and *Whitton* of Beverley. Under the tower on the ne pillar is a brass with full-length effigy of Anthony Bannister, the promoter of the Hull & Withernsea Railway, d.1878, and at e end of the n aisle a fine bronze wall plaque with portrait of Frederick Blunt, first Bishop of Hull, by *L. Merrifield*, 1912.

What little there is to see of architectural interest in the older part of the town lies to the n and w of the church. On **Vicarage Lane** the house with the full-height round-headed blank arch was built as a Wesleyan Methodist chapel, 1813. Further n the former **vicarage**, red brick with stone details and tile-hung gable by *Botterill, Son & Bilson*, 1885–6, with later additions and also the mid-C18 **North Lodge**. Directly w of the Anglican church, and trying to outdo it with another showy spire, is the yellow brick **Methodist church**, Tower Hill, by *William Botterill*, 1875–6, the adjoining **schoolroom** by *Runton & Barry*, 1911. Opposite on **Northgate** some of the oldest properties in the town, Nos. 7–9, a pair of early C18 brick and pantile cottages, one storey and attics with lobby-entry plan. No. 36 is early C19, grey brick with hipped slate roof. Further n off Northgate on **Swanland Road** the **Cemetery** opened 1865. It has two simple Gothic **chapels** in grey brick and at the ne corner the delightful small Gothic **mausoleum** erected for J.R. Pease in 1866 [145]. Also on Swanland Road **Our Lady of Lourdes church** (R.C), 1950, simple, red brick with corner tower.

Back down Northgate and to the right on **The Weir** a mid-C19 grey brick terrace, Nos. 16–22, and to the n, of the same date, Nos. 24–26, a larger semi-detached pair with simple porticos with slender columns and Ionic capitals. Then **Ferriby Road** with the rather dull red brick former police station, **Peeler House**, by *Smith & Brodrick*, 1875, and Victorian terraced housing to n and s. From here Ferriby Road forms the n boundary of the most architecturally rewarding area of the town, filled with substantial Victorian and Edwardian middle-class homes.

With the opening of the Hull to Selby railway in 1840 the area to the n of the station was a target for development, but with no immediate success. Already **Southfield House**, off Greenway, had been built *c.* 1838. It was soon joined by **Cliff House**, w of the station, a typical stuccoed villa with pediments and round-headed windows, built 1840–1 for John

Gresham, one of the promoters of the railway. Then came an inn, the Coburg Hotel (dem.), built just s of the station in 1842, which with its bowling green, quoit ground, skittles and parties taking tea in 'Chinese bowers' in the pleasure gardens, was the objective of evening train rides from Hull in the summer months.

In 1847 *Cuthbert Brodrick* produced plans for a villa estate on **West Hill** for Hull Charterhouse but it was not until twenty years later that a syndicate of Hull businessmen took out long leases on this land on the w side of Woodfield Lane. Four houses were built 1867–9, three at least designed by *William Botterill*: West Hill House (dem.) for the starch manufacturer Francis Reckitt, **Mentone** for his brother James, and **Woodleigh**. **The Chestnuts** next door, of red brick with a large two-storey bow, clustered chimneystacks and a Gothic stone entrance, was designed by *Smith & Brodrick*, 1875 for Claud Hornstedt, ship-owner.

E of Woodfield Lane a much larger estate, **Southfield**, was laid out *c.* 1867. By the early 1870s around twenty houses had been built, a mixture of good cream brick Victorian villas and semi-detached houses. Many were probably by *Botterill* who designed **Rydal Villas**, Nos. 51–53 Southfield, just N of the station, in 1867. Amongst the grander houses are **Woodfields** (Emmanuel Residential Home) and **York Lodge**, No. 30, which has particularly elaborate bargeboards and Gothic hood-moulds to the windows. By the First World War there were fifty houses on Southfield; the later houses include three pairs of semis on the s side by *Runton & Barry*, 1901–3.

Runton & Barry, later the architects of James Reckitt's Garden Village (*see* Walk 9, p. 174) were active in the development of the adjoining **Davenport Estate**, comprising Davenport Avenue, Chestnut Avenue and the s side of Ferriby Road. Laid out *c.* 1894, it was largely complete by 1905. It is a period piece, a tree-lined enclave of middle-class villas and semi-detached houses exhibiting all the hallmarks of minor Late Victorian and Edwardian suburban architecture. There are elements of Queen Anne, Jacobethan and vernacular revival with half-timbered and tile-hung gables, rendering, pargetting, decorative friezes and bargeboards. Terracotta finials abound, including a pair of dragons. The last are on **Davenport Avenue**, Nos. 67–69 by *Runton & Barry*, 1901, who also designed Nos. 57, 65, 68–84 and 88, **Woodside**, the best house in the street, and **Quarry Bank** on the corner with Woodfield Lane.

Gelder & Kitchen designed No. 2 **Chestnut Avenue**, 1901, as a private school. Towards the w end of **Ferriby Road** are a group of Arts and Crafts-style houses by *Runton & Barry*. A contrast to No. 93, also Arts and Crafts, by *John M. Dossor*, 1901, large, rendered and gabled with decorative plasterwork. Opposite on the corner of Woodfield Lane is a single-storey **lodge** to Hesslewood Hall (*see* below), a diminutive villa of grey brick with overhanging eaves. Built 1840–1, probably by *H.F. Lockwood*.

By far the best of the local Arts and Crafts houses, **Beacon Garth** [146], lies to the s of the station on the corner of **Redcliff Road** and **Cliff Road**. Designed by the Scarborough architect *Frank A. Tugwell* in 1896 for a marine engineer, Charles F. Amos. Irregular, Tudor-style of dark red brick with stone details, half-timbering, tile-hanging, tall stacks, large mullioned-and-transomed windows, a great variety of leaded glazing and battlements. Inside are plenty of original tiled fireplaces and a fine Arts and Crafts staircase leading off a large central hall. On the opposite side of Cliff Road the overtly Victorian **Dykes House** of the mid 1860s.

Cliff Road leads down to the Humber foreshore where there is the six-storey tarred brick tower of a **whiting mill** built *c.* 1810. It was used for crushing chalkstone from the great quarry to the N, which with its dramatic steep cliffs and woodland has been a popular resort, known as Little Switzerland, since the late C19. Above soars the magnificent **Humber Bridge** (*see* below).

146. Beacon Garth, Redcliff Road, by Frank A. Tugwell, 1896

147. Humber Bridge, by Freeman, Fox & Partners, 1972–81

Hesslewood Hall, now a business centre and its grounds an office park, ½ m. w of the village, was the earliest and the grandest of the merchants' mansions. Built 1784–91 for the merchant Joseph Pease, to the designs of *Charles Mountain sen.*, the cream brick and slate house was altered and enlarged in the C19 and C20. Handsome five-bay, two-storey and attic main block linked by single-storey, three-bay wings to two-storey pedimented pavilions set back to left and right.

The **Humber Bridge** [147] is one of the great engineering and architectural triumphs of late C20 Britain. Work began in 1972. At the time of opening in 1981 it was, at 4,626 ft (1,410 metres), the longest single-span suspension bridge in the world. The consulting engineers were *Freeman, Fox & Partners* (Partner in charge: *Bernard Wex*), with *R.E. Slater* as architectural adviser.

Engineering considerations dictated the form and elegance of the bridge, but details such as the rounding of the corners of the tower legs, the decorative treatment to the massive concrete anchorage blocks and the colour of the suspended steel structure were introduced for aesthetic reasons. On either side of the river are two reinforced concrete towers consisting of two tapering piers with horizontal braces, standing 520 ft (158.5 metres) above high water. The deck, which carries a dual two-lane carriageway with footpaths and cycle tracks, is made up of 124 hollow steel box sections suspended from the main cables by inclined high-tensile steel spiral strands. The administration building, by *Parker & Rosner*, is a sleek horizontal design with a band of continuous tinted glazing sandwiched between a sloping wall of vitreous enamel panels. Pedestrian access to the bridge is via the visitor car park and viewing area off **Ferriby Road**.

Cottingham and West Hull Villages

From the C18 the villages to the w of Hull were considered by Hull's prosperous merchants as ideal locations for a country residence. Extensive C20 development, much of it on the former grounds of these mansions, has transformed these once rural settlements into popular suburbs.

Cottingham

With its medieval market and fairs, which lasted until the C17, and its long-time role as a dormitory for Hull, Cottingham has always been more of a town than a village. In the late C18 it became the 'favourite place of residence for the more opulent portion of the merchants of Hull' and it could boast of having 'many handsome country houses, gardens and pleasure gardens'.

The large parish church of **St Mary the Virgin** [149], Hallgate, is an impressive cruciform building with nave, chancel, transepts and a dominant crossing tower. There was a church here by the mid C12 but the earliest parts now are the nave, with flowing tracery in the windows, and transepts, both Dec of the early C14. The chancel, all Perp except for a doorway in the N wall, was rebuilt in 1374 by the rector, Nicholas of Louth. Tall tower also Perp, the upper stages probably of the C15. At some stage, possibly in the C18, it was found necessary to strengthen the

148. Cottingham

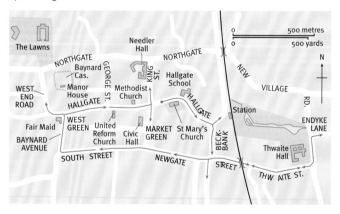

149. St Mary, Cottingham, nave early c14; tower c15

tower by inserting rather clumsy support arches. Eight pinnacles were added in 1744. At the NE corner an impressively sheer staircase turret, almost detached. The church was restored in 1844–5 with further alterations 1895–6 by *Smith, Brodrick & Lowther*. **Stained glass**. Fragment of medieval glass in SW window of S aisle, otherwise so much by *J.B. Capronnier* of Brussels 'that for moments one feels transported into a French church' (Pevsner). Other Victorian and later glass by *H. Dobbelaere*, Bruges, *Hardman & Co.* and *Kempe*. **Monuments**. Brasses to Canon Nicholas of Louth (de Luda) d.1383, and to John Smith d.1504 and wife. A great array of C18–C19 monuments commemorating the numerous merchant families of the parish. The best are at the W end of the nave to members of the Burton family of Hotham Hall and Hull Bank House including one to William Burton d.1764, attributed to *Henry Cheere*.

On the S side of the churchyard is a block of three early Victorian Gothic buildings: **Arlington Hall** built for vestry meetings in the late 1850s; **Church House** with mid-C19 rendered façade and Gothic porch, originally built in 1729 as a workhouse, and **Mark Kirby's School** rebuilt in 1861.

From the church go E along **Hallgate**, on the N side of which is a splendid red brick former **Board School** by *John Bilson*. The date, 1892, is given on an elaborate cartouche of carved brick in the S gable. Three pretty cupolas. Further along several houses of the 1870s with good details including tiled porch surrounds and carved keystones. NE of the junction of Hallgate and Beck Bank is the **Railway Station** of 1846 by

G.T. Andrews with contemporary **station master's house** and **goods shed**. On **Beck Bank** Nos. 24–28, on the E side, form an attractive row of single-storey brick and pantile cottages of the early C18, largely rebuilt 1992–3. Then left into **Thwaite Street**. On the N side several large merchants' houses. **Tudor House**, 1780s, refronted *c.* 1830. Stuccoed façade with pilasters and balustrade. **Green Wickets**, also 1780s with Ionic porch of *c.* 1820 and bay window of *c.* 1900. **Holtby House**, 1871, later the family home of Winifred Holtby. **Southlands**, cream brick, built in the 1860s. On the opposite side Nos. 100–102, a late C18 farmhouse. Behind a high brick wall **Cleminson Hall** built as The Bungalow *c.* 1896 for Charles Wilson, ship-owner, by *Smith, Brodrick & Lowther*. Large, red brick with tile-hanging and half-timbered gables. Finally, on the N side again **Thwaite Hall** built *c.* 1805 (*see* University of Hull, p. 83). The extensive grounds now known as Thwaite Gardens, formerly the University Botanic Gardens, with a great range of trees and plants, are open to the public. Around the corner is **New Village Road**, so called because between Middledyke Lane and Endyke Lane twenty smallholdings were set out on church land in 1819–25 by the Overseers of the Poor for poor families. Originally known as Paupers' Gardens it was called **New Village** by 1830. Most of the original cottages have been rebuilt in recent years although No. 25 **Endyke Lane**, little changed, is still attached to a smallholding.

Return along Thwaite Street, which becomes Newgate Street at the junction with Beck Bank. Directly opposite lies **Snuff Mill Lane**, with **Eastgate House** of the 1780s on the corner. Red brick with graduated Westmorland slate roof. Further down the lane is **Snuff Mill House**, *c.* 1760, a tall narrow building of red brick under a double-span pantile roof with parapet. The watermill which adjoined has been demolished. Continuing along **Newgate** the best house is on the s side, the elegant **Newgate House** built *c.* 1784 for Hull merchant John Thornton. Cream brick with stone dressings and slate roof. Two-storey, five-bay main range flanked by one-bay wings, both originally single-storey. Central door with semicircular porch carried on columns. At the junction with King Street the road becomes **South Street** and the most prominent buildings are on the N side. **Cottingham Memorial Club** (originally Elmtree House), with stone façade, built by Hull draper John Hebblewhite, by 1820; **South Street House** *c.* 1800 and at the w end **Southwood Villa**, early C19.

Right into Baynard Avenue takes us to the triangular **West Green**. (At this point a detour can be made along **West End Road**, opposite the end of which is **The Lawns**, University halls of residence (*see* University of Hull, p. 84). The three-storey **Fair Maid** (formerly Westfield House) facing **West Green** was built *c.* 1778 for William Hall, with a two-storey C19 s extension. Impressive brick garden wall, an arcade of twenty-three blank arches. In the front gardens of Nos. 274–286 **Hallgate** on the N side of West Green can be seen the remains of the outer ditch of the medieval fortified manor house or **castle**. The inner ditch surrounds a

150. Southwood Hall, off Burton Road, Cottingham, *c.* 1660

mound on which stands, hidden from view, the C17 timber-framed **Manor House**, two-storey, four-bay with a simple structure of posts with braces curving up to wall-plate. Continue E along Hallgate. On the N side No. 266, **The Beeches**, is of *c.* 1830, grey brick with bays. On the opposite side Nos. 247–253, a row of late C18 single-storey cottages. The middle section of **Hallgate** is the principal shopping street and most of its older buildings have been drastically altered. What stand out are the two chapels. On the s side **Zion United Reformed Church** and adjoining **Manse**, 1819, by *Appleton Bennison* of Hull. One of the finest Nonconformist chapels in the East Riding. Grey brick, three bays with a three-bay pediment. Round-headed windows in two tiers. Lower

151. Castle Hill Hospital, Cottingham, Oncology and Haemotology Unit, by HLM Design, 2008

entrance bays, left and right, with curving-up parapets. Unspoilt interior galleried on three sides with original pews. Further along on the N side the more showy Italianate **Methodist church**, 1878–9, by *William Ranger* of London.

Turn left at the junction with **King Street**. No. 188, on the E side, is a mid-C18 one-and-a-half-storey brick and pantile cottage with lobby-entry plan. On the opposite side, on the corner of Northgate, is the late C18 **Needler Hall** (*see* University of Hull, p. 84). Back to the Hallgate junction and s along King Street takes us to the **Market Green** and one of Cottingham's earliest buildings, the **Duke of Cumberland**, late C17 with distinctive shaped gables and pronounced band. Adjoining to the w is an excellent row of unspoilt single-storey brick and pantile early C18 **cottages** with steeply pitched roof.

Cottingham's best house, **Southwood Hall** [150], lies to the sw of the village on the N side of Burton Road, surrounded by modern housing. An exceptional red brick and pantile house of *c.* 1660 with Artisan Mannerist details. Of five bays with a central three-storey gabled porch with round-headed opening flanked by pilasters, and a triangular moulded brick pediment over the first-floor window. Fine C17 interior.

On the outskirts of Cottingham is **Castle Hill Hospital** on the site of the large castellated mansion known as **Cottingham Castle**, which was built by a Hull banker, Thomas Thompson, 1814–16. It was gutted by fire in 1861 and subsequently demolished. All that remains is the octagonal **Prospect Tower**, erected in 1825, which stands beside the Beverley–Hessle road. The latest addition to the hospital site, the impressive **Oncology and Haemotology Unit**, 2008 by *HLM Design* [151], with its terrace of low tile buildings, looks like an East Riding version of an Italian hillside village when viewed from the N. Further N, on the E side of the road, is **Skidby Mill**, 1821, now a museum.

Anlaby

Described in the 1790s as 'a pleasant country village'. Of the seven large mansions built in the late C18–early C19 only Anlaby House survives.

St Peter, Church Street, 1864–5 by *William Kerby* of Hull, was declared unsafe and rebuilt 1885, except for the s wall and chancel arch, to the designs of *Smith & Brodrick*. Red brick with blue and white brick detail and stone trim, with a fancy bell-turret with small spire.

The Old Hall, Pryme Street. Brick and tile seven-bay house set in walled grounds near the centre of the village. Although its plain sash-windowed façade suggests a rebuilding of the late C18–early C19, the clustered chimneystacks, two-storey entrance porch, and plan reveal late C17 origins.

Anlaby House, Beverley Road, for John Boyes, Hull merchant, in the 1790s. A large yellow brick and slate three-storey house with stuccoed bands between the floors. N (entrance) front with large Tuscan portico.

Almost opposite Anlaby House are the former **entrance gates** and **lodge house** of Tranby Croft, 1874.

Tranby Croft (Hull Collegiate School). Built 1874–6 to designs of *C.R. Chorley* of Leeds for Arthur Wilson, a Hull shipping magnate. Extended 1888–9. Large three-storey Italianate yellow brick mansion with a 72-ft (22-metre)-high corner tower topped by balustrade. Two-storey bays on three fronts and a large stone entrance porch. Ornate late Victorian interior. **Stable block** of 1874 with clock tower and at the NE corner a high water tower in Italianate style.

Kirk Ella

A dozen handsome mansions were erected at Kirk Ella by 'opulent merchants' in the late C18–early C19. Some have been demolished whilst most of the others have had their former extensive grounds developed with typical large suburban houses of the inter-war period.

St Andrew, Church Lane. Stone, but described as being mostly of brick by John Warburton in 1730. Medieval brick to upper part of s chancel wall. The church is basically E.E. with a striking Perp w tower of white magnesian limestone. The tower was begun in 1450 and completed 1454. The contrasting dark pinnacles are of the restoration by *Smith & Brodrick*, 1882–3. A major reconstruction of the church took place 1859–60 when the aisles were rebuilt, doubling their width, the clerestory taken down and remodelled and the chancel restored. E.E. chancel with six lancet windows to s. The N chapel, paid for by the Sykes family, and organ chamber are of 1860. The E.E. style arcade and the re-set lancets in chancel N wall are however of 1886–7 by *F.S. Brodrick*. **Screens**. Under the tower, and w of the N chapel part of a Dec screen, reconstructed 1886 by *James Elwell* to designs of *F.S. Brodrick*. The screen to the N chapel, 1900, also by *Brodrick* and *Elwell* who were responsible for most of the chancel **fittings** 1891–2. **Stained glass**. One s window in the chancel by *C.E. Kempe*, 1900. The rest of the chancel

and s aisle windows, 1860–4, and w window, 1846, by *William Wailes*, 1860–4. N chapel 1878 by *Clayton & Bell*. N aisle E 1897, possibly the best, artist unknown. **Monuments**. They are plentiful in Kirk Ella church, and the most spectacular is that of Joseph Sykes d.1805. It is by *Bacon*, 1809 [152]. Sykes rises from his coffin amid shattered rocks. There are some good **wall-tablets**, two signed by the architect *Appleton Bennison*, 1819–23, and another to Joseph Sykes d.1857 with portrait medallion by *W.D. Keyworth jun.* Large churchyard with good C19 **table tombs**.

On the w wide of **Packman Lane**, opposite the church, No. 1, early C18 brick and pantile. Further N the single-storey Tudor Cottage, No. 11, was built as the **Infants' School** in 1838. On the E side the **Wheatsheaf Inn**, rebuilt 1870 by *William Hawe*. **Vesper Lodge**, 1912, by *Runton & Barry* for J.W. Hellyer, Hull trawler owner. Typical sub-Arts and Crafts rendered façade with large bays. **Western Lodge**, *c.* 1905, half-timbered to first floor, brick with stone mullioned windows. **Victoria Cottage**,

153. Kirkella Mansions, Church Lane, present façade *c.* 1855

1897, half-timbered gables with decorative panels. Further up Packman Lane is **Kirkella Hall** (Hull Golf Club). An existing house considerably enlarged in 1778–9 by William Kirkby, a Hull solicitor and white lead manufacturer. Further alterations in the 1790s and early C19. Grey brick with hipped slate roof, seven bays and two storeys with first-floor band and projecting porch.

To s of the church along **Church Lane**, the emphasis is on Early Victorian Tudor. **Kirkella Mansions** [153], No. 6, originally two cottages, given the present façade *c.* 1855. Rendered with rusticated quoins and mullioned-and-transomed windows with hoodmoulds. Adjoining to the left No. 8, **The Acorns** (former vicarage) is very similar but in red brick with stone dressings. Dated 1839, it is said to by *H.F. Lockwood*. The N elevation is largely by *Smith & Brodrick*, 1887–8. On the s side **The Old Hall**, No. 10, rebuilt *c.* 1760 with major alterations and additions probably undertaken for Fewster Wilkinson, a Hull merchant and ship-owner who lived there 1828–56. Stuccoed, long mid-C19 street elevation with windows in moulded surrounds. The garden front has a Doric porch between large two-storey bays. **Kirk Ella House**, built *c.* 1778 by John Stephenson, Hull merchant. Stuccoed, of five bays with a slightly projecting central bay with pediment. Stylish pedimented outbuilding, *c.* 1800, to left. **Elm Lodge** was associated with The Elms (dem.). Early C19, grey brick with stone band. Recessed entrance with Doric columns. **Wolfreton Hall** and **Wolfreton Grange**, off the N side of Church Lane, were one house. Late C18, red brick, refronted in grey brick *c.* 1810 with three-storey canted bays by William Williamson, Hull merchant.

Wolfreton House, **Beverley Road**. Built *c.* 1810 by John Cankrien, Hull merchant. Grey brick with stone details and a hipped slate roof. Pedimented stable block with cupola.

West Ella

Although West Ella [154] has its share of C20 suburban housing, at its heart is a picturesque former estate village.

West Ella Hall, a large but undistinguished stuccoed brick and slate house set in fine grounds, was the home for almost fifty years of Joseph Sykes (d.1805), Hull merchant. The modest original mid-C18 block of two storeys, four bays, has rusticated quoins and a projecting square porch of C19. Large two-storey canted bays were added to each end of the s front by the 1770s, and the original rear wing was extended and a further large canted bay added *c.* 1800. Many later alterations and additions.

The restraint the Sykes family showed in the architecture and embellishment of their home was dispensed with when it came to the adjoining **village**. The short main street is lined with picturesque whitewashed houses and cottages, many set back from the road in large hedged gardens. Some have a circular pigsty. Most exhibit simple Gothic detail with arched openings, mullioned-and-transomed windows with Tudor hoodmoulds and latticed casements, and ornamental bargeboards.

154. West Ella, mid-c19 estate housing

Although the houses have a unity of style there is a great variety of composition reflecting that they range in date from the mid c18 to the late c19. One is dated 1753, another 1864. West Ella was Gothicized by Richard Sykes (d.1870), whose obituary in *The Gardeners' Chronicle* records that 'On inheriting the demesne of West Ella in 1832 he commenced a work which became the principal occupation and delight of his life. From a poor dingy country village he transformed that of West Ella into one of the prettiest and most picturesque in the country.'

It is unusual to find in such a closed estate village that the only place of worship is a small yellow and red brick Gothic **Methodist church** (Wesleyan). 1895 by *Freeman & Gaskell*.

Willerby

To the N of Kirk Ella lies Willerby, chiefly a suburban settlement of the c20 but with a couple of early houses.

Willerby Hall. A handsome building, described as lately built in the early c18, but how much of it is original? Brick with stone quoins and keystones. Five bays, two storeys and attics. It has shaped end-gables and the central bay projects slightly with quoins and has a Dutch gable with stone coping. The shaped gables were seemingly rebuilt in 1878 by *William Botterill*.

The Beeches, No. 99 Main Street. Built *c.* 1730 with early to mid-c19 additions at the back. Fine ashlar front with quoins. The centre bay breaks forward slightly and is pedimented. Doric porch with triglyph frieze and pediment.

East of Hull: Hedon and Burton Constable

The excursion to the E of the city includes the historic town of Hedon, and the large Elizabethan country house at Burton Constable.

Hedon

Less than 2 m. from Hull's docks and western boundary, Hedon has managed to retain its independence and its charming small town character. It was a medieval 'new town' that initially flourished, gaining borough status *c*. 1170, but by the late C13 it was in decline. Hedon continued as a market town with some tanning, brewing and milling, and had until 1832 the right to return two M.P.s. It expanded rapidly in the later C20 and had a population of 6,322 in 2001.

St Augustine's church, standing majestically on Market Hill, is the only one of Hedon's three medieval churches to survive and is one of the largest and grandest parish churches of the East Riding, a reminder

155. Hedon

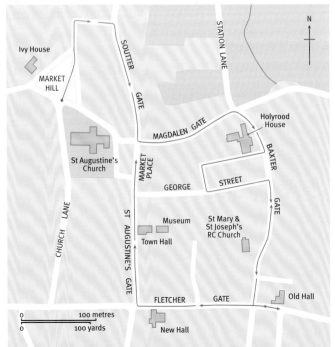

156. St Augustine, Hedon, nave, early c14

of the town's former importance. It is cruciform, 165 ft (50 metres) long, with a splendid crossing tower 129 ft (39 metres) high. The chancel and transepts are E.E. of the late c12–early c13, the nave is Dec, early c14, and the tower is Perp, early c15. The E aisles of the transepts and a chapel on the s side of the chancel were demolished before the c18. Major restoration by *G.E. Street*, 1868–77.

Exterior: The N side of the **chancel** has tall single-shafted lancet windows with single lancets to the clerestory with blank arcading between. On the mutilated s side are lancet windows and a Perp two-storey vestry incorporating the E wall from the demolished chapel. The large E window of the chancel, for which there was a bequest in 1451, is also Perp. Now the **transepts**. The end wall of the s transept is largely by *Street*, who replaced a large Perp window with two rows of lancets and a rose window above. The s door with its three orders of colonnettes and a round arch is original. The N transept is slightly later; here the N door has a pointed arch and much dogtooth. The two tiers of lancets above are original but the top tier and the gable are of Street's restoration. The aisles on the E side of the transepts have been removed but on the w side the two tiers of lancets are largely original. The aisle windows of the first three bays of the five-bay **nave** [156] have the same lively tracery of *c.* 1300. The windows in the westernmost bay have flowing tracery which suggests a completion of the nave around 1320 or later. The great w window and flanking aisle windows are Dec. Finally the crossing **tower**, high and proud, with one tier of big three-light blind windows, then yet taller three-light bell-openings, an openwork parapet, and sixteen pinnacles. Money was left for its building in 1428.

Interior: The appearance of the **chancel** is not enhanced by the blocked remnants of the demolished transept aisles and the two-bay s chapel. A pretty doorway leads into the vestry which has beautiful E.E. wall arcading on the w wall, possibly from the demolished s chapel. On the N side of the chancel is a blocked entrance into the now demolished N transept aisle and an odd length of blank arcading. The chancel clerestory has a wall passage screened by detached arcading.

The arches to the **central crossing** have traces of steeper arches for an earlier tower. In the **transepts** are the blocked arches of the former E aisles and the clerestories have arcading inside, like the chancel. For part of its length the N transept w clerestory is replaced by a strange wooden gallery. The arches from the transepts to the nave aisles are E.E. The arcades are Dec, of five bays, tall, with four major filleted and four minor keeled shafts.

Furnishings and fittings: Excellent Dec **font**, polygonal, with much decoration, a smaller version of the font in Holy Trinity, Hull. Two **royal arms**, an unusual Elizabethan arms in plaster, 1584, and the usual painted board of 1741. Good Victorian floor **tiles**, *Minton*, 1844, in choir and sanctuary, *Godwin*, 1869, in s transept. Plenty of Victorian **stained glass**, not helping the interior appearance, some of it good. E window 1900 by *Clayton & Bell*. s aisle, third from the E, *Wailes, Son & Strang*, as late as 1877 but reminiscent of the 1850s. N aisle E by *Harry J. Stammers*, 1951, nice Festival of Britain style, w by *M.F. Pawle*, Bristol, 1966. Of the **monuments** the most interesting are the imposing black stone slab in the N transept, late C13–early C14, with a cross in relief, and the mid-C14 figure of a civilian in the chancel. Some good Georgian **wall-tablets**, the best to Ann Watson d.1721, a lovely Rococo cartouche with cherubs.

Our walk begins N of the church on **Market Hill**, a triangular open green where the market was originally held. Prominent on the w side is **Ivy House**, late C18. In the garden architectural fragments which the lawyer James Iveson collected in the early C19 at the destruction or restoration of various local churches. Some pieces have been used to build an eccentric Gothic summerhouse. On the E side No. 4 has a mid-C19 front and a late C18 rear and Nos. 6–8 are of the late C18. Go past the former **Board School**, 1874, by *J.T. Webster* and along **Wayfbain Lane** and turn right into **Soutter Gate**, the best street in the town, lined with good C18–C19 buildings. On the E side the finest house in the street **Burnham House**, built for a tanner, *c.* 1785. Five bays with pretty pedimented doorcase. Opposite Nos. 47–51, **Painter's Cottages**, former almshouses founded 1562, rebuilt 1777, one storey, brick and pantile. Nos. 9 and 15 have excellent early to mid-C19 shopfronts. The latter has lions' heads to the gutter brackets and a decorative rainwater head.

At the s end of **Soutter Gate** turn left into **Magdalen Gate**. Former **Baptist chapel** (now the British Legion Club), 1801. Brick with a hipped pantile roof. Central round-headed window, and round-arched doorways to left and right. Further E is **Magdalen House**, early C19 with large rectangular bays and a columned porch of *c.* 1860.

Right into **Baxter Gate**, and on the w side **Holyrood House**. At its core are two houses of *c.* 1820 refaced and greatly extended in 1885. The original houses were the only part completed of James Iveson's planned elegant square, **Holyrood**, down the turning on the right, with the 20ft-high C15 **Kilnsea Cross** as its centrepiece. It was erected here in 1828.

To the w **King's Place**, a pleasant secluded terrace of three houses, *c.* 1820, with splendid lettering to street sign. No. 17 **George Street** is part of the same development. George Street was laid out *c.* 1820 but undeveloped on its s side until 1888 when the terrace of twenty-eight red and yellow brick cottages was built. Go E along George Street then turn right into **Baxter Gate** past the mid-C18 **Shakespeare Inn** to **St Mary and St Joseph's R.C. church** [157]. Built 1803–4. A plain rectangular brick building with hipped pantile roof and round-arched windows, just like a contemporary Methodist chapel. The interior has a delightful uncluttered simplicity with painted benches and at either end an apse under a basket arch with contemporary pilastered architrave. At one end the altar with frescoes by *Henry Immenkamp*, 1897, behind, at the other a bowed gallery. Adjoining is the late C18 **Presbytery**.

Continue on to **Fletcher Gate**, to the left the **Old Hall**, built *c.* 1700 for Henry Waterland, attorney. Brick, double-pile, five bays, two storeys, the centre bay breaks forward and there are residual full-height pilasters at the corners. w along **Fletcher Gate** on the s side of which is **New Hall**. Built *c.* 1735 for Jacob Dawson, town clerk. The N front has an over-large pedimented Tuscan porch. Grand entrance hall with mid-C18 staircase and moulded plaster ceiling. Opposite a pair of pedimented buildings of the 1840s. On the next corner a mid-Victorian house built by a stonemason, with an elaborate stone doorcase and carved heads as keystones to every window.

157. St Mary & St Joseph's R.C. church, Baxter Gate, 1803–4

158. Burton Constable Hall, E front, 1560s, altered by Timothy Lightoler, 1757–68

Turn right into **St Augustine's Gate**, the principal shopping street with many altered façades. Good early C19 bowed shopfronts at Nos. 1 and 21. On the E side the **Town Hall**, built 1693 at the expense of Henry Guy, M.P. for Hedon. Brick, the façade rendered in the late C19 and the ground floor rusticated. Three bays, two storeys; the centre bay breaks forward slightly with pediment above. Inside a fine closed string staircase with heavy vase-shaped balusters and newels with ball finials. In the Council Chamber are late C17 doorcases and seats with bolection panelled backs and a rail with vase-shaped balusters.

The walk ends in **Market Place**. The present rectangular area may be the result of replanning after one of the serious fires that beset Hedon in the C17. On the E side Nos. 2–8, built 1828–9 by George Sawyer, surgeon, form a handsome block of four three-storey buildings, gable-end to the road with the roof-lines masked by a stuccoed parapet with anthemion decoration in corners. No. 12, mid C18, has a later Doric doorcase with unusual overlight.

Burton Constable Hall

Burton Constable Hall, the grandest country house in the East Riding, stands alone in the Holderness countryside just over 7 m. from the centre of Hull, and only 3 m. from the city boundary. The village of Burton Constable was deserted in the Middle Ages but Abercrombie proposed a satellite town of 60,000 people here in his post-war development plan for Hull. Luckily nothing came of this.

It was probably *c.* 1500 that the Constable family built a manor house here, of which the present N tower and N wing were part. The rest of the house is the result of a number of building phases from the mid C16 to late C18. The major changes were made by William Constable in the years 1755–85. Constable, barred from public office by his Catholicism, went on two 'Grand Tours' and devoted his life and fortune to the pursuit of the arts and sciences. A galaxy of architects, landscape gardeners, artists and craftsmen were employed to transform his home and its setting. Further alterations were made by Sir T.A. Clifford Constable and his first wife in the 1830s–40s. There have been few changes since the mid C19 and the house has a great collection of Georgian and early Victorian furnishings and fittings. The Hall, the home of John Chichester-Constable, is the property of the Burton Constable Foundation who in 1992 began a major scheme of restoration, conservation and interpretation. The contents are in the care of Leeds City Art Gallery.

The first impression of the **house** when approached across the open parkland from the E is the strongest [158]. The long principal front is built of brick with stone details, and has the eminently English irresistible grid of vertical and horizontal, mullion and transom. The vast house is rectangular, with a small central courtyard, and two wings projecting to form a large entrance court. At each end of the central range are square castellated towers. The apparent near-symmetry is however the result of several building phases. The N tower is late medieval in origin, of brick with a stone base from an earlier tower, and a vaulted ceiling to the ground floor. Much of the two-storey long projecting wing that abuts to the E appears to be contemporary with the tower. The present E (entrance) front, running S from the medieval tower, was built by Sir John Constable in the 1560s replacing an older, probably timber-framed, building. Also of this date are the S projecting wing and S tower. The S section of the W (garden) front including the present gallery were probably completed in the late C16.

A painting of the entrance (E) front *c.* 1700 shows it as it would have been in the early C17. In the foreground was an outer brick-walled courtyard with on the W side a two-storey Jacobean entrance gate with four ogee-capped corner turrets. This led into the inner courtyard flanked by the two wings much as they are today. However changes were made to the E side 1757–68 by *Timothy Lightoler*. The dates are given on rainwater heads. The gatehouse and courtyard walls were removed. The E **front** remained Tudor in character but was regularized. A central cupola disappeared and the present top storey with two-light mullioned windows was added. The ogee caps were taken from the corner stair-turrets and placed on top of the canted bays. The off-centre entrance was replaced by a mullioned window, and a large central bay by the present entrance prominent displaying the Constable arms under a triangular pediment. The stone entrance has pairs of Doric columns with a triglyph frieze and above the first-floor window has a

159. Burton Constable Hall, Great Hall, by Timothy Lightoler, 1765–9

segmental pediment. Constable also had the whole building coated in yellow ochre to emulate stonework. This was removed in the C19.

The handsome **w front** although it looks Jacobean only gained its present unified appearance in the mid C19. Again it is of brick with stone quoins and large stone mullioned-and-transomed windows. In the centre is a big canted bay. The right-hand block up to and including the central bay has diaper brickwork probably of the late C16. The rest of the w front is of *c.* 1770 including the attic storey of the projecting block to the s and the entrance door to the centre bay. This C18 work is a successful copy of the earlier building but without the diaper patterning to the brickwork. However, until the mid C19 there were three sash windows to the ground floor on either side of the centre bay.

The **s side** of the house is the service side. The courtyard by *Capability Brown*, 1772 has a modest gateway with a concave open pediment and to either side two-storey outbuildings ending in squat battlemented towers.

Interior: One enters straight into the splendid **Great Hall** [159], a remarkable Jacobean revival replacement of the original Elizabethan hall by *Lightoler*, 1765–9. The plaster ceiling is by *James Henderson*, the stone chimneypiece by *Thomas Atkinson*, and intricately carved wooden overmantel by *John* and *Samuel Fisher*. To the right the **Dining Room**, part of the Elizabethan structure, but now a striking Neoclassical room designed by *Lightoler* in 1767 with a ceiling by *Giuseppe Cortese,* doorcases by *Jeremiah Hargrave* of Hull and relief and free-standing sculpture by *William Collins*. *Lightoler*'s large but uneventful **Staircase Hall** of the 1760s has an impressive cantilevered staircase leading up to the **Long Gallery**. The gallery, first mentioned in 1610, has late c17 bolection moulded panelling, bookcases of the 1740s and a crude Neo-Jacobean stucco frieze and ceiling of the 1830s. The main fireplace is of elaborate Scagliola by *Domenico Bartoli, c.* 1765.

The **Chapel** on the ground floor was designed in 1774 by *Atkinson* as a billiard room. Adjoining is the **Great Drawing Room** by *James Wyatt*, 1775 with doorcases by *Jeremiah Hargrave*, mirror frames by *Thomas Chippendale* and ceiling by *Cortese*. Across the Staircase Hall the **Blue Drawing Room** designed by *Atkinson* in 1783 has a bow with a domed plaster ceiling of the 1820s by *Charles Mountain jun*. At the s end of the w front is the exotic **Chinese Room** of the 1840s with fantastic gilded dragons by *Thomas Brooks*.

To the sw of the house is the delightful **Orangery**, 1788, by *Atkinson*, with urns, pineapples and statues, all of *Coade* stone. To the SE is the massive red brick **Stable Block**, 1768, by *Lightoler*. The stables, coach houses and riding school are arranged around two quadrangles, the main front of nine bays.

The **landscaped park** was laid out by *Capability Brown*, 1772–82. He created the large lake which is divided by a dam cleverly disguised as a five-arched **bridge** with a handsome balustrade. The **Menagerie**, a charming pavilion at the N end of the lake, was designed by *Thomas Knowlton c.* 1762. To the sw a Gothic **gatehouse** and **lodge** by *James Wyatt*, 1786.

Also worth a visit is the **Holy Sacrament R.C. church** at Marton. The small brick and pantile church stands alone with the adjoining former presbytery and a burial ground in a tranquil spot just off the road going N a mile from Burton Constable. Built 1789 by *Thomas Atkinson* for William Constable it has a fine simple interior with a w gallery, remains of box pews and a monument to Mary Chichester, d.1813, by *Tyley* of Bristol, with mourning female figure.

Beverley

8.5 m. from central Hull

Beverley is one of England's most attractive country towns, and deserves to be better known. Its historic core, with medieval street plan, is remarkably intact. The town has many fine houses, predominantly Georgian, a rare medieval brick gateway, a handsome market cross, and a superb Guildhall, but its greatest architectural works are the Minster and St Mary's. No other town in England can boast two parish churches of such exceptional quality.

Beverley flourished in the Middle Ages, its prosperity based on textiles, tanning, brickmaking and its role as a centre of pilgrimage and sanctuary. In the C14 it was the tenth most populous town outside London. Economic decline began in the late C15 but the town's fortunes revived in the C18 when it became the administrative and social capital

160. Beverley

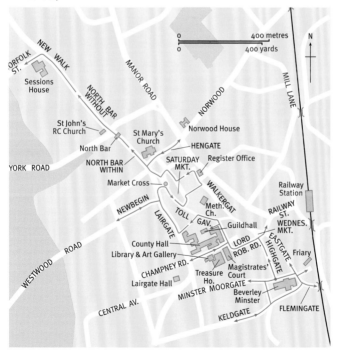

of the East Riding. Substantial houses were built, assembly rooms and a theatre provided, and a tree-lined promenade was laid out N of the town. In the Victorian period Beverley became a minor industrial town, with tanning, shipbuilding and agricultural implement works, but is now chiefly residential. In recent years the population has grown rapidly (approaching 30,000 in 2005) with large-scale housing estates on all sides except to the W where development is mercifully constrained by the common pastures of Westwood and Hurn. This open space, with its striking views of the W towers of the Minster, provides the best approach to this delightful town.

Any exploration of the town should start at the Minster, where the history of Beverley really begins. Bishop John of York, who founded a monastery on the site of the Minster in the early C8, was canonized as St John of Beverley in 1037, and it was the development of his cult which encouraged the growth of a town to provide for the needs of pilgrims and churchmen.

Beverley Minster

Beverley Minster is one of the great Gothic churches of Europe. It is of cathedral size, 330 ft (100 metres) in length. The medieval Minster was a collegiate church served by a body of some fifty clergy but at the Reformation it became just a parish church with two clergy.

Nothing of the monastery founded here by St John or of the Minster rebuilt after his canonization, other than reused masonry, survives. In 1188 the church was badly damaged in a fire and in 1213 the central crossing tower collapsed. It was then that the building we see today was begun, starting at the E end by 1221 and extending to the main transepts and the first bay of the nave by the middle of the century. The rebuilding of the nave began *c.* 1310 and the magnificent W front with its twin towers was probably completed by the 1390s. Although built over two centuries the Minster has throughout a uniformity in style found in few great churches. The choir and transepts are of oolitic limestone from nearby Newbald, the nave of magnesian limestone from the Tadcaster area, with C14 brick used for the nave vaulting.

In great decay by the early C18, it was well restored by *Nicholas Hawksmoor* and *John Thornton* of York, 1717–31. Thornton skilfully saved the front of the N transept from collapse. Further restorations took place in the 1820s by *Thomas Rickman* and others and in 1866–78 by *Sir George Gilbert Scott*.

Exterior. Commencing at the E **end** which is dominated by the great nine-light Perp E **window**, glazed *c.* 1416–20, and the **Percy chapel** of *c.* 1490. From here to the main transept the **s side**, with the exception of the Perp S choir aisle and E transept aisle windows, is all E.E. There are three tiers of paired lancet windows to the narrow E **transept**, and two

161. Beverley Minster, w front, *c.* 1390

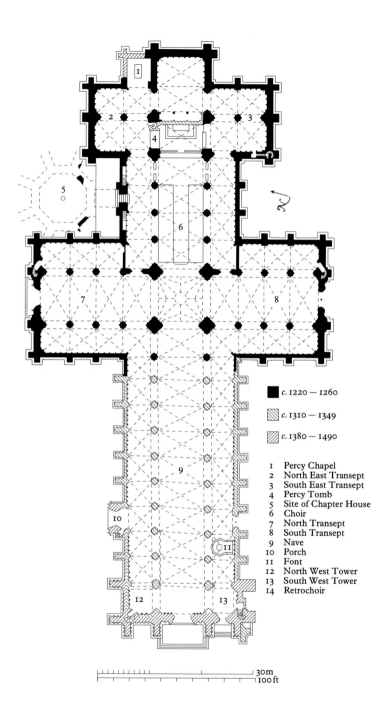

■ *c.* 1220 — 1260

▨ *c.* 1310 — 1349

▨ *c.* 1380 — 1490

1   Percy Chapel
2   North East Transept
3   South East Transept
4   Percy Tomb
5   Site of Chapter House
6   Choir
7   North Transept
8   South Transept
9   Nave
10 Porch
11 Font
12 North West Tower
13 South West Tower
14 Retrochoir

30m
100 ft

162. Beverley Minster, plan

rows of three lancets then a gable with a rose window to the **main transept** and single lancets with small rose window above to the transept aisles. The windows in the **clerestory** are flanked by blank lancets. The pattern is repeated on the N side, and with the exception of the N main transept, there are flying buttresses throughout to support the stone vaulting inside.

In the centre the low crossing **tower** built in 1721 by *Hawksmoor* who gave it an ogee-shaped cupola, removed in 1824. Now the **nave** where the change to Dec can be seen in the aisle windows. On the N side they have reticulation units, mouchettes and mouchette wheels, on the s side a leaf motif. The tracery of the **clerestory** windows is transitional between Dec and Perp, perhaps of *c.* 1360. To the w of the N porch the aisle windows are Perp. On the s wall is a Gothick doorway by *Hawksmoor*. Here was the N wall of the church of St Martin, demolished 1548.

The Perp **w front** [161] is a remarkably successful composition with the great w window, dated to 1388–96, flanked by the monumental but graceful towers. The tall bell-openings are of three lights, and above the towers end in fourteen pinnacles. The buttresses are panelled and have niches for **statues**, though on the whole w end there is only one original figure, that of Henry Percy, 1st Earl of Northumberland, on the N side. The rest are of the late C19–early C20 by *Robert Smith*. So too are the statues on the imposing two-storey early C15 N **porch**, the main entrance to the Minster. Here the doorway has an ogee hood enclosed in a steep gable, cusped beneath and rising through blank panelling topped by a frieze of images and high pinnacles.

Interior. On going **inside** one is immediately struck by the splendour of the high well-lit nave and the view along the whole length of the church [164]. The choir, nave and transepts all conform to the same system, tall piers, a low triforium, a tall clerestory and quadripartite rib-vaults and blank wall arcading. The choir, transepts and first bay of the nave have a profusion of Purbeck-like marble shafts. In the choir and retrochoir the clerestory has one lancet in each bay, in the centre of a composition of five stepped lancet arches. The triforium has two layers of arcading, the front trefoiled and the back much lower and pointed. The choir piers consist of substantial shafts, some with fillets in the main direction, but keels in the diagonals. In the N **choir aisle** is the elegant early C13 double **staircase** that led to the octagonal chapter house destroyed at the Reformation.

The pattern of the E end was carried on into the first bay of the **nave**, and then work stopped. When it was resumed *c.* 1310 it was decided to continue with the minimum of change. The shape of the piers remains, but they have capitals with foliage, figures, faces and monsters and angel and human musicians as hoodmould stops. The triforium is repeated but the clerestory now has one wide opening between two small ones and ballflower decoration. On the s side the wall arcading retains its pointed trefoiled form, but with new knobbly leaf capitals; on

163. Beverley Minster, detail from the Percy Tomb, early C14

164. Beverley Minster, nave looking E, C14

the N side it has changed to thickly crocketed ogee arches with figures of musicians as hoodmould stops. Finally the panelled w wall with tiers of figures by *Percy Baker*, 1910 and the door with the Evangelists and their symbols by *Thornton, c.* 1720.

Furnishings and fittings: The stone **frith-stool**, possibly late C7 by the high altar. **Font** C12 of Frosterley marble, elaborate wooden cover by *Thornton*, 1726. **Reredos**, an exquisite piece of Dec stone and Purbeck marble, statues and mosaics of 1897. The E face has three open arches and rib vaulting. **Choir stalls** of *c.* 1520 with 68 misericords. **Organ** by *John Snetzler*, 1769, much altered. **Organ screen** by *Scott*, carved by *James Elwell* of Beverley, 1878–80. Lead **statues** of St John and King Athelstan by *William Collins*, 1781.

Most of the medieval **stained glass** that survives was incorporated in the great E window in the 1720s, including glass attributed to the workshop of *John Thornton* of Coventry, *c.* 1416–20, the principal artist of the E window at York Minster. Most of the rest of the windows are by *Hardman & Co.* 1857–1921, with others by *Clayton & Bell*, *Powell* of Whitefriars, and most recently a striking window in the retrochoir by *Helen Whittaker*, 2004.

The **Percy Tomb** [163], because of the fortunate survival of its superb canopy sculpture, is considered the most splendid early C14 monument in England. It possibly commemorates Lady Eleanor Percy d.1328. Amongst other medieval **monuments** are the effigy of Nicholas Huggate, provost, d.1338, a canopy probably from the tomb of Lady Idonea Percy d.1365 and the tomb-chest of the 4th Earl of Northumberland, murdered by a mob in 1489.

165. Ann Routh's Hospital, Keldgate, by James Moyser, 1749

The best of the post-Reformation monuments are to members of the Warton family in the retrochoir and include the splendid memorial to Sir Michael Warton, the great benefactor of the Minster, by *Peter Scheemakers*, 1728–32. There are plenty of good Georgian wall-tablets and an unusual *Coade* stone monument to Major-General Bowes, 1813.

Walk A Beverley Minster to Saturday Market

On leaving the Minster by the N porch turn left, then glimpse down **Minster Moorgate** which has a number of neat mid-to-late C18 brick and pantile cottages on the s side. Some retain sliding-sash windows as does **Charles Warton's Hospital** on the N side, near the end of the street. Built in 1689 for six poor widows, single-storey raised to two in the C19. Now left into **St John Street**, in the shadow of the great w towers of the medieval church. Until the Reformation the Minster was surrounded by buildings where the prebendaries or canons and other clergy lived. None have survived but Nos. 9–11 St John Street incorporate the lower part of a substantial medieval stone wall that was part of the communal dwelling of the *berefellarii* or parsons of *c.* 1400. The present cottages, together with No. 8, were built as one house *c.* 1701 by the master of the Grammar School (which originally stood in the sw corner of the churchyard) and retain many fittings of that date. Before turning left into Minster Yard South turn right to explore the E part of **Keldgate**. The best building, on the N side, is **Ann Routh's Hospital** [165] of 1749 by *James Moyser*. Handsome front of three bays with giant blank arches and a top pediment with a cartouche of arms. Opposite, **Keldgate Manor** (No. 31), early C18 with early C19 alterations, has a good s façade but presents a dismal public face. Further w No. 51, *c.* 1700, has a large attached music room of *c.* 1740. On the N side No. 54 (**Old Grammar School**), a grand seven-bay house, built *c.* 1696. Back to **Minster Yard South** where the open space called Hall Garth marks the site of the medieval manor house of the Archbishops of York who had an extensive park s of the town. In the early 1980s the controversial **Lurk Lane housing complex** by the *York University Design Unit* (*David Crease*) was built alongside Hall Garth. From the SE corner of the Minster **Flemingate** leads towards Beckside, the location of Beverley's medieval port and site of its third medieval church of **St Nicholas**, demolished in the C17, and the present church built 1879–80 by *F.S. Brodrick*. Large, in Dec style with prominent tower, of stone with brick to the interior walls. Directly opposite the Minster is the **Sun Inn** with a jettied timber front, possibly C16–C17. A little further along Flemingate, on the same side, No. 15, which adjoins the Lord Nelson inn, has exposed timber-framing and a good late C15 crown-post roof.

Return to the Minster and N onto **Eastgate**, on the E side of which is **Friars Lane**. This leads to the former Dominican **Friary** (YHA), a significant remnant of a wealthy friary established in 1240. Following the dissolution in 1539 the surviving building became a private house which from the late C16 to early C19 was owned by the Warton family and their descendants. The E section, chiefly of stone, stands on C14 footings and has buttresses and a C14 doorway. The brick W wing and porch, both with tumbled gables, are post-Reformation. Inside are remains of C17 wall paintings including some in the wing with religious symbols, almost certainly added following Michael Warton's marriage to Everilda Creyke, an ardent Catholic.

The building was restored in the early 1980s and is now a youth hostel. The early C16 stone gateway in the grounds was originally at the Guildhall. The brick and ashlar precinct wall has an early C17 brick gateway. Another was resited on the W side of **Eastgate** in the 1960s. Near the Friary, fronting Eastgate, is one of Beverley's more imaginative developments, of the late 1980s by *Lazenby, Needler & Sangwin*. Two- and three-storey houses loosely grouped around attractive courtyards. They occupy the site of Hotham House and its gardens, a magnificent Palladian mansion by *Colen Campbell* for Sir Charles Hotham, built 1716–21 and demolished some fifty years later.

From Eastgate turn into **Minster Yard North**. On the right the **Old Vicarage**, 1704, red brick refronted in grey brick *c.* 1820. Next door is the former Minster Girls' School, now the **Minster Parish Hall**, 1885 by *F.S. Brodrick*. Gothic, red brick with tile-hung bellcote. Then comes **Highgate**, formerly known as Londoners' Street, for until the early C18 London merchants attending the annual fairs had their shops here. On the W side, at right angles to the street, is the former **Bluecoat School**, built in 1745 as a private house. The grander houses are on the E side including Nos. 25–25A, built 1756, originally one six-bay, three-storey house lived in by Colonel Oliver de Lancy, an American loyalist refugee from New York in 1785. The inappropriately renamed **Monks Walk** (formerly the George and Dragon) has an c18 brick façade which hides a late medieval timber-framed building and at the rear on the left of the passageway an unexpected stretch of whitewashed brick wall with Artisan Mannerist details, dated 1671. On the w side No. 2 is of 1759, one of the earliest houses by *William Middleton*, Beverley's leading Georgian builder-architect.

Highgate takes us into **Wednesday Market**, the smaller and probably the older of the two market places. On the s side the rustic-looking No. 15, late c17 and earlier, contrasts with No. 13 of *c.* 1790. On the e side **Railway Street**, laid out by *Edward* and *Gregory Page* in the late 1840s, leads to the handsome **Railway Station**, 1846, by *G.T. Andrews*, single-storey, fifteen bays with three-bay arcades to each end. Back on **Wednesday Market**, No. 8 was described as newly built in 1785. Nos. 6–7 have a c17 plan with large central stack and through passage, Nos. 3–4 have a staircase of *c.* 1700, and No. 1 is late c18. To the n is **Butcher Row**.

On the w side of **Wednesday Market** stands **Highgate House**, a fine mid-c18 house, once larger. Two bays were demolished in 1909 for the construction of **Lord Robert's Road**. On the left side of this street, just before the bend, is the former **Baptist Chapel** of 1910 by *G.F. Pennington* of *Garside & Pennington*, an entertaining building of red brick in stone in a Free Gothic style with Art Nouveau touches. It is dwarfed by the recent **Magistrates' Court** by *Austin Smith:Lord*, 2001–2.

Turn left into **Champney Road** for more large public buildings. The s side is dominated by the **Treasure House** (Archives and Local Studies), opened 2007, by *East Riding of Yorkshire Council Architects*, large and functional in brick enlivened by a corner tower. It is linked to the original and more charming **Public Library and Art Gallery**, 1906 by *John Cash* with an addition by *H.W. Cash*, 1928, all in an attractive Flemish Renaissance style. The Art Gallery has a collection of early c20 paintings by Fred Elwell (son of James Elwell). Opposite the end of Champney Road, on **Lairgate**, is **Lairgate Hall**, now offices. Built *c.* 1760 but the large dining and drawing rooms to the w front and two-storey canted bays to the s front were added *c.* 1770 for Sir James Pennyman, probably by *John Carr*. The stone centrepiece with a porch of pairs of Doric columns with tripartite window over is early c19. Good stucco ceilings to the former dining and drawing rooms. Back along Champney Road, past the 1980s and later additions to **County Hall** on the n side and left into **Cross Street** which was laid out *c.* 1827 to the plan of *Edward Page*. Some of the Neoclassical buildings erected there soon after have been demolished but the former **Subscription Rooms** (now part of County Hall) with two giant Greek Doric columns *in antis* remains, as does the delightful stuccoed villa, No. 11, opposite, by *Edward Page*, *c.* 1834. Next to the Subscription Rooms is *Smith & Brodrick*'s **County Hall** of 1890–1, Flemish Renaissance style, red brick with stone details, built for East Riding County Council. Extended 1906–8 by *B.S. Jacobs*. Round the corner in **Register Square** is the large Greek Doric portico of the **Guildhall**, by *Charles Mountain jun.*, 1832–5,

166. Guildhall, Register Square, court room by William Middleton, 1762; plasterwork by Giuseppe Cortese, 1762–3

which disguises its earlier origins. Inside are the timber-framed remnants of the house acquired by the governors of the town in 1501, and a court room and council chamber added by *William Middleton* in 1762. The elegant court room is a great surprise with its gorgeous Rococo ceiling by the plasterer *Giuseppe Cortese*, 1762–3 [166]. The magistrates' room on the first floor, built as a council chamber, has a rare collection of early C17 civic furniture.

To the left from Register Square is **Toll Gavel**, the most altered of Beverley's older streets. At the junction look right to No. 65, built *c.* 1706 by the bricklayer *Thomas Ellinor*. Unspoilt interior. Now turn left; on the w side of Toll Gavel No. 44 has an unusual former chemist's **shopfront** of *c.* 1830. The doorway has narrow Doric columns entwined by cast-iron snakes, symbol of Aescupalius, god of medicine. Nothing then of note until we reach, on the opposite side, **Toll Gavel Methodist and United Reform Church** of 1890–2 by *Morley & Woodhouse* of Bradford. Set well back from the street, of red brick with grand Italianate stone front and large portico, it has a fine galleried interior.

Across the street go down the narrow entry to **Landress Lane** which leads to **Lairgate**. On the w side Nos. 72–74, an imposing semi-detached pair, of *c.* 1797 by *William* and *John Middleton*. Further N the **Lairgate Hotel**, late C17, remodelled *c.* 1780 when the top storey was added. Nos. 26–28, with Ionic pilasters with large pediment over, were built as a **Savings Bank**, 1843. Those who extend the walk by turning left into **Newbegin** will be amply rewarded. Firstly along the s side, the modest C18 façade of No. 5 (**Skipwith Place**) hides substantial timber-framing, the remains of a C15 merchant's house. No. 3, completely rebuilt *c.* 1750, was originally part of the same property. Stones at each end of the block inscribed 'St M Ch Py' denoting former ownership by St Mary's church. Similar stones can be seen around the town. No. 9 was built *c.* 1700. At the end of the street, where one of the original gates to the town stood, is **Newbegin Bar House**. Built 1745–6 by *William Wrightson*, at a cost of £315, it incorporates a sedan chair house, now altered internally but still marked by double doors in the rear wing. Now for the N side of **Newbegin**. The finest house is Nos. 14–16 (**Newbegin House**), built *c.* 1689 for Charles Warton. Seven bays, two storeys and attics with hipped roof and a doorcase with bold shouldered architrave. No. 10 (also known as **Newbegin House**) was described as 'lately erected' in 1746. The house was heightened and refronted in the early C19. The porch added to the w elevation *c.* 1826 incorporates columns from *Hawksmoor*'s early C18 gallery from Beverley Minster. Nos. 6 and 8, probably by *William Middleton*, were built as a matching pair *c.* 1780 but the symmetry has been spoilt by the addition of another storey to No. 6.

Back on Lairgate continue N and turn right into **Saturday Market**, the focal point of which is the particularly handsome **Market Cross** [167], the showpiece of the Georgian town. It is an extremely successful version of the traditional type of open shelter, square with canted corners and eight Roman Doric columns supporting a jolly cupola roof of fanciful outline. This is topped by a square glazed lantern which in turn is surmounted by an obelisk and weathervane. The cross was erected in 1711–14, partly at the expense of the town's two M.P.s, Sir Charles Hotham and Sir Michael Warton, whose arms, along with those of the borough and the crown, are displayed on cartouches. It was designed by *Theophilus Shelton* of Wakefield. The vases by *Crabtree & Rushworth* were added in 1797.

The large market place, roughly rectangular, is surrounded by a great medley of C17–C19 buildings, only a few of which are described here. Opposite the Market Cross is a neat group, Nos. 14–27, known as the **Dings** or **Butterdings**, largely built as a speculation in the 1750s. On the N side of Saturday Market the best building is No. 1 of the 1760s–70s,

167. Market Cross, Saturday Market, by Theophilus Shelton, 1711–14

typical of the work of the builder-architect *William Middleton*. The w side is dominated by more overtly commercial Victorian buildings including No. 60, **NatWest Bank**, built for the Yorkshire Banking Co., 1864, with its ostentatious Italianate façade. The architect was *William Hawe*. The s side of the square is largely taken up by the eight-bay **Yorkshire Bank**, an enforced reconstruction of a fine 1760s building which was demolished in the early 1970s. On the e side of the market square the first building is the mid-c18 **King's Head**, altered in the early c19. At the opposite end is the least-altered building in Saturday Market, No. 28, a narrow three-storey shop of *c.* 1765 with wood modillion eaves cornice and a tripartite sash to the first floor. Close by, **Browns department store** was the former Corn Exchange and Public Swimming Baths, designed by *Samuel Musgrave*, built in 1886. Elaborate Flemish Renaissance façade of red brick with decorative terracotta details. Some internal details have been retained in the successful conversion by *Jonathan Hobson* of *Ingleby & Hobson*, 2009–10.

168. St Mary, Beverley, N chapel, *c.* 1330

Dyer Lane, on the E side of Saturday Market, leads to **Walkergate**, named after the fullers who 'walked' cloth in Walkergate Beck, the winding culverted stream that runs along its w side. At the N end of Walkergate are two large houses, **The Grosvenor Club**, an unusual three-storey house of the early C18, extended at the rear and re-fitted in 1833 and **Walkergate House**, *c.* 1775, five bays, three storeys, with hipped flat-tile roof. The latter is surely by *William Middleton* who often used flat tiles in preference to pantiles, the usual choice in Beverley by this date. Across the road No. 62, a delightful two-storey brick building with low hipped pantile roof, moulded eaves cornice and blank arcade façade, was built as **Tymperon's Hospital**. The date may be *c.* 1731, soon after the death of William Tymperon, the apothecary who endowed it. The façade is similar to that of **Ann Routh's Hospital**, Keldgate, and also possibly by *James Moyser*. At this point turn left into Dog and Duck Lane and right into **Ladygate**, a narrow street which has some of the earliest buildings in the town. Nos. 19–21, timber-framed but fronted in brick in the early C19, has an excellent C15 crown-post roof.

Return to **Saturday Market** by turning left into **Sow Hill** which was cut through Ladygate in the mid 1960s, demolishing the C17–C18 Globe Inn and destroying the enclosure of the N end of the market place.

To the N of Saturday Market, on the E side of **North Bar Within**, is **St Mary's church**. It was established in the mid C12 as a daughter church of the Minster, to serve the townspeople. It is 197 ft (60 metres) in length and one of the most beautiful parish churches in England but the awkward corner site does not do it justice. The earliest part is of local oolitic limestone but the rest magnesian limestone from near Tadcaster. The mid-C12 church consisted of nave and chancel, possibly with a central tower. Nave aisles and transepts had been added by the mid C13, but rebuilding began in earnest in the late C13. A large chapel was added to the E side of the N transept and *c.* 1300 the E aisle of the S transept was widened and a S aisle added to the chancel. In the early C14 the nave aisles were widened and *c.* 1330 the superb chapel with luscious tierceron-star vaulting and sacristy were built on the N side of the chancel with rooms above [168]. The splendid Perp w front with polygonal turrets is of *c.* 1400 when the nave clerestories were built. Next in time come the early C15 chancel clerestory and S porch and the reconstruction of the transepts in the mid C15. Bequests for rebuilding the w end of the nave aisles were made 1458–1500 but much of this work was undone when in 1520 the central tower collapsed and 'overwhelmed' some of the worshippers. It could have been an even greater disaster had not, as Sir Thomas More reported, many of the townspeople been at a bear baiting. The nave and tower were soon rebuilt. Major restorations by *A.W.N. Pugin*, 1844–52, particularly the w front where he replaced the turrets, *E.W. Pugin*, 1852–60, who added the flying buttresses to the S transept, and *Sir George Gilbert Scott*, the nave 1864–7 and chancel 1875–6.

The **interior** is full of interest. There is a fine series of **ceilings**, the best in the chancel consisting of panels with C15 paintings (restored) of forty English kings originally ending with Henry VI. Over 600 carved **bosses**, many of them on the early C16 nave ceiling. The rebuilding of the nave arcades after 1520 was paid for by the merchant community and guilds and the hood-mould stops are in the form of demi-figures bearing scrolls within inscriptions telling who gave the money for the piers, including the 'good wives of Beverley'. Most famous is the **Minstrels' pillar** [169] with its group of five musicians. Almost as well-known is the **pilgrim rabbit**, a hood-mould stop to the sacristy

169. St Mary, Minstrels' pillar, 1520s

door in the N choir aisle. The **choir stalls** with 28 **misericords** date from
c. 1425–50. Large octagonal **font** of Derbyshire marble, c. 1530. Gothic
alabaster **pulpit**, c. 1865, by *Scott*. Elaborate **reredos**, 1880–1 by *John
Oldrid Scott*, executed by *James Elwell*. The **Priests' Room** is a treasure
trove of bits and pieces including sections of medieval **screens** and a
maiden's garland dated 1680.

Most of the **stained glass** is by *Hardman & Co. c.* 1850–1924 and
includes the W window designed by *Pugin c.* 1850. E window, 1877 by
Clayton & Bell. Numerous **monuments**, the best to members of the
Warton family – three, all early C18, attributed to *William Woodman sen.*
Of the Georgian wall-tablets, a fine one to Bridget Pennyman d.1775 by
Edmund Foster of Hull, and another to the actor-manager Samuel
Butler d.1812. On the exterior of S chancel aisle an oval memorial tablet
to two Danish soldiers d.1689.

Walk B St Mary's Church to New Walk

On leaving St Mary's church turn left along **Hengate**. Adjoining the
church are the **Memorial Gardens** with **War Memorial**, 1921, by *R.H.
Whiteing*, carved by *Vincent Hill* of Beverley. Two fine houses on the N
side of Hengate, both with the usual Beverley four-bay façade with off-
centre entrance, No. 3 of 1778 by *William Middleton*, and No. 7, built for
Henry Spendlove, attorney, 1708–9. The latter has a staircase with bar-
ley-sugar balusters and panelled rooms on the first floor. The S side of
Hengate is dominated by the curving façade of the **White Horse Inn**
('Nellie's'), fronted in brick in the C18 but with timber-framing exposed
at the back. Three-storey rear wing of the 1830s. The building retains a
remarkable array of C19 pub fittings. The arched doorway of **Arden's
Vaults** (No. 16), early C18, leads to an extensive brick vaulted cellar.

Across the wide and unsightly junction at the E end of Hengate is
Norwood, and on the N side **Norwood House** [170], arguably Beverley's
best Georgian domestic building. It was built c. 1760 for Jonathan
Midgley, attorney, almost certainly by *Thomas Atkinson* of York. The
house is of five bays and three storeys, linked to low projecting wings.
Brick with painted stone dressings. The main front has a pediment
right across with a round window in an elaborate wooden Rococo cartouche with trailing chains of husks. Rusticated ground floor with a
prominent entrance doorway with a Gibbs surround. Inside is an
uncommonly fine drawing room of the late 1760s with a stucco ceiling
and fireplace with elaborate overmantel.

Return via Hengate to **North Bar Within** (which begins at the N end
of Saturday Market), the widest street in the medieval town. Many
noteworthy buildings. On the E side, on the corner of Hengate, No. 22,
early C18, raised in the mid C18. Dummy windows on top floor and a
bowed early C19 shopfront. Nos. 18–20, of c. 1700, has an C18 doorcase
with pedimented canopy with boldly carved consoles. Opposite, Nos.
7–9, an apothecary's shop from the C18, contains earlier timber-fram-

170. Norwood House, Norwood, attributed to Thomas Atkinson, *c.* 1760

ing, exposed in the N gable, and a triple-arched Georgian shop-divider with Doric columns and segmental arches. No. 15 has a handsome frontage with stuccoed window surrounds and mansard roof of *c.* 1870 by *William Hawe* which masks the remnants of the early C18 town house of the Boyntons of Burton Agnes. Just beyond is a narrow entry which leads into **Wood Lane** and **Woodlands**, streets lined with a pleasant mixture of mid-to-later C19 artisan and middle-class housing ending at *William Hawe*'s grand entrance arch of 1895 to the **Westwood Hospital**, built 1860–1 to the designs of *J. B. & W. Atkinson* of York as the Beverley Union Workhouse.

Back on **North Bar Within** No. 19, *c.* 1750, with a contemporary staircase. No. 21 is by *William Hawe*, 1886. The most prominent building on this side is the **Beverley Arms Hotel**, formerly the Blue Bell Inn, rebuilt 1794–6 by *William Middleton* as the premier inn of the East Riding. A

171. North Bar, 1409–10 and Bar House, altered by William Hawe, 1866

pleasing simple brick façade, three storeys with parapet, sill-band to first floor. Originally of seven bays, extended by three bays in 1966–7 to incorporate the site of No. 25. Stone entrance portico with iron balcony above reached from a round-headed first-floor window. Behind a 1960s mini-tower block (part of the hotel), a great intrusion on the townscape of Beverley when viewed from the w. No. 35 is a typical *William Wrightson* house of *c.* 1740, five bays, two storeys and attics. Nos. 37–39 (**Pizza Express**), a large Italianate three-storey red brick block with arched windows and stone imposts, by *Cuthbert Brodrick*, 1861.

N of St Mary's, set back behind a brick wall and tall trees, is **St Mary's Manor**, a large stucco-fronted Regency villa with characteristic hipped slate roof, bracketed oversailing eaves and Doric porch. It was rebuilt for Henry Ellison *c.* 1803, retaining an early C18 three-bay service wing and also the N wall and other features of the late C17 house of the Moyser family. Interior remodelled *c.* 1828 when the entrance hall was enlarged and the grand staircase with Ionic colonnaded landing was introduced. The architect was probably *Charles Mountain jun.* The wrought-iron landing balustrade formed part of the early C18 altar rails at the Minster designed by *Hawksmoor*. Massive extension to the rear in the 1990s as part of a conversion to flats.

On the E side between St Mary's Manor and North Bar is a range of C18 properties, some with remnants of earlier timber-framing. Nos.

32–36 were refronted in brick by *Peter Duke*, joiner, *c.* 1736. Nos. 34 and 38 have early C19 bowed shopfronts. The three-storey red brick **Bar Chambers** adjoining the North Bar was built by *William* and *John Middleton*, 1793–4. Another late use of flat tiles in Beverley. Pedimented doorcase with slender Doric columns and a decorative fanlight. The block goes through into **North Bar Without** where No. 2 is of the same date and has a similar doorcase.

Back to the w side of **North Bar Within**, where the eleven-bay block, Nos. 41–47, formed one of the principal buildings of Georgian Beverley, the Tiger Inn, built *c.* 1740. It rivalled the nearby Beverley Arms as a meeting place and centre of administration for the East Riding until the early C19. Nos. 49–51 (**St Mary's Court**) is the best surviving timber-framed building in Beverley, C15 with a much altered façade. The s end, which retains original timbering and a blocked timber mullion window, jetties out into Tiger Lane. Adjoining is the **Coronation Garden**, formerly St Mary's burial ground, with ornamental cast-iron railings, gates and gatepiers dated 1829, from *William Crosskill's* newly estab-lished Beverley foundry. Nos. 55–63, five three-storey red brick houses forming a terrace, built for Charles Pelham, 1st Lord Yarborough, *c.* 1780, possibly by *William Middleton*. Nos. 65–67 (**Bar House**) prob-ably incorporates part of the late C17 town house of the Wartons of Beverley Parks. The property was altered by *William Hawe* in 1866, and given its stuccoed façade and Italianate belvedere tower. To the N, outside the Bar, are the remnants of the C17 garden wall and resited gate pillars.

The **North Bar** [171] is the earliest English town gate built of brick and the sole survivor of Beverley's medieval gateways. Rebuilt in 1409–10 at a cost of *c.* £100, it is two-storey with a room over the arch-way. The battlements are probably of the later C17 when the arms and crest of the Warton family were placed on the N side.

North Bar Without is another unusually wide street. On the E side No. 4 and Nos. 6–8 were rebuilt by the woodcarver *James Elwell*, *c.* 1882 and 1893 respectively. Half-timbered, with a great array of excellent carved figures, and two panels over the doors with cartoon scenes about Disraeli and Gladstone. On the opposite side, at the corner of York Road, which leads to the common pastures called Westwood and Hurn, more mock timber-framing on the **Rose and Crown** of *c.* 1930. Next door is **St John's R.C. church**, 1897–8, by *Smith, Brodrick & Lowther*. There are many pleasing houses in North Bar Without. On the w side, No. 29, **The Elms**, set back from the street, was built *c.* 1744, probably by *William Wrightson*. A third storey was added *c.* 1800. No. 39, 1769, with a later top storey and Edwardian bay windows, is by *William Middleton*. **Oak House** (No. 43), dated 1880, was designed by *Smith & Brodrick* for James Elwell and has good examples of *Elwell's* woodwork inside. *Elwell* designed the house to the N, No. 45, dated 1894. A carved panel over the door depicts a scene from Charles Dickens's *The Cricket on the Hearth*. On the E side of North Bar Without No. 48, *c.* 1730, with contemporary staircase and panelling.

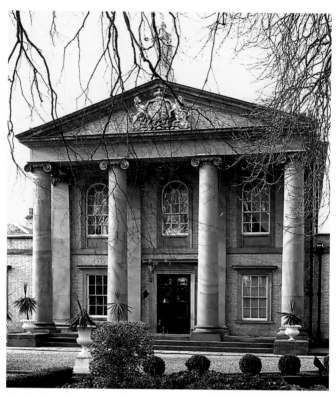

172. Sessions House, New Walk, by Charles Watson, 1805–10

No. 56, *c.* 1766, three storeys, has a splendid doorcase with an elaborate frieze. It is set back from the street, as is No. 62 (**Ash Close**), built *c.* 1732, a most attractive two-storey red brick house with Westmorland slate roof and slightly projecting central bay with rounded-headed arched doorway.

The continuation of North Bar Without is **New Walk**, a tree-lined promenade laid out in the 1780s. The large Victorian houses, some with mansard roofs and elaborate French classical detailing, are chiefly by *William Hawe* and *Smith & Brodrick*. In 1805–10 the handsome former **Sessions House** [172], designed by *Charles Watson* of Wakefield and supervised by *Appleton Bennison*, was built at the end of the promenade, on the w side. The classical building, of grey brick with stone dressings, has a large Greek Ionic stone portico with four unfluted columns and a pediment. Royal arms in pediment and a figure of Justice in *Coade* stone above. Round the corner, in **Norfolk Street**, is what remains of *Watson's* early C19 House of Correction, which was converted to houses (Nos. 5–13) by *M.L. Whitton* in 1880. The e block housed the treadmill, the central octagon was the turnkey's house, and the w block contained the men's cells.

Further Reading

The best **overview** of the history and architecture of Hull is provided by K.J. Allison (ed.), *Victoria County History (VCH), Yorkshire East Riding Vol. 1: The City of Kingston upon Hull* (1969), which has sections on secular buildings by Sandy (A.G.) Chamberlain and Ivan Hall and on parish churches by Edward Ingram. The **development** of the city is succinctly dealt with in Derek Spooner's *Kingston upon Hull* (2005) in the Geographical Association's excellent *Discovering Cities* series, and in M.T. Wild's 'The geographical shaping of Hull from pre-industrial to modern times' in Stephen Ellis and David Crowther (eds), *Humber Perspectives* (1990). Much background material can be found in Susan Neave and Stephen Ellis (eds), *An Historical Atlas of East Yorkshire* (1996).

The older histories of Hull by Gent (1735), Hadley (1788), Tickell (1796), Frost (1827) and Sheahan (1864) remain valuable contemporary accounts but have been superseded by the *VCH* volume cited above and E. Gillett and K.A. MacMahon, *A History of Hull* (2nd edn, 1989).

For the **medieval** and **early modern** periods *The Changing Plan of Hull 1290–1650* (1978) by Rosemary Horrox uses the corporation's extensive collection of early deeds and leases to chart the development of the Old Town. The buildings of the period are examined in 'Urban Domestic Architecture in the Lower Hull Valley in the Medieval and Early Post-Medieval Periods' by David H. Evans (2001), one of a series of articles that he has contributed to the periodic *Lubecker Kolloquium zur Stadtarchaologie im Hanseraum* (M. Gläser, ed.). The others deal with the archaeology (1997), trade (1999) and infrastructure (2004) of the town and port up to 1700. For **building materials** see F.W. Brooks, 'A medieval brick-yard at Hull', *Journal of the British Archaeological Association* (1939) and David Neave, 'Pantiles: Their early use and manufacture in the Humber region' in D. Tyszka, K. Miller and G. Bryant (eds), *Land, People and Landscapes* (1991).

The town's **fortifications** are covered by David H. Evans and Brian Sitch, *Beverley Gate: The Birthplace of the English Civil War* (1990) and Audrey Howes and Martin Foreman, *Town and Gun: The 17th-Century Defences of Hull* (1999). David Neave's *The Dutch Connection: The Anglo-Dutch Heritage of Hull and Humberside* (1988) and 'Artisan Mannerism in North Lincolnshire and East Yorkshire: The Work of William Catlyn (1628–1709) of Hull' in C. Sturman (ed.), *Lincolnshire People and Places* (1996) concentrate on Hull's distinctive architecture of the later 17th century. This is the starting point for *Georgian Hull* (1979), the splendidly illustrated and researched account of **eighteenth** and **early nineteenth-century** buildings by Ivan and Elisabeth Hall. More on the architecture of the period occurs in the *Transactions of the Georgian Society for East Yorkshire* (1937–63) with Gordon Jackson, *Hull in the Eighteenth Century* (1972) providing a detailed economic and social background.

For the **Victorian** period there is Ian. N. Goldthorpe's detailed *Architecture of the Victorian Era of Kingston upon Hull* (ed. M. Sumner) (2005) based on a thesis written in 1955, and there are two articles surveying Hull's contemporary architecture in *The Builder*, 6 July 1861 and 2 April 1898. Victorian religious buildings, many destroyed in the Second World War and most of the rest demolished later, are recorded in B.W. Blanchard's thesis, 'Nonconformist Chapels in the Hull District' (1955) and David Neave, *Lost Churches and Chapels of Hull* (1991). More of the lost buildings and streetscapes of the Victorian and Edwardian city are illustrated in the two volumes of F.S. Smith's drawings *Images of Victorian Hull*, ed. Caroline Aldridge (1989) and Chris Ketchell (1990) and *Hull Then & Now* (2008) by Paul Gibson. C.A. Forster, *Court Housing in Kingston upon Hull* (1972), traces the origin and development of the city's distinct working-class housing which is well-illustrated in G. Wilkinson and G. Watkins, *Forgotten Hull: A seleloction of photographs from the Hull Corporation Health Department Collection 1890s–1930s* (1999).

Little has been written on the city's **twentieth-century architecture** but there is much information in the *York and East Yorkshire Architectural Society Yearbook* (1927–63), continued as *Perspective East Yorkshire* (1964–7), and *The Guild of Building Review* (Hull, 1931–81). B.C. Skern, *Housing in Kingston upon Hull between the Wars* (1986) is a useful but brief survey, whilst E. Lutyens and P. Abercrombie, *A Plan for the City & County of Kingston upon Hull* (1945) provides a snapshot of the city at the end of the Second World War. The first stages of the postwar rebuilding are detailed in articles in the *Architects' Journal*, 2 July 1953 and *Municipal Journal*, 3 Dec 1954; the former has a most useful account of the city's architectural firms. Later developments are charted in the published annual reports of the Town (later City) Planning Officer 1956–76.

Of major **twentieth-century buildings** Robin Diaper has written about 'The Guildhall' in *East Yorkshire Historian* 10 (2009) and the development of the **university** is dealt with in T.W. Bamford, *The University of Hull: The First Fifty Years* (1978), with individual buildings examined in L. Martin, *Buildings & Ideas 1933–83: From the Studio of Leslie Martin and His Associates* (1983), and R. Proctor, 'Social Structures: Gillespie, Kidd & Coia's Halls of Residence at the University of Hull', *Journal of Society of Architectural Historians*, vol. 67, no. 1 (2008). The Deep is discussed in Jane Tobin, *Ten years, ten cities: the work of Terry Farrell and partners, 1991–2001* (2002) and Hugh Pearman, *The Deep* (2002).

The detailed descriptions from the *List of Buildings of Special Architectural or Historic Interest: City of Kingston-upon-Hull* (revised 1994 with later additions) and Hull City Council 'Local Buildings List' (compiled 2006–7) are available online as are a number of most useful character appraisals of some of the city's 26 Conservation Areas.

Areas of Hull have been the subject of detailed accounts including Robert Barnard, *High Street, Hull 1673–1798* (2002); Paul Gibson, *The Anlaby Road* (2007); Chris Ketchell (ed.), *An illustrated history of the Avenues and Pearson Park, Hull* (1989); Mary Fowler, *Holderness Road* (1990); B.N. Reckitt, *The Garden Village, Hull* (2002); Merrill Rhodes, *Sutton, Bransholme and Wawne* (2006) and the *New Sutton Walk* (revised 2009).

For the **villages** to the west of the city see especially Keith Allison's *'Hull Gent. Seeks Country Residence' 1750–1850* (1981) and *Cottingham Houses* (2001). A number of merchants' villas are illustrated in David Neave and Edward Waterson, *Lost Houses of East Yorkshire* (1988). **Hedon** is dealt with in vol. 5 (1984) of *VCH, Yorkshire East Riding* (ed. K.J. Allison) and works by Martin Craven and John Markham. **Burton Constable Hall** is well covered in studies by Ivan and Elisabeth Hall (1991), Arthur Credland (ed. 1998), and David Connell and Gerardine Mulcahy (2002).

For the history and architecture of Beverley see K.J. Allison (ed.) *VCH, Yorkshire East Riding Vol. 6* (1989), Keith Miller et al., *Beverley: An Archaeological and Architectural Study* (1982) and the well-illustrated *Historic Beverley* (1973) by Ivan and Elisabeth Hall.

For **Beverley Minster** the most comprehensive account is Rosemary Horrox (ed.), *Beverley Minster: An illustrated history* (2000). See also Paul S. Barnwell and Arnold Pacey, *Who built Beverley Minster?* (2008) and relevant chapters in C. Wilson (ed.), *Medieval Art and Architecture in the East Riding of Yorkshire* (1989).

There is a good coverage of Hull **architects** in Howard Colvin, *A Biographical Dictionary of British Architects, 1600–1840* (4th edn, 2008) and excellent accounts of H.F. Lockwood by Jon Burgess in his thesis on 'Lockwood & Mawson' (De Montfort, PhD, 1998) and Cuthbert Brodrick in Derek Linstrum, *Towers & Colonnades* (1999). Local architects are included in Arthur Credland's wide-ranging *Artists and Craftsmen of Hull and East Yorkshire* (2000) which has a most useful chapter by Gerardine Mulcahy on the two families of Hull sculptors, the Earles and Keyworths. The early work, locally, of the Hull-born builder George Myers is covered in Patricia Spencer-Silver, *Pugin's Builder* (1993).

There is a wealth of **primary sources** in the Hull History Centre including records of the city engineer's and architect's departments and building control and other plans.

For buildings in Hull and areas not covered in this volume see Nikolaus Pevsner and David Neave, *The Buildings of England: Yorkshire: York and the East Riding* (1995).

Glossary

Acanthus: *see* [2D].

Aedicule: architectural surround

Ambulatory: aisle around the *sanctuary* of a church.

Angle buttress: one set at the angle or corner of a building.

Antae: simplified *pilasters*, usually applied to the ends of the enclosing walls of a *portico* (called *in antis*).

Anthemion: *see* [2D].

Apse: semicircular or polygonal end, especially in a church.

Arcade: series of arches supported by *piers* or columns (cf. *colonnade*).

Arch: for types *see* [4].

Architrave: *see* [2A], also moulded surround to a window or door.

Art Deco: a self-consciously up-to-date interwar style of bold simplified patterns, often derived from non-European art.

Ashlar: large rectangular masonry blocks wrought to even faces.

Atlantes: male figures supporting an *entablature*.

Atrium: a toplit covered court rising through several storeys.

Attic: small top storey within a roof. Also the storey above the main *entablature* of a classical façade.

Back-to-back houses: with a shared rear (spine) wall.

Baldacchino: solid canopy, usually free-standing and over an altar.

Balusters: vertical supports, often of outward-curved profile, for a handrail, etc.; the whole being called a balustrade.

Ballflower: globular flower of three petals enclosing a small ball.

Baroque: bold, free and emphatic European classical style of the C17–C18, revived in the late C19.

Barrel vault: one with a simple arched profile.

Basement: lowest, subordinate storey; hence the lowest part of a classical elevation, below the *piano nobile*.

Bay: division of an elevation by regular vertical features such as columns, windows, etc.

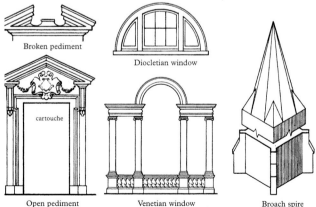

Broken pediment

Diocletian window

cartouche

Open pediment

Venetian window

Broach spire

1. Miscellaneous

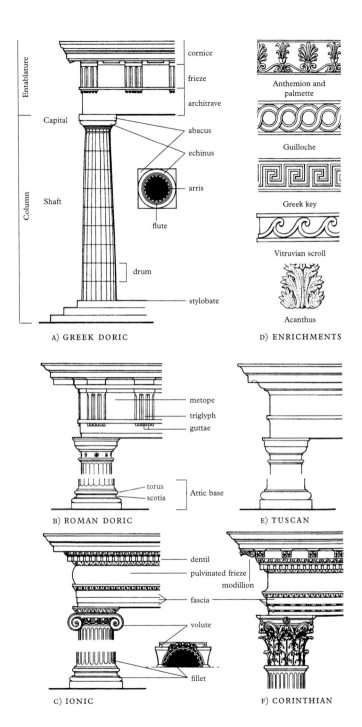

A) GREEK DORIC

Entablature
Column

cornice
frieze
architrave
Capital
abacus
echinus
arris
Shaft
flute
drum
stylobate

B) ROMAN DORIC

metope
triglyph
guttae
torus
scotia
Attic base

C) IONIC

dentil
pulvinated frieze
modillion
fascia
volute
fillet

D) ENRICHMENTS

Anthemion and palmette

Guilloche

Greek key

Vitruvian scroll

Acanthus

E) TUSCAN

F) CORINTHIAN

2. Classical orders and enrichments

Bay window: one projecting from the face of a building. *Canted:* with a straight front and angled sides.

Beaux-Arts: a French-derived approach to classical design, at its peak in the later C19–early C20, marked by strong axial planning and the grandiose use of the *orders*.

Bellcote: small gabled or roofed housing for a bell or bells.

Bolection moulding: convex moulding covering the joint between two different planes.

Brise-soleil (French): a sunscreen of projecting fins or slats.

Broach spire: *see* [1].

Bucrania: ox skulls used decoratively in friezes on classical buildings.

Campanile (Italian): free-standing bell-tower.

Cantilever: horizontal projection supported at one end only.

Capital: head feature of a column or *pilaster*; for classical types *see* [2].

Cartouche: *see* [1].

Castellated: with battlements.

Catslide: a roof continuing down in one plane over a lower projection.

Chancel: the E part or end of a church, where the altar is placed.

Chapter house: place of assembly for the members of a monastery or cathedral.

Choir: the part of a great church where services are sung.

Clerestory: uppermost storey of an interior, pierced by windows.

Coade stone: ceramic artificial stone, made 1769–*c.* 1840 by Eleanor Coade and associates.

Coffering: decorative arrangement of sunken panels.

Colonnade: range of columns supporting a flat *lintel* or *entablature*

Corbel: projecting block supporting something above.

Composite: classical order with capitals combining Corinthian features (acanthus, *see* [2D]) with Ionic (volutes, *see* [2C]).

Corinthian; cornice: *see* [2F; 2A].

Cottage orné: artfully rustic small house.

Cove: a broad concave moulding.

Crenellated: with battlements.

Crocket: leafy hooks decorating the edges of Gothic features.

Crown-post: a vertical roof timber starting centrally on a tie-beam and supporting a collar *purlin*.

Crypt: underground or half-underground area, usually below the E end of a church.

Cupola: a small dome used as a crowning feature.

Dado: finishing of the lower part of an internal wall.

Decorated (Dec): English Gothic architecture, late C13 to late C14.

Dentil: *see* [2C].

Diaper: repetitive surface decoration of lozenges or squares flat or in relief. Achieved in brickwork with bricks of two colours.

Diocletian window: *see* [1].

Doric: *see* [2A, 2B].

Dormer: *see* [3].

Drum: circular or polygonal stage supporting a dome.

Dutch or Flemish gable: *see* [3].

Early English (E.E.): English Gothic architecture, late C12 to late C13.

Embattled: with battlements.

Entablature: *see* [2A].

Faience: moulded *terracotta* that is glazed white or coloured.

Fleurons: carved flower or leaf.

Flying buttress: one transmitting thrust by means of an arch or half-arch.

Freestone: stone that can be cut in any direction.

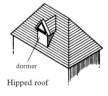

dormer

Hipped roof

Mansard roof

Flemish or Dutch gable

3. Roofs and gables

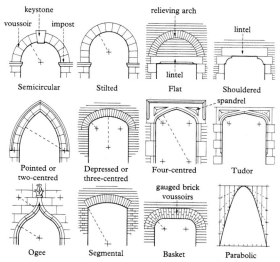

4. Arches

Frieze: middle member of a classical *entablature*, see [2A, 2C]. Also a horizontal band of ornament.

Geometrical: of *tracery*, a mid-C13–C14 type formed of circles and part-circles; *see* [6].

Giant order: a classical *order* that is two or more storeys high.

Gibbs surround: C18 treatment of an opening with blocked architraves, seen particularly in the work of James Gibbs (1682–1754).

Gothic: the style of the later Middle Ages, characterized by the pointed arch and *rib-vault*.

Half-timbering: non-structural decorative timberwork.

Herm: head or bust on a pedestal.

Hipped roof: *see* [3].

Hoodmould: projecting moulding above an arch or *lintel* to throw off water.

Hyperbolic paraboloid: of a roof, built to a double-curved profile suitable for thin shell construction.

Impost: horizontal moulding at the springing of an arch.

In antis: (Latin) of columns, set in an opening (properly between simplified *pilasters* called *antae*).

Ionic: *see* [2C].

Italianate: a classical style derived from the palaces of Renaissance Italy.

Jack arches: shallow segmental vaults springing from iron or steel beams.

Jamb: one of the vertical sides of an opening.

Kingpost roof: one with vertical timbers set centrally on the *tie-beams*, supporting the ridge.

Lancet: slender, single-light pointed-arched window.

Lantern: a windowed turret crowning a roof, tower or dome.

Light: compartment of a window.

Lintel: horizontal beam or stone bridging an opening.

Loggia: open gallery with arches or columns.

Louvre: opening in a roof or wall to allow air to escape.

Lucarne: small gabled opening in a roof or spire.

Machicolation: openings between *corbels* that support a projecting *parapet*.

Metope: *see* [2B].

Mezzanine: low storey between two higher ones.

Moderne: of 1930s design, fashionably streamlined or simplified.

Modillion: *see* [2D].

Moulding: shaped ornamental strip of continuous section.

Mullion: vertical member between window *lights*.

Narthex: enclosed vestibule or porch at the main entrance to a church.

Newel: central or corner post of a staircase.

Nogging: brick infilling of a timber frame.

Norman: the C11–C12 English version of the *Romanesque* style.

Œil de bœuf: small oval window, set horizontally.

Ogee: of an arch, dome, etc., with double-curved pointed profile.

Orders (classical): for types *see* [2].

Oriel: window projecting above ground level.

Overthrow: decorative fixed arch above a gateway.

Parapet: wall for protection of a sudden drop, e.g. on a bridge, or to conceal a roof.

Pargeting: exterior plaster decoration, either moulded in relief or incised.

Patera: round or oval ornament in shallow relief.

Pavilion: ornamental building for occasional use; or a projecting subdivision of a larger building (hence *pavilion roof*).

Pediment: a formalized gable, derived from that of a classical temple; also used over doors, windows, etc. For types *see* [1].

Penthouse: a separately roofed structure on top of a multi-storey block of the C20 or later.

Perpendicular (Perp): English Gothic architecture from the late C14 to early C16.

Piano nobile (Italian): principal floor of a classical building, above a ground floor or basement and with a lesser storey overhead.

Pier: a large masonry or brick support, often for an arch.

Pilaster: flat representation of a classical column in shallow relief.

Pilotis: C20 French term for pillars or stilts that support a building above an open ground floor.

Plinth: projecting courses at the foot of a wall or column, generally chamfered or moulded at the top.

Polychromy: the use of contrasting coloured materials such as bricks as decoration, particularly associated with mid-C19 Gothic styles.

Porte cochère (French): porch large enough to admit wheeled vehicles.

Portico: porch with roof and (frequently) *pediment* supported by a row of columns.

Portland stone: a hard, durable white limestone from the Isle of Portland in Dorset.

Postmodern: idiom associated with the 1980s that references older styles, notably classicism, not always reverently.

Presbytery: a priest's residence.

Purlin: horizontal longitudinal timber in a roof structure.

Quatrefoil: opening with four lobes or foils.

Queen Anne: the later Victorian revival of the mid-C17 domestic classical manner, usually in red brick or terracotta.

Queenpost: paired upright timbers on a tie-beam of a roof, supporting purlins.

Quoins: dressed or otherwise emphasized stones at the angles of a building; *see* [5].

Rainwater head: container at a *parapet* into which rainwater runs from the gutters.

Reeded: decorated with small parallel convex mouldings.

Render: a uniform covering for walls for protection from the weather, usually of cement or *stucco*.

Reredos: painted and/or sculpted screen behind and above an altar.

Reveal: the inner face of a jamb or opening.

Rib-vault: masonry framework of intersecting arches (ribs) supporting vault cells.

Rock-faced: masonry cleft to produce a natural, rugged appearance.

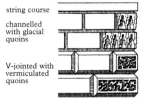

string course

channelled with glacial quoins

V-jointed with vermiculated quoins

5. Rustication

lancet

transom

Geometric   Intersecting   Reticulated

Panel

6. Tracery

Romanesque: round-arched style of the C11 and C12.

Rood: crucifix flanked by the Virgin and St John, carved or painted.

Rubble: of masonry, with stones wholly or partly rough and unsquared.

Rustication: exaggerated treatment of masonry to give the effect of strength; *see* [5].

Sacristy: room in a church used for sacred vessels and vestments.

Saddleback roof: a pitched roof used on a tower.

Sanctuary: in a church, the area around the main altar.

Sedilia: seats for the priests in the *chancel* wall of a church or chapel.

Sexfoil: a six-lobed opening.

Shaped gable: with curved sides, but no pediment (cf. Dutch gable, [3]).

Spandrel: space between an arch and its framing rectangle, or between adjacent arches.

Splayed: angled; (of an opening) wider on one side than the other.

Stanchion: upright structural member, of iron, steel or reinforced concrete.

Stiff-leaf: carved decoration in the form of thick uncurling foliage; originally late C12–early C13.

Strapwork: decoration like interlaced leather straps.

Stringcourse: horizontal course projecting from a wall surface.

Stripped classicism: buildings whose proportions conform to classical precedent but where the usual classical decoration is implied or removed altogether.

Stucco: durable lime plaster, shaped into ornamental features or used externally as a protective coating.

System building: system of manufactured units assembled on site.

Terracotta: moulded and fired clay ornament or cladding (cf. *faience*).

Tie-beam: main horizontal transverse timber in a roof structure.

Tile hanging: overlapping tiled covering on a wall.

Trabeated: having a post-and-beam structure, i.e. not arched.

Tracery: openwork pattern of masonry or timber in the upper part of an opening; *see* [6].

Transept: transverse portion of a church.

Transom: horizontal member between window lights; *see* [6].

Trefoil: with three lobes or foils.

Triforium: middle storey of a church interior treated as an arcaded wall passage or blind arcade.

Truss: braced framework, spanning between supports.

Tunnel vault: one with a simple elongated-arched profile.

Tuscan: *see* [2E].

Tympanum: the area enclosed by an arch or *pediment*.

Undercroft: room(s), usually *vaulted*, beneath the main space of a building.

Vault: arched stone roof, sometimes imitated in wood or plaster. See also Barrel vault.

Venetian window: *see* [1].

Vitruvian scroll: wave-like classical ornament.

Volutes: spiral scrolls, especially on Ionic columns (*see* [2C]).

Voussoir: wedge-shaped stones forming an arch.

Wagon roof: with the appearance of the inside of a wagon tilt.

Wainscot: timber lining of a room (cf. Panelling).

Index
of Artists, Architects and Other Persons Mentioned

The names of architects and artists working in the area are given in *italic*, with entries for partnerships and group practices listed after entries for a single name. Page references in italic include relevant illustrations.

Abbey Hanson Rowe Partnership 112
Abercrombie, Sir Patrick 29, *30*, 33
Abernethy, James 119
Abraham, Henry R. 128
Accrington Brick & Tile Company 110
Adams, Robert 121
Adams & Kelly 19, 166
Adamson, J. 179
Aikman, William 159
Alder, George 186
Alderson, Dr John 47, 66, 163
Alec-Smith, Rupert 47, 190
Allderidge & Clark 26
Aluminium Bungalows 32
Amos, Charles F. 192
Andrew, A. 73
Andrew, Harry 28
Andrews, G.T. 134, *135*, 138, 196, 220
Appleton, C. 189
Appleyard, John 47
Architects' Co-Partnership 78, 81
Arcon Industries 32
Arminge, Hugh 46
Atkinson, T.B. 132, 133
Atkinson, Thomas 160, 210, 226, *227*
Atkinson (J.B. & W) 227
Aumonier, William 173, *174*
Austin-Smith:Lord 110, 220

Bacon, John jun. 47, *200*
Bacon (Percy) & Bros. 190
Bailey, E.H. 190
Baines (George) & Son 22, *142*
Baker, Percy 216
Bakewell, Robert 90
Ballantine, James 45
Bannister, Anthony 66, 190
Bannister, John 52
Barker, Rev. John 52
Barry, William E. 23, *175*
Bartoli, Domenico 210
Bawden, Edward 81
Beckman, Martin 118

Bedford, Henry 186
Behnes, William 47
Beilby, Jonathan 52
Belasyse, John, Lord 90
Bell, William 70, 114, 134, 138
Bellamy & Hardy 17, 91, 144
Bennett (T.P.) & Son 29, 134
Bennison, Appleton 126, 197, 200, 230
Berry, Henry 14
Bilson, John 18, 19, 22, 28, 100, 125, 150, *151*, 166, 171, 179, 180, 183, 195
Bingley, W.H. 137, 150, 159
Binks, H. Percival 23, 139
Binks, Thomas 42
Blackmore, Alfred C. 26
Blackmore Sykes & Co. 26, 160, 161
Blanchard, Wheatley & Houldsworth 161
Blaydes, Benjamin 52, 95
Blomfield, Sir Reginald 24
Blunt, Frederick, Bishop of Hull 190
Boden, Hubert 166
Bodley, G.F. 19
Bond Bryan Partnership 143
Botterill, William 18, 19, 22, 88, 98, 99, 100, 107, 110, 131, 138, 143, 149, 160, 190, 191, 202
Botterill & Bilson 18, 19, 126, 143, 144, 153, 172
Botterill (W.) & Son 92
Botterill, Son & Bilson 138, 150, 190
Boulton, Gilbert 51
Bowes, Major-General 218
Bown, Henry E. 178
Boyes, John 199
Boyson, Alan 132, *133*
Brandon-Jones, John 134
Brangwyn, Frank 58
Breuer, Marcel 29
Broadley, Miss 44
Brodrick, Cuthbert 16–18, 19, 53, *54*, 68, 100, 120, 125, 129, 148, 150, 189, 191

Brodrick, Frederick Stead 18, 39, 149, 182, 199, 219
Brodrick, Lowther & Walker 22, 28, 88, 97, 98, 100, 123, 137, 161, 189
Bromsgrove Arts Guild 139
Brooks, Thomas 210
Brown, Capability 209, 210
Brunton (John) & Partners 34, 139
Bryant, J. 118
Bryson, John 144
Building Design Partnership 36, 98, 99
Burlington, Richard Boyle, 3rd Earl 11, 90
Burlison & Grylls 159
Burmantofts Pottery 151
Burton, Ralph 160
Burton, Richard 160
Burton, William 195
Butler, Samuel 226
Byll, Richard 46

Cadbury, George 174
Campbell, Colen 219
Campbell Tile Co. 144
Cankrien, John 201
Capronnier, J.B. 195
Carmichael, Ian 156
Carr, John 220
Carrick, Rev. George M. 131
Carter, Kenneth 121
Cartlidge, H.I. 16
Carvill, G.B. 173
Cash, H.W. 220
Cash, John 220
Casson, Hugh 186
Castle, Park, Dean, Hook 80
Catlyn, John jun. 108–10
Catlyn, John sen. 9, 130
Catlyn, William 90, 92, 93, 130
Chalmers, Sir George, Bt. 74
Chambers, Sir William 13, 73–4, 76
Chancellor, Fred 22
Chapman, William 14, 111, 112
Charles I, KIng 9
Cheere, Sir Henry 90, 195
Cheers, H.A. 143
Chermayeff, Serge 29
Chetwood Associates 88
Chichester-Constable, John 208
Chippendale, Thomas 210
Chorley, C.R. 199
Christie, David 95
Christmas 46
City Architect's Department 32

City Land Syndicate 170
Citybuild 36
Clamp, Robert 104, 149
Clapham, Madame 129
Clark, John 121
Clarke, Rev. John 131
Clay, James 66
Clayton & Bell 45, 46, 51, 200, 205, 216, 226
Collins, William 210, 216
Colquhoun, Ian 91
Constable, Sir John 208
Constable, T.A. Clifford 208
Constable, William 208, 210
Cooke (S.N.) & E.C. Davies 24, 68, 69
Cooper, Edwin 21, 22, 53, 57, 58, 59
Cooper, John Scott 19, 157
Cortese, Giuseppe 91, 92, 210, 221
Courtenay, Tom 33
Cowles-Voysey, C. 29, 134
Cox, Oliver 115
Crabtree & Rushworth 222
Crane, Walter 45, 46
Crease, David 219
Creyke, Everilda 219
Cromie (R.) and W.B. Wheatley 129
Crosskill, William 229
Crouch, Butler & Savage 22, 82, 83
Crowle, George 11, 88, 89
Czaky, John 116

Dale, Peter G.H. 36
Dale, Thomas 171
Dalton, Thomas 46
Dannatt, Trevor 31, 78, 84
Dawson, Jacob 206
Defoe, Daniel 10
Delamotte, Jane 146
Denman, Thomas 190
Dewjoc Architects 36
Dibb, William T. 131
Dix, Arthur J. 166
DLA Architecture 36, 105, 113, 123
Dobbelaere, H. 195
Dobson, Alderman William 52
Donald Hamilton Wakeford & Partners 29
Dossor, John M. 22, 23, 139, 140, 158, 161, 166, 192
Dreyer, C.A. 42
Dunn & Watson 102
Dykes, Rev. Thomas 131

Earle, E. Haworth 46

Earle, George 56, 183
Earle, John 14, 47, 52, 56, 105, 146
Earle, John jun. 113, 114, 126
Earle, Thomas 46, 47, 56, 58, 66, 75, 76, 103, 146, 147
East Riding of Yorkshire Council Architects 220
Edward I, King 4, 39, 58
Edward III, King 5, 6
Edward VII, King 22, 51
Edwards, J.C. 110
Eland, John 44
Ellinor, Thomas 221
Elsworth Sykes Partnership 34, 110, 171
Elwell, James 44, 199, 216, 226, 229
Evetts, L.C. 190
Eyton, H.M. 138

Farman, A.L. 104
Farrell, Terry 3, 36
Farrell & Clark 83
Farrell (Terry) & Partners 116
Fehr, H.C. 60, 139
Ferens, Thomas R. 24, 68, 77, 173, 174, 179
Ferres, Thomas 9, 47, 71
Field, Patricia 58
Fisher, John and Samuel 210
Fisher, Hollingsworth & Partners 98
Foale, William 74, 75, 105, 107, 137
Forrest, J.B. 122
Forsyth, William A. 24, 77–8, 79, 82
Forsyth & Maule 77
Forsyth & Partners 77, 80, 81, 84
Foster, Edmund 46, 226
Foster & Partners 136
Freeman, William 18, 157, 165
Freeman & Gaskell 202
Freeman, Fox & Partners 193
Freeman, Son & Gaskell 23, 95, 112, 144, 151, 184
Frith, Thomas 51, 63, 182
Fry, Drew and Partners 34, 125

Gabo, Naum 29
Gale, Benjamin 5
Gammond Evans Crichton Ltd. 82, 83, 139
Garbutt, David Parkinson 156
Garnier, Richard 90
Garside & Pennington 220
Gaskell, Peter 133
Gee, William 9, 108
Gelder, Sir Alfred 19, 20, 23, 53, 95, 104, 108, 140, 158, 165, 166, 173, 174, 179

Gelder, Edward 27
Gelder & Kitchen 19, 22, 27, 95, 101, 103, 126, 132, 133, 140, 143, 150, 151, 153, 156, 158, 192
Gibberd, Frederick 30–1, 34, 121, 122
Gibson, J.S. 22, 60, 125, 126
Gillespie, Kidd & Coia 30, 31, 84
Gillinson, Barnett & Partners 34
Glossop, William 159
Goch, Giliad 47
Goddard, Edward 179
Godwin 205
Gomme, Sir Bernard de 118
Gravill, Captain John 150
Gray, John 47
Gresham, John 191
Grundy, John 14
Guy, Henry 207
Gwyther, W.W. 102

Habron, G. Dudley 28, 161
Habron & Robson 23, 161
Hadlock, Neil 113
Hagen, F.W. 149
Haigh Foundry Wigan 114
Hall, Ivan 65
Hall, William 196
Hamilton, James 92
Hammond & Riddell 51
Hardman, John 45, 46, 190
Hardman & Co 195, 216, 226
Hardman (John) & Co. 46, 166
Hare, Henry T. 22, 169
Hargrave, Jeremiah 13, 72, 73, 74, 210
Hargrave, Joseph 13, 130, 131
Harrison (Samuel) & Son 46
Hartford, Kate 120
Hartley, John B. 14, 95, 111, 112, 117
Hartshorne, Robert 46, 47
Harvey, David 25, 26–7, 126
Haryson, Alderman John 51
Hawe, William 200, 223, 227, 229
Hawksmoor, Nicholas 212, 215, 222, 228
HBG Construction Ltd. 143
Head, Charles 52
Heard, Michael 81
Hebblewhite, John 196
Hellyer, J.W. 200
Henderson, James 210
Hendra (Robert) & Geoffrey Harper 178
Henry VIII, King 9, 118
Hepworth, Joseph 101
Hildyard, Robert 51

Hill, Vincent 226
Hillier, Joe 83
Hirst, Joseph H. 21, 23, 25, 65, 67, 83,
103, 104, 107, 129, 144, 145, 153, 158,
161, 166, 167, 168, 170, 171, 173, 178,
179, 180
HLM Design 198
H.M. Office of Works 97
Hobson, Jonathan 179, 223
Hodge, Albert H. 53, 55, 56
Holder Mathias Architects 36, 136
Hollar, Wenceslaus 7, 9
Holt, Luke 14
Holtby, Winifred 196
Hornstedt, Claud 191
Horth, Frederick J. 28
Horth and Andrews 131
Horth (F.J.) & H. Andrew 137, 169
Hotham, Sir Charles 222
Hotham, Sir John 9
Howard, Richard 184
Hudson, John 169
Huggate, Nicholas 216
Hughes, H. 183
Hughes, Robert 79
Hughes, T. Harold 134
Hull and Barnsley Railway Co. 15
Hull Dock Company 64
Hull Forward 36
Hull Property Design Practice 92
Huntington, John 46
Hutchinson, Miss 46
Hutchinson, Charles 163
Hutchinson, William 159

Illingworth, J. 179
Immenkamp, Henry 128, 206
Ingleby & Hobson 179, 223
Iveson, James 206

Jackson, George 164
Jackson, William 179
Jacobs, B.S. 22, 70, 89, 98, 107, 110,
163, 220
Jalland, B.M. and J.E. 174
Jarratt, John 128
Jenkin, David 33
John of Beverley, St 212
John of York, Bishop 212
Johnson, Amy 156
Johnson, Francis 31, 45, 90, 130–1
Jones, Alfred Garth 139
Jones & Willis 166
Jopling & Wright 27, 158

Kelsey, A.E. 122
Kemp, Rev. Henry W. 131
Kempe, C.E. 180, 183, 195, 199
Kent, William 90
Kerby, William 144, 185, 199
Keyworth, Joseph 56
Keyworth, William Day jun. 56, 57, 58,
66, 91, 92, 93, 98, 107, 115, 138, 146,
200
Keyworth, William Day sen. 47, 56,
131, 183
King & Co. 110
Kirk, Thomas 183
Kirkby, Mark 47
Kirkby, William 201
Kitchen, Llewellyn 19, 103, 159
Kitching, W.H. 19, 98
Knowlton, Thomas 210

Lambert, Anthony 47
Lambert, George 47
Larkin, Philip 150, 161
Lazenby & Priestman 31, 121
Lazenby, Needler & Sangwin 219
Leake, Albert 165
Lee, Charles 169
Leeds Fireclay Co. Ltd. 110, 120
Leeds Marble Works 134
Leland, John 6
Lever, W.H. 175
Lightoler, Timothy 207, 208, 209, 210
Lockwood, Henry Francis 15–16, 17, 39,
44, 75, 76, 125, 136, 141, 151, 173, 192,
201
Lockwood & Mawson 104, 162
Loft, James 52, 66
Lofting (E.E.) & E. Priestley Cooper
178
Longley, Clifford 45
Lowther, Arthur 19, 158
Lucas, W.H. 110
Lutyens, Sir Edwin 29, 30
Lyons, Israel & Ellis 32, 179

McAslan (John) & Partners 79
McDowell & Benedetti 36, 88
McGeoch, J. McLardie 161
Macmillan, Andrew 31, 84
Maister, Henry 11, 47, 90
Maister, Nathaniel 47
Maister, William 46
Martin, Bruce 32
Martin, Sir Leslie 28–9, 30, 31, 78, 79
Martin (Hugh) & Partners 35, 69,
105

Marvell, Andrew 56, 130
Matcham, Frank 66
Matthewson, John J. 47
Maw & Co. 64, 190
Mawson, William 16
Merrifield, L. 190
Metzstein, Isi 31, 78, 84
Michael of Canterbury 39
Middleton, John 222, 229
Middleton, William 220, 221, 222, 223, 224, 226, 227, 229
Midgley, Jonathan 226
Midland Architectural Metal Workers Co. 64
Miller Partnership 36, 167
Milner, H.V. 51
Milner, Rev. Joseph 47
Milner and Craze 27
Milner (W.) & R.B. Craze 178
Minghella, Anthony 156
Minton 205
Mitchell, William 122, 123
Moore, Leslie T. 27, 52, 145, 179
Moore, Temple 19, 22, 50, 51, 145, 158, 179
Moore (Temple) & Moore 52
Morley & Woodhouse 222
Moro, Peter 31, 78
Moro (Peter) & Partners 81–2
Morris & Co. 190
Mountain, Charles jun. 14, 103, 107, 129, 210, 220, 228
Mountain, Charles sen. 13, 103, 123, 124, 193
Moyser, James 218, 224
Mumby, G.H. 144
Musgrave, Benjamin 164
Musgrave, Samuel 110, 137, 143, 223
Myers, George 15
Myers & Wilson 15

Napper, Jack 31
Napper Architects 82
Napper Collerton Partnership 82
Needler (confectioners) 15
Niall McLaughlin Architects 36, 119
Nicholas of Louth 194, 195
Nicholls, G.B. 149
Nicholson, Ben 29
Nicholson, Sir Charles 22
Niven, James 146
Northumberland, Henry Percy, 4th Earl 216

Page, Edward 220

Page, Gregory 220
Page, Joseph 11–13, 73, 74, 90, 96, 107
Parker, George 44–5
Parker, John 47
Parker & Rosner 193
Parkin 183
Parmentier, James 44
Pawle, M.F. 205
Peadon, A.R. 83, 124
Peak, E.A. 178
Pearson, J.L. 15
Pearson, Zachariah 146, 147, 148
Pease, Joseph 52, 94, 193
Pease, J.R. 13, 123, 190
Peck, George 44
Pennington, G.F. 220
Pennyman, Bridget 226
Pennyman, Sir James 220
Percy, Lady Anne 190
Percy, Lady Eleanor 216
Percy, Lady Idonea 216
Philip, John Birnie 42
Pickering, Christopher 170, 171
Pole, Michael de la 42, 56, 58
Pole, Richard de la 44, 46, 47
Pole, William de la 6, 44, 46, 115, 129
Pope & Parr 98
Potter, Douglas 156
Potts, W. 97
Powell (of Whitefriars) 216
Priestman, Thomas 186
Pringle Richards Sharratt 35, 36, 128, 129
Prior, E.S. 161
Prosser, Thomas 138
Pryme, Abraham de la 10
Pugin, A.W.N. 15, 225
Pugin, E.W. 225
Pycock, George 13–14, 103, 133

Ramsden, John 46
Ranger, William 198
Rank, J. Arthur 174
Rank, Joseph 15, 27, 95, 174, 179
Rankine, Andrew 33, 34, 83, 126
Ratcliffe-Springall, C. 36
Ravetz, Alison 34
Reckitt family 15, 173
Reckitt, Francis 191
Reckitt, Frank N. 173
Reckitt, Frederic I. 178
Reckitt, Sir James 23, 174–5
Reed (Kenneth W.) & Associates 141
Reeves, William 148–9
Reeves, W.K. 112

Reid, Dick 47
Rennie, John 14, 111, *112*
Rickards, E.A. 22, *139*
Rickman, Thomas 212
Riddell, Thomas 13, 103
Robinson, H. Conyers 27
Rogers, John 118
Roltenhering, John 44
Rowntree, Joseph 174
Runton, Percy T. 23, *175*
Runton & Barry 23, 143, 169, 170, *174*,
     175, *177*, 179, 190, 191, 192, 200
Rushworth, William 73
Russell, Gordon 58
Russell, Cooper, Davis & Mallows 53

Salviati 190
Sawer, George 207
Sayers, Dorothy L. 156
Scarlett & Ashworth 24, *136*
Scheemakers, Peter *109*, 110, 218
Scoles, J.J. 126, *127*
Scott, Sir George Gilbert 39, 40, 42, 44,
     48, 49, 50, 51, 52, 212, 216, 225, 226
Scott, George Gilbert jun. 19, *157*
Scott, Sir Giles Gilbert 32
Scott, Rev. John 52
Scott, John Oldrid 226
Seale, Gilbert 66
Shankland Cox Associates 35, *115*
Sharpe, Joseph Fox 149, 167, 178
Shaw, W.H. 47
Shelton, Theophilus 222
Shepeard Epstein Hunter 79
Sherrin, George 22
Shields, John 150
Simpson, Edward 159
Simpson & Malone 15, 44
Sims, Ronald 47
Sissons, William 128
Skayll, William 39
Skinner, William 46
Slater, R.E. 193
Smith, B.J.A. 161
Smith, F.S. 8, *10*
Smith, John (d. 1504) 195
Smith, John (d. 1875) 47
Smith, Richard George 18–19, 96, 147,
     150, 179, 182, *189*
Smith, Robert 215
Smith & Brodrick 19, 98, 99, 108, 110,
     125, 126, *127*, 148, 150, *152*, 159, *159*,
     182, 190, 191, 199, 201, 220, 229, 230
Smith, Brodrick & Lowther 69, *70*, 162,
     195, 196, 229

Smith & Nephew (medical goods) 15
Snetzler, John 216
Snowden, Thomas 98, 107
Soukop, Willi 81
Sparrow, J. Silvester 46
Spendlove, Henry 226
Spooner, Ltd 32
Spooner (J.L.) 33
Spruce, E. Caldwell 69, 144
Stammers, Harry J. 45, 46, 159, 205
Standidge, Sir Samuel 52
Stangroom, M. 76
Stephenson, John 201
Street, G.E. 15, 19, 204
Stuart, James 174
Suffolk, Michael de la Pole, 1st Earl 6,
     129
Suffolk, William de la Pole, 1st Duke 6
Summerson, Sir John 90
Sutton, Sir John de 182, *183*
Swan, Alderman Thomas 51
Sykes family 199, 200, 201, 202
Sykes, Daniel 66
Sykes, Joseph (d. 1805) 201
Sykes, Joseph (d. 1857) 200
Sykes, Richard 202
Sykes, Wilfred E. 26

Tarran Industries 32
Tasker, Sidney S. 98
Taylor Young Partnership 163
Thew, Robert 14
Thomas, D. 36
Thompson, Robert 146, 183
Thompson, T.B. 98, 158, 179
Thompson, Thomas 198
Thomson, William 46
Thorarinsdottir, Steinunn 115
Thornton, John (merchant) 196
Thornton, John (of Coventry) 216
Thornton, John (of York) 212
Thorp, David 18, 143, 179
Thorpe, George 158
Tickell, J. 5
Tiffen, Joseph 123
Tugwell, Frank A. 192
Tyley of Bristol 210
Tym (Roger) & Partners 36
Tymperon, William 224

Underwood, John 63

Voysey, C.F.A. 23, 176

Wailes, William 200

Wailes, Son & Strang 205
Wakeford, Kenneth 29, 69
Walker, James 14
Walker, W.S. 22, 97, 98, 100
Waller, F. Runton 177
Walsh & Nicholas 104
Walter of Hereford 42
Ward, A.L. 46
Ward, Thomas 46
Ward & Hughes 183
Warton family 226
Warton, Sir Michael 218, 219, 222
Waterhouse, Alfred 70
Waterland, Henry 206
Watson, Charles 230
Watson, Harry 58
Webster, J.T. 19, 180, 205
Weekes, Henry 56
Wellsted, W.H. 21–2
Wellsted, Dossor & Wellsted 160, 161
Welsh, Edward 111, 112
Westmacott, Richard jun. 163
Wex, Bernard 193
Wheatley & Houldsworth 139, 161
Whincop, Thomas 46
Whitaker, J.R. 166
Whiteing, R.H. 226
Whittaker, Helen 216
Whitton of Beverley 190
Whitton, M.L. 230
Wicksteed 178

Wilberforce, William 11, 56, 92
Wilkinson, A.L. 58
Wilkinson, Fewster 201
Wilkinson, Philip 52
Wilkinson Eyre 36, 134
Williams, J. 101
Williams, Sleight & Co. 166
Williamson, William 201
Wilson, Arthur 199
Wilson, Charles 196
Wilson, Christopher 40n, 42
Wilson, Harry 104
Wilson, Joseph 91
Wilson Mason & Partners 99
Windross, A.I. 179
Womersley, Peter 78, 82
Wood, Derwent 97
Woodman, William sen. 226
Woolley, William 47
Wray, Christopher G. 17, 60, 63
Wright, Joseph 19, 185
Wright & Wright 36, 136, 137
Wrightson, William 222, 228, 229
Wyatt, James 210

Yates, Cook & Darbyshire 173
York University Design Unit 219
Yorke, Rosenberg & Mardall 34, 162–3
Yorkshire Design Group (YDG) 33–4
Young, Gordon 87n
Young & Pool 146

Index
of Localities, Streets and Buildings

Principal references are in **bold** type; page references including relevant illustrations are in *italic*. 'dem.' = 'demolished'

Age Concern Healthy Living Centre **139**
Ainthrope Primary School 27
Albemarle Music Centre 36, *136*
Albert Dock 15, **113–14**
Albert House, Pearson Park *148-9*
Albion Independent chapel (dem.) 16
Albion Street 13, *124*
Alexandra Dock 15, **119**, 180
Alexandra Hotel 162
Alfred Gelder Street **20**, 21, *95*
All Saints, Hessle 44, *189–90*
All Saints (dem.) 19
Allders (now Primark) 34
Anlaby 6, 25, **199**
Anlaby Park Estate 23, *169–70*
Anlaby Road 13, 15, 34, **138**, 139, *162–4, 167–9*
Anlaby Road (Thornton) estate **33–4**
Ann Routh's Hospital, Beverley *218*
Ann Watson's Hospital, Sutton-on-Hull **185**
Annison Building 172, *172*
ARC Building 36, *119–20*
ARCO National Distribution Centre **36**
Arden's Vaults, Beverley **226**
Ariel Chambers **132**
Artisan Mannerist style 10, **90**, 99
Askew Avenue estate 25
Assembly Rooms (former) 14
Astoria Cinema (former) **179**
Avenue, The, Bishop Lane **89–90**
Avenue, The, Sutton-on-Hull 184–5
Avenues, The 15, 19, 23, *154–8*
Avenues Adult Education Centre, The 18, 158

Baker Street 13, *126*
Bank, The 179
Bar House, Beverley *228*, **229**
Baxter Gate, Hedon **206**
Bayles House **88**
Beacon Garth, Hessle *192*

Beck Bank, Cottingham **196**
Belgrave Terrace **137**
Beverley 6, *211–30*
Beverley Arms Hotel **227–8**
Beverley Gate and town walls **5**, 104
Beverley High Road 26
Beverley Minster *212–18*
Beverley Road 13, 15, *141–6*, 159
Beverley Road Baths 21, **144**, *145*
BHS **132**, *133*
Bilton Grange 33
Bishop Lane **89**
Bishop Lane Staith **89**
Blaydes House 12, *95–6*
Blundell Street School 18, 143
Blundell's Corner 141
Board Schools **18**
BOCM Garden Village **179**
Bond 31 **88**
Bond Street 34, 125
Boots, Whitefriargate **103**
Boulevard **166**
Bowlalley Lane **98**, *99*
Bowling Circle 179
Bransholme 34, 36
Bricknell Avenue 25
bricks **6**
Britannia **104**
Britannia House 137
British School 173
Broadway, The 179
Brook Chambers *24*, *29*, *136*
Brough 15
Brown's Department Store, Beverley **223**
Brunswick House 143
Bull Inn *144*
Burnett Avenue **88**, 89
Burton Constable Hall *207–10*
Burtons
    Hessle Road 165
    Whitefriargate **104**
Butcher Row, Beverley **220**

Canton Place *167*

Carlton Theatre 26
Carmelite House **107**
Carnegie Library (former) 21, *168*
Carr Lane 34
CASPON houses **33**
Castle Hill Hospital, Cottingham *198*
Castle Street 29, 111
Cecil Cinema (former) *140*
Cenotaph 134
Central Fire Station 129
Central Library 22, *125–6*
Central Police Station 21, 31, 121
Chamberlain's Hospital, Sutton-on-Hull **185**
Champney Road, Beverley **220**
Chanterlands Avenue 161
Charles Warton's Hospital, Beverley **218**
Charlotte Street 13
Charterhouse Hospital 3, 6, 9, 10, 13, 90, *129–31*
Charterhouse Lane School 18, **131**
Chesters Learning Resource Centre 123
Christ Church Schools 16, **129**
Church Lane, Kirk Ella **201**
Church Mount, Sutton-on-Hull 183
Church Street, Sutton-on-Hull *183–4*
Citadel 10, *118*, 119
City Cemetery *180*
City Hall 3, *20*, 21, 22, **65–7**
City Hotel **97**
City Treasury **123**
Claremont House **144**
Clarence Mill 27, **95**
Cliff Road, Hessle **192**
Clyde Terrace **167**
Cogan House **98**
College of Art (former) 22, **139**
College Street, Sutton-on-Hull **185**
Colonial Chambers 105
Coltman Street 35, *164–5*
Conservancy Buildings 103
Corn Exchange (former) 17, **91**
Cottingham 15, 25, *194–8*
Cottingham Road *158–9*
council housing 23, 25–6, 32–4, 179
County Hall, Beverley 19
court housing *16*
Criterion **165**
Cross Street, Beverley **220**
Crowle House **88–9**, 90
Crown, The 179
Crown Chambers **98**
Crown Court 36, **98**, 99

Crown House 29, **136**

Dagger Lane *10*, 107
Danish Buildings **88**
Dansom Lane **173**
Davenport Estate, Hessle **191–2**
David Lister High School **32**, 179
Dawson House 159, *159*
De la Pole Avenue 16
Deaf Institute 28
Deep, The 3, 36, 114–15, *116*
Derek Crothall Building **124**
Derringham Bank estate 25, **26**, 28
Dock Office (former) 17, **96**
Dock Office Row **96**
Dock Street **124–5**
docks 13–14, *14*, 15, 35, *111–20*
Dram Shop, The **125**
Drypool Bridge 94
Duke of Cumberland, Cottingham **198**
Dunwell's Forge **89**

Eagle Inn 164
East Hull Baths *173–4*
East Hull estate 25
East Park *178*
East Park Baptist Church 179
Eastern Cemetery **27**
Eastgate, Beverley **219**
Elim Pentecostal Church **150**
Ella Street **158**
Ellerburn Avenue 26
Empress Hotel **104**
Endeavour High School **143**
Endike Primary School **27**
Endlike Lane estate 25
Endyke Lane, Cottingham **196**
Essex House 99
Europa House 34, **139**
Exchange (former) **98**

Ferens Art Gallery 24, **68–9**
Ferens Haven of Rest 179, *179*
Ferensway *24*, 36, *134–7*
Ferensway House 136, **140**
Ferres Almshouses (former) **105**
Ferriby Road, Hessle **190**, *192*, 193
Festival House 29, **134**
Fish Street Congregational School 110
Flemingate, Beverley **219**
Fletcher Gate, Hedon **206**
Foredyke Primary School 27
Fountain House **153**
Francis Reckitt Institute **173**

Frederic Reckitt Homes of Rest 177
Freedom Quay 112–13
Friars Lane, Beverley **219**

Gaiety Picture House **110**
Gaol, Mytton Gate (dem) 14
Garden Village 23, *174–7*
General Cemetery 16
General Post Office (former) 22, *97–8*
George Hotel **98**
George Street 13, 34, *123–4*, **125**
George Street, Hedon **206**
George Yard 8
Georgian Houses **92**
Gipsyville 25
Glad Tidings Hall **143–4**
Goose, The 125
Granville Terrace **143**
Great Thornton Street Chapel (dem)
  16, *17*
Greatfield 33
Green Bricks **120**
Grimston Street **129**
Guildhall, Beverley **220–1**
Guildhall and Law Courts 3, 9, 21, *21*,
  22, *53–9*, 90

Halifax House **125**
Hall Road Primary School 27
Hall Street 137
Hallgate, Cottingham **195**, **196–8**
Haltemprice 6
Haworth Arms 27, 159
Haworth Hall **160**
Hawthorn Avenue 16
Hedon **203–7**
Hedon Road **179–80**
Hengate, Beverley **226**
Hepworth's Arcade 19, *101–2*
Hessle 6, 15, 25, *188–93*
Hessle Cemetery **190**, *191*
Hessle Road 15, 34, **162**, **165–6**, 170–1
Hesslegate Buildings 120
Hesslewood Hall, Hessle **13**, **193**
High Street 4, **8**, 10, 11–13, *86–96*
Highgate, Beverley **219–20**
Holderness House 174, **174**
Holderness Road 15, 16, *172–4*, **178–80**
Holiday Inn **112**
Holy Sacrament R.C. Church,
  Marton 210
Holy Trinity 3, *4*, 6, 10, 19, *38–47*, 112
Hope House **163**
Horncastle Media and Performing
  Arts Centre 123

House of Fraser 29, *134*
HSBC Bank, Whitefriargate **104**
Hull and East Riding Museum 8, 17,
  91
Hull and Sculcoates Dispensary
  (former) Baker Street **126**
  Boulevard **166**
Hull Atelier of Architecture **28**
Hull Botanic Garden 163
Hull Brewery (former) **128**
Hull Castle 118
Hull College 30–1, 34, *122–3*
  Park Street Centre **138**
Hull Community Church 158
Hull Daily Mail Office **141**
Hull Exchange 19
Hull General Cemetery **150**
Hull General Infirmary (dem.) 14
Hull History Centre 35, 36, **129**
Hull Medical School **128**
Hull Prison **179–80**
Hull Royal Infirmary 34, *162–3*
Hull Savings Banks (former) **28**, 143
Hull School of Architecture **28**
Hull School of Art 28
Hull Truck Theatre 36, *137*
Humber Bridge *193*
Humber Dock (The Marina) 5, 14, **14**,
  35, **111**, *112–13*, 120
Humber Place **114**
Humber Quays 36, **113**
Humber Street **120**
Humberside Police Authority
  Headquarters **89**
Hutt Street 151
Hymers College 19, *150–1*

Imperial Chambers 98
Ings Road estate **33**
Institute for the Deaf **137**

James Reckitt Public Library (for-
  mer) *173*
Jameson Street 20, **132**, **133–4**
Jarratt Street 13, *126–8*
John Street **129**
Juliette Reckitt Haven of Rest 177

KC Stadium 36, *167*
Keldgate, Beverley **218–19**
King Albert Chambers **133**
King Edward Street 20, 22, **132**
King George V Dock 119
King Street 107, 108
King William House 34, **110**

King's Head 8
King's Head, Beverley **223**
King's Place, Hedon **206**
Kingston, The **107**
Kingston Chambers 98
Kingston House 34, **125**
Kingston Square **128–9**
Kingston Theatre Hotel **129**
Kingston Wharf **112**
Kingston Youth Centre **141–2**
Kingswood College 36
Kirk Ella 6, 25, *199–201*
Kirkella Mansions, Kirk Ella *200*, **201**

Laburnum Avenue 178
Ladygate, Beverley **224**
Lair, The **138**
Lairgate, Beverley **220**, **222**
Lambert Street Primitive Methodist Church 158
Land of Green Ginger 98
Landress Lane, Beverley **222**
Law Courts *see* Guildhall and Law Courts
Lee's Rest Houses 22, *169*
Lilac Avenue 176
Linnaeus Street **163–4**
Lloyd's Bank, Lowgate (former) **100**
Longhill 33
Lord Robert's Road, Beverley **220**
Lowgate 22, 97, **98**, 100
Lowgate, Sutton-on-Hull **184**, **185**

Magdalen Gate, Hedon **205**
Magistrates' Court **110**
Magistrates' Court, Beverley **220**
Maister House *11–12*, **90–1**
Malet Lambert school **26**
Malton Street Board School 172
Manchester Arms **88**
Manor Street 98–9
Marfleet **180**
Marfleet Church (dem.) 14
Marina, The *see* Humber Dock
Marine View 114
Maritime Buildings 22, **97**
Maritime Museum 17, *61–5*
Mark Kirkby's School, Cottingham 195
Market Cross, Beverley **222**, *223*
Market Green, Cottingham 198
Market Hall 21, *106*, **107–8**
Market Hill, Hedon **205**
Market Place 23, 100, **101**, 110
Market Place, Hedon 207

Marks & Spencer
   Silver Street **102**
   Whitefriargate **104**
Marlborough Avenue **156**
Masonic Hall, Sutton-on-Hull 185
Masters Bar **133**
Mayfair Cinema (former) 26
Mercantile Marine Offices (former) **107**
Merchants Warehouse **108**
Mersey Street School 18
Methodist Central Hall **132**
Methodist Church, Sutton-on-Hull *184*
Midland Street 138
Mill, The (pub) *179*
Minerva Hotel **114**
Minerva Pier 114
Minerva Terrace **114**, **137**
Minerva's Freemasons' Lodge **107**
Minster Moorgate, Beverley **218**
Minster Parish Hall, Beverley **219**
Minster Yard North, Beverley **219**
Minster Yard South, Beverley **219**
Mint, The **100**
Mission, The **107**
Monument Buildings **70**
Municipal Training College (former) 22, 82–3
Museum of Fisheries and Shipping (former) **171**
Museums Quarter **91**

National Picture Theatre **143**
National Provincial Bank, Lowgate (former) **100**
NatWest Bank, Beverley **223**
Nautical College (former) 32
Nelson Street 14, 114
Neptune Inn (former) *13*, **103**
New Bridge Road 23
New George Street 26
New Northbridge House 96
New Theatre 14, **129**
New Village Road, Cottingham **196**
New Walk, Beverley **230**
Newgate, Cottingham **196**
Newington Primary School 18
Newland 159
Newland Avenue 16, 158
Newland High School 21, 83
Newland Homes *159*
Newland Methodist Church **27**, 158
Newland Park 15, 23, 26, 28, *160–1*
Newtown 26